Widening Participation in Post-Compulsory Education

WIDENING PARTICIPATION IN POST-COMPULSORY EDUCATION

Liz Thomas

CONTINUUM
London and New York

Also available from Continuum:

Jim Smith and Andrea Spurling, *Lifelong Learning*
Richard Teare, David Davies and Eric Sandelands, *The Virtual University*
Linda Evans and Ian Abbott, *Teaching and Learning in Higher Education*
Lovemore Nyatanga, Dawn Forman and Jane Fox, *Good Practice in the Accreditation of Prior Learning*
Stewart Ranson, *Inside the Learning Society*
Kangmin Zeng, *Dragon Gate: Competitive Examinations and their Consequences*

Continuum

The Tower Building   370 Lexington Avenue
11 York Road   New York
London SE1 7NX   NY 10017–6503

First published 2001

British Library Cataloguing-in-Publication Data
A catalogue record for this book is available from the British Library.

ISBN 0-8264-7908-1 (paperback)

Typeset by YHT Ltd, London
Printed and bound in Great Britain by Biddles, Guildford and King's Lynn

Contents

Acknowledgements

I would like to take this opportunity to acknowledge the help and support of a number of people without whom this book would not have been possible. First, I would like to thank Professor Christine King, Vice-Chancellor of Staffordshire University, and Professor David Jary, formerly Dean of the Graduate School, for initiating the Institute for Access Studies and for providing me with the opportunity to work in this field. Second, I would like to thank Jan Thomas for assisting with the typing, and Peter Thomas, Robert Jones and Kim Slack for reading and commenting on my manuscript, without whose guidance this would be a far less eloquent read. I would also like to thank everybody who has assisted with, or participated in, the research that informs much of this book. Finally, I would like to thank Anthony Haynes of Continuum for encouraging me throughout the process of writing.

CHAPTER 1

An Introduction to Widening Participation in Post-compulsory Education

Introduction

This book is written at a time when widening participation in post-compulsory education seems to be undergoing something of a renaissance. It is therefore necessary to seize this opportunity to ensure that the nature of post-16 learning opportunities is radically changed to overcome elitism and exclusion. Similar sentiments are shared by others, including for example Dick Taylor (2000) who calls for the development of a 'transformed higher education system emerging from the concepts and practices of continuing education and lifelong learning' (p. 14; see also Watson and Taylor, 1998).

I am not claiming that this book should serve as a blueprint for change. This is, for me, primarily because a single, detailed agenda for reform cannot hope to meet the diverse needs of a broader constituency of learners. Such groups must be involved in the processes of change. Rather, this book has three primary aims: first, to examine some of the reasons underpinning the renewed interest in access, widening participation and lifelong learning; second, to categorize and explore the barriers to wider participation in formal learning by so-called 'non-traditional' students; and third, to promote a strategic approach to widening participation that involves potential students in addressing the various barriers to access and progression. This will promote genuine institutional and social change.

Expansion and participation

The first part of the book (Chapters 2 to 4) examines expansion and participation in post-compulsory education in the latter part of the twentieth century. This is attempted partly through the consideration of contemporary research, policy and practice, and also by reference to some of the older literature and seminal works, which should not be neglected as we all rush to 're-invent the wheel' in this renaissance period.

In the late 1980s and the 1990s there has been a huge expansion in participation in post-16 education in the UK and much of the developed world. In the UK participation rates in post-compulsory education in the 1950s, 1960s and 1970s were comparatively low, accounting for less than 20 per cent of school leavers, with no more than 5 per cent of the relevant age group entering higher education in the 1950s. These numbers have subsequently risen dramatically, and now more than 70 per cent of school leavers go on to some form of further education and training (Gleeson, 1996). Indeed, the National Advisory Council for Education and Training Targets (NACETT) reported, in 1996, that in the UK more than 80 per cent of 16-year-olds participated in some form of education or training (full-time, part-time or work-based training), and, similarly, about 60 per cent of 18-year-olds participated (NACETT, 1996). Including adults, there are now approximately 5 million post-16 learners, in England alone, involved in a wide range of post-compulsory education (Kennedy, 1997, p. 9). Almost 4 million people in England participate in further education, and about 80 per cent of these are adults (Sand, 1998, p. 30).

Although in the UK only about 25 per cent of post-16 learners are in higher education, this sector has also expanded significantly. In 1985/86 there were 599,000 full-time students in higher education; in twelve years the number more than doubled to 1,230,400 in 1997/8 (DfEE, 1998a). In the 1950s, in the UK, no more than 5 per cent of the age group entered higher education, but now this figure is approximately one third of the age group (API), and in Scotland the API is 45 per cent (Ward and Steele, 1999, p. 198). Indeed, the UK higher education system is now described as a 'mass' system. Martin Trow (1970) has argued that at around 15 per cent participation 'elite' standards and patterns of provision cannot be sustained across the national HE system. Instead, a mass system of higher education is said to exist, although this is often more differentiated than the traditional elite system, even in a nominally 'unitary' system as there is in the UK now. The UK government has set the target of a 35 per cent participation rate amongst 18–21-year-olds by 2002 and 50 per cent by 2007, and 50 per cent of under-30-year-olds to have participated in higher education by 2010. Hence, the trend towards a mass system of higher education is set to continue in the UK.

Phenomenal rates of expansion in higher education have been

witnessed in many post-industrial countries. All European Union member states have increased participation in higher education, especially female participation (Green *et al.*, 1999). In Japan and the USA, participation exceeded 50 per cent at the start of the 1990s. In Ireland there was an eleven-fold increase in enrolments in higher education between 1950 and 1990 (Clancy, 1995). Similarly, in Australia in the ten-year period between 1987 and 1997, the number of students in higher education rose by 67 per cent (DETYA, 1997).

In each of these countries the impetus for expansion has largely come from the government. For example, in the United States, the GI Bill, introduced at the end of the Second World War, had a profound effect on participation rates. It gave millions of returning service men and women the opportunity to go to college, many of whom were the first in their families to go, and who have subsequently ensured that their children have also benefited from a college education. This legislation promoted broader participation in tertiary education in the USA far earlier than in other countries, and recent efforts have focused on gaining equal representation of students from different ethnic and cultural groups.

In Australia, *A Fair Chance for All: Higher Education That's Within Everyone's Reach* (DEET, 1990) was a government initiative to increase access, participation, retention and success in higher education of targeted 'equity groups'. These were listed as Aboriginal and Torres Strait Islander people, people with disabilities, people from low socio-economic backgrounds, people from rural and isolated areas, people from non-English-speaking backgrounds and women in non-traditional subject areas.

More recently, in Ireland the government published the White Paper *Charting Our Education Future* (Department of Education, Ireland, 1995), and the Green Paper *Adult Education in an Era of Lifelong Learning* (1998), the former of which, particularly, emphasized education and training as a necessity for economic development.

In the UK the government has produced or supported a number of reports that contribute to its agenda on expanding and widening participation in post-compulsory education, including:

- The Report of the National Committee of Inquiry into Higher Education (NCIHE), usually referred to as the 'Dearing Report', July 1997;
- *Learning Works: Widening Participation in Further Education*, by Helena Kennedy and produced by the Further Education Funding Council (FEFC), 1997a;

- *The Learning Age*, Green Paper (England), April 1998;
- *Learning is for Everyone*, Green Paper (Wales), April 1998;
- *Opportunity Scotland*, Green Paper (Scotland), September 1998; and
- *Lifelong Learning: A New Culture for All*, Northern Ireland consultation paper, February 1999.

Within the political agendas of European countries, two broad types of drivers can be identified as contributing to the push for expansion, relating to economic and 'non-economic' returns to education. First, economic factors, such as unemployment caused by industrial decline, and the perceived need by governments to develop a 'knowledge economy' or a 'learning society' to ensure success in the 'global' market. The economic argument is premised on theories of human capital and the requirement to invest in human resources, primarily through education and training. During the industrial and manufacturing period, investment was made in plant and machinery to enable heavy industry to operate, but today, so it is argued, the investment must be in human capital. This sentiment is made apparent in the UK government's Green Papers on lifelong learning. In *The Learning Age* it states:

> The Industrial Revolution was built on capital investment in plant and machinery, skills and hard physical labour. British inventors pushed forward the frontiers of technology and our manufacturers turned their inventions into wealth ... Our history shows what we are capable of, but we must now apply the same qualities of skill and invention to a fresh challenge. The information and knowledge-based revolution of the 21st century will be built on a very different foundation – investment in the intellect and creativity of people. (DfEE, 1998a, p. 9)

This assertion raises questions. A fundamental issue is the extent to which higher levels of education and training are genuinely required from the labour force for economic competitiveness, compared with the distortions of spiralling 'qualifications inflation' caused by credentialism on the part of employers. Credentialism denotes the primacy of qualifications, rather than the form or content of the education, or the skills possessed by candidates. These facets of the economy and labour market are explored in Chapter 2.

The second broad type of expansionary drivers relates to the 'non-economic' returns to education – the intrinsic value of education to individuals and society, and an associated desire for greater social equity. These ideas are found in the Green Paper for England, *The Learning Age* (DfEE, 1998a) and the OECD report *Overcoming Exclusion Through Adult Learning* (1999): 'Learning is about opening access to economic activity and resources, and for promoting many aspects of social, cultural and personal life' (OECD, 1999a, p. 20).

The motivation to 'share' these benefits of education may be based on a moral imperative, or simply the pragmatic desire to minimize the risk of social unrest and disturbance (which in turn may disrupt the economy). Extending learning opportunities to social groups who have not traditionally participated may be a covert attempt to subsume people into the dominant culture and, consequently, to 'normalize' and control them (see, for example, Woodrow, 2000 and Preece, 1999b). Alternatively, it may stem from a genuine belief in the personal and social returns of education. The latter, however, will involve changing the form and content of the education available to meet the needs of new and diverse learner groups. Irrespective of the debates regarding the purpose and content of learning, there is no doubt that education is perceived as a major tool in the attempts of UK and European governments to overcome what has been termed 'social exclusion' (see Thomas and Jones, 2000, and Leney, 1999). These issues are discussed further in Chapter 3.

The needs of the economy and concerns with personal development and social justice are broad and complex but, to some extent, interconnected issues. Jary and Thomas (1999, p. 4) note that employment often contributes to personal fulfilment, and, through the income and status it brings, is often a prerequisite for the achievement of other goals such as participation in cultural and leisure activities and 'active citizenship'. For the sake of clarity of analysis, however, economic and non-economic drivers are examined critically in turn. In brief, non-economic motivations for access to further and higher education require that participation is *widened*; in other words, that a greater diversity of people participate in formal education and other learning activities. The economic arguments require an *expansion* in the numbers of people participating in education (and gaining qualifications), but diversity is of secondary or no importance. So although the economic and non-economic returns to education may be correlated, there are also tensions in the access agenda(s): it can be described as 'a mixed bag of a social movement' (*ibid.*, p. 3).

These tensions in the access movement are recognized by Beverly Sand (1998). In a review of government policies and commissioned reports relating to lifelong learning, she identifies three broad attitudes towards education and the expansion of opportunities to non-traditional learners (based on the work of Stephen Ball, 1990). These positions are identified as 'modernizers', 'progressives' and 'cultural restorationists' (Sand, 1998, p. 18). Modernizers emphasize the value of education and training to the *economy*; progressives are liberals, citing the role of education and learning in promoting *social justice* and *self-realization*; while cultural restorationists are reactionaries seeking to preserve *traditional values* and *academic standards*.

The agendas of the economy and personal and social development are represented, but these may be tempered by those claiming that access is about 'dumbing down' (the perceived decline in academic standards, c.f. Jordan, 2000). Although this is an oversimplified view of positions informing policy debates and formulation, it assists with understanding the tensions in the field of access and provides an analytical tool for examining government and institutional approaches to widening participation. In reality, as both Sand (1998) and Williams (1997) point out, policies and practices often span more than one of these positions.

Having reviewed the drivers expanding post-compulsory education and training, particularly in developed countries, Chapter 4 examines the patterns of participation by 'non-traditional' student groups. It disaggregates participation rates, paying particular attention to the *level* and *forms* of participation in relation to socio-economic class, ethnicity, disability, gender, age and entry qualifications, using examples from further and higher education in the UK, and higher education in Australia and Ireland. It shows that despite the numerical expansion in student numbers, this does not necessarily mean that there has been an increase in diversity, or that groups who have traditionally not participated in post-compulsory education are now equally represented. It is therefore important to clarify the distinction between 'increasing' participation and 'widening' participation, as various authors have sought to do. The Kennedy Committee has, arguably, discussed this differentiation most comprehensively. The report says:

> Recent policies to increase participation and achievement in learning have achieved some success, but mainly in providing opportunities for those who have already achieved to continue to do so ... We must widen participation not simply increase it. Widening participation means increasing access to learning and providing opportunities for success to a much wider cross-section of the population than now. (Kennedy, 1997, p. 15)

It is perhaps most helpful to view the distinction as an attempt to move beyond the policies and ideological tendencies of the 1980s, which, through the implementation of the 1988 Education Reform Act and the 1992 Further and Higher Education Act, saw the introduction of market forces to education.

Others have made similar points. For example, Peter Scott (1995) has argued that higher education has expanded not so much by reaching out to new student constituencies, but by exploiting existing constituencies more fully (from Taylor, R., 2000, p. 15). Maggie Woodrow warns of the potential contradiction between widening participation and lifelong learning, unless priority in the latter is given to the former, but current trends in Europe are increasing individual financial responsibility for post-compulsory education, which means that lifelong learning will not be available to everybody (Woodrow, 1999a, p. 11).

A further issue for consideration is 'participation in what?' This book is entitled *Widening Participation in Post-compulsory Education*, and this, to me, is important, as it is not focusing exclusively on one form of learning, such as higher education. In particular, I want to emphasize the importance of working with further education and other forms of tertiary education. This is for two reasons: alternative forms of post-compulsory education often provide routes or ladders of progression into higher education; secondly, the boundaries between educational providers are blurred. For example, in the UK in 1997/98 there were a total of 2,031,103 higher education-level enrolments. 1,800,064 were at higher education institutions and 231,039 were at further education institutions. A final argument should also be noted, that higher education is not necessarily the pinnacle that all students are, or should be, aiming for; some forms of education are more suitable than others at various stages in students' lives. Thus to focus exclusively on widening participation in higher education actually contributes to and reinforces its position at the top of a hierarchy, with other forms of adult and post-compulsory education occupying more lowly positions.

Barriers and opportunities

The second aim of the book is to categorize and explore the different types of 'barriers' that contribute to low participation rates in post-compulsory education by some sectors of society, and the opportunities for access, with a particular focus on students from low socio-economic groups. The term 'barrier' is used to refer to factors that discourage or prevent participation in post-compulsory education. In this book, four categories of barriers are identified. First, there are those related to the education system; second, those linked to income and the labour market; third, the influence of social and cultural factors is considered; and finally, the notion that individual 'deficits' are to blame for non-participation is critiqued. It can be difficult to disentangle the impacts of the education system, the labour market, social and cultural norms, and individual issues, but to aid thinking about barriers to participation the above categories are utilized.

One particular benefit of the utilization of these categories is to raise awareness of, and explore, the assumptions that underpin explanations of non-participation in post-compulsory education and, subsequently, the solutions that are proposed (if indeed, low participation rates are perceived to be problematic). Assumptions tend to vary between individuals, and particularly between different stakeholders, such as potential learners and education providers. If assumptions made by education providers are not in line with the perceptions of the intended beneficiaries, efforts to widen participation can be, at best, ineffective and, at worst, detrimental. The aim of this book is to stimulate thinking about the range of barriers that can impede participation, and so avoid overly focused attention on one set of issues. Once assumptions are identified, they can be critically investigated and analysed, and, if necessary, re-conceptualized. This can best be achieved via participatory planning and implementation processes involving a range of stakeholders, especially those who are expected to benefit from new policy or practice that is being developed.

Chapter 5 explores the notion of assumptions and seeks to demonstrate how the best approaches to widening participation are based on consultation and the involvement of beneficiaries. Although this theme is returned to in Chapter 11, this book does not explore participatory approaches in detail (for further discussion about participatory approaches and applications, see Atweh and Bland, 1999; Atweh, Kemmis and Weeks, 1998; Powell, 1999; and Thomas, 2000). The aim is to encourage policy makers, practitioners, researchers and other 'interested parties' to engage in the process of thinking about assumptions and barriers – and to involve other stakeholders in this process.

Chapters 6 to 10 examine barriers to participation, and related opportunities for access, utilizing the case of students from lower socio-economic groups, and supplemented by examples and issues relating to other groups that are identified in Chapter 4 as under-represented in post-compulsory education. First, Chapter 6 turns to the impact of the compulsory education sector. Schools help to determine the future participation of pupils in further and higher education, partly through educational achievement, as this facilitates progression to the next educational level, and by contributing to the images pupils have of themselves in relation to learning. The chapter looks first at qualifications and achievement, and secondly at attitudes towards learning, and thus the barriers that may be attributable to the compulsory education system.

Chapter 7 considers some of the ways in which the post-compulsory education system inhibits and limits participation in further study by some students, and examines some attempts to overcome these barriers. The state and/or individual institutions determine the structure and operation of the post-compulsory education sector, and, accordingly, have the power to promote or curtail learning opportunities for under-represented groups. Using the example of the UK, in particular, the chapter illustrates how government policy can stimulate participation in post-compulsory learning for non-traditional students, but can also create barriers. A second major barrier to participation for many potential learners is cost, both direct and indirect cost. Further structural barriers that are considered are entry requirements and the role of alternative admission routes, the need for appropriate and flexible learning opportunities, the role of academic and support services and the importance of a receptive institutional culture. The importance of institutional culture is central to the arguments in Chapter 7, as this is crucial in determining the flexibility of the institution, its willingness to change and the extent to which it embraces or suppresses diversity.

Chapter 8 examines some of the ways in which the economy and the labour market inhibit participation in post-compulsory education and training. First, the chapter considers the 'opportunity cost' of post-compulsory education, which is the opportunities or alternative courses of action that must be forgone in order to pursue education. Of particular significance is remuneration from the labour market, in the form of either wages or welfare benefits. A second potential barrier created by the labour market is related to surplus income and the ability to 'invest' in education and training. Family income levels and entitlement to benefits will influence this for both dependent and independent students, as will the direct and indirect costs of education. Opportunities for employment in conjunction with studying, may also be important considerations. Finally, this chapter considers the influence of rates of return from the labour market on participation in post-compulsory education; these are determined by the demand for qualified labour, wages paid and whether or not employers discriminate against some sectors of society.

Chapter 9 focuses on social and cultural barriers to participation and draws on the work of Pierre Bourdieu (Bourdieu and Passeron, 1977), particularly the concepts of *habitus* and *cultural capital*. These notions explain why some social and cultural groups opt not to participate in post-compulsory education, especially higher education. Some forms of tertiary education are both outside of their experience, or habitus, and, secondly, of little value to them, as they do not possess the relevant cultural capital. The chapter considers the relevance of prior experience of post-compulsory education, and of accruing debt to finance post-compulsory education, in shaping the decisions people make about participation. It also revisits the need to develop curricula that are of value to the intended beneficiaries.

Chapter 10 turns to the last category of barriers that is addressed in this book: barriers that are said to exist at the level of the individual. Although it is the case that there are individuals from all walks of life that have overcome disadvantages and successfully accessed education to the highest level, such a position disregards the other issues that affect participation which are discussed in this book. While it is acknowledged that some activities at the level of the individual can be beneficial, this chapter is averse to the notion that individuals are to blame for non-participation in learning. It is therefore critical of initiatives and policies that *only* seek to change the behaviour of individuals, and not the structures of institutions. Consequently, it starts to demonstrate the importance of integrated approaches to widening participation. The chapter utilizes the example of a scheme designed to raise the aspirations of all pupils aged 13 and 14, to illustrate that educational, labour market and social and cultural advantages help to determine the extent to which different pupils benefit from an initiative. The second part of the chapter considers the provision of information, guidance and awareness-raising. There is a clear need for more information, but the aim of such initiatives must not be to blame individuals for not having sufficient information, but to view it as a link or a bridge between the world that potential students inhabit and that of education. Hence, there is a need to recognize the other types of barriers that exist, and target recipients carefully, a theme that is developed in Chapter 11.

Developing a strategic approach to widening participation

Having discussed both the expansion of post-compulsory education and the different types of barriers that can inhibit some learners from participating, the final part of the book considers the need to develop a strategic approach to widening participation. Chapter 11 explores the ideas of creating a 'strategic' approach to widening participation, both at the level of the project and, more broadly (such as within institutions) regionally or nationally. Three elements of the term 'strategic' are considered. The first is the inter-relationship of the different types of barriers to participation *within* a single policy or project. This is illustrated by reference to a scheme that is trying to recognize the range of issues confronting young people who come from families and schools without a tradition of participation in third-level education. The second is the development of coherence and complementarity *between* different policies and projects. Again, an example is used, this time of an Australian university that has attempted to develop an institution-wide approach to widening participation. The third issue is the need for longer-term sustainability, including financial autonomy, ownership by stakeholders (particularly those who traditionally lack authority), the extent to which the capacity of stakeholders is developed and evidence of institutional learning and change.

Of paramount importance in the creation of a strategic approach is to consider *who* is involved; this relates to the discussion in Chapter 5 regarding the assumptions underpinning policies and practice, and that assumptions made, for example by a provider, may not coincide with those of the intended beneficiary group. In which case a policy or initiative founded on assumptions, rather than consultation and research, may be, at best, less effective, and at worst, damaging.

In order to help to promote awareness of a broad range of barriers facing potential entrants, and to assist with strategic thinking, at the end of each chapter (5–11) some 'key questions' are posed. These are not intended to act as a checklist, but to stimulate thinking, and, in particular, they could be used in participative planning processes to initiate discussions.

Chapters 12, 13 and 14 present three case studies of initiatives from institutions in Sweden, the UK and Ireland that are intended to widen participation to under-represented groups in communities that are socially and geographically marginalized from post-compulsory education and training. Each case study provides a necessarily subjective description of the initiative based on data from a range of sources. These examples are not presented as 'best practice', but are meant to provide an opportunity to use the framework of analysis advocated in this book to think about 'real world' initiatives. The assumptions that underpin each case study are reviewed, as is its effectiveness in relation to the four categories of barriers discussed in the preceding chapters. Finally, the extent to which a widening participation strategy, rather than a short-term and marginal project, has been implemented is reviewed. This is not to evaluate each initiative, and thus pronounce its utility and effectiveness, but to seek to illustrate the different assumptions that can underpin outreach work, and the potential benefits of moving towards strategic thinking, involving a range of stakeholders.

At the end of each chapter is a grid listing the main issues (culled from the questions posed at the end of Chapters 5–11 and presented in Appendix 1), and a 'score' of how well I think the scheme rates in relation to these issues. This is *not* an objective score, and, as such, is of no value. Instead, the *process* of completing the grid is perceived to be of value, particularly when it is undertaken as a group activity and used to stimulate reflection and debate between stakeholders. The scores indicated in the grids relate to my perceptions and are based on my limited and necessarily biased information about the projects.

Chapter 12 focuses on a distance-learning programme using information and communication technology (ICT) and video-conferencing to deliver higher-education modules in one province in Sweden. Chapter 13 considers an initiative providing outreach education in the UK, centred on the employment of education-community link-workers to raise awareness about educational opportunities, to assess needs and to make arrangements for community-based course provision. The final case study in Chapter 14 is a programme of higher-education courses in Community Education and Development, which are delivered in outreach locations in the south-east of Ireland by an institute of technology and community group partners. The form and content of the courses are strongly influenced by the participants.

The concluding argument is that to acknowledge only one category (especially one particular barrier), is unlikely to be the most effective way of addressing the complex issues surrounding non-participation by some sectors of society. To recognize and remedy only one of the barriers to access may even be counter-productive, as non-traditional students may enter education but be unable to complete, as other obstacles remain in place. For example, providing education in a more accessible location, without offering appropriate personal and support services, may be insufficient and may result in withdrawal. This experience, which could be perceived as 'failure' (whether by students or institutions), may discourage or prohibit future involvement in formal learning. As a result, it is suggested that an effective strategy to widen participation among under-represented groups of students must take account of the different barriers that exist, and must seek to develop a participatory approach that engages with as wide a range of factors as possible.

CHAPTER 2

Modernizers and the Economic Drive for Expansion

Introduction

This chapter examines and questions the economic arguments and motivations for expanding third-level education and training. It considers the contentions of modernizers regarding the needs of post-industrial economies, particularly the necessary investment in 'human capital', the notion that more education and training improves people's ability to generate an economic return. These economic claims are then questioned by reference to the notion of 'qualifications inflation', and inequalities in the labour market.

Economic decline and the development of a post-modern economy

Within government circles *economic* motivations, rather than those of personal development and equity, dominate and subsequently steer the expansion of post-compulsory education. This is reflected in government policy statements, and in the way that further and higher education is funded. David Blunkett, when UK Secretary of State for Education and Employment stated, in the preface to *The Learning Age* Green paper:

> Learning is the key to prosperity – for each of us as individuals, as well as for the nation as a whole. Investment in human capital will be the foundation of success in the knowledge-based global economy of the twenty-first century. (DfEE, 1998, p. 7)

A government committed to widening participation in post-compulsory education for predominantly non-economic or liberal reasons is unlikely to adversely change the funding mechanisms, as can be witnessed in both the further and higher education sectors in the

UK. There are restrictions on the funding further education colleges can access in respect of participants on courses who are not deemed to enhance labour market participation. These are so-called 'leisure courses' that do not lead directly or indirectly to qualifications. (This was an outcome of the Further and Higher Education Act, 1992; see Kennedy, 1997, p. 33.) Secondly, the changes in the funding arrangements in higher education affect students directly, through the introduction of fees and the replacement of maintenance grants with loans. This system *expects* graduates to reap economic returns via their participation in the labour market, and this is evinced by the student loan system itself – older students are not entitled to student loans, irrespective of their personal circumstances. This, one can only conclude, is due to the reduced employment opportunities available to this age group (see DfEE, 1998b).

The dominance of economic arguments for the expansion of tertiary education and lifelong learning is perpetuated in other developed countries. Woodrow *et al.* (2000) examined lifelong learning policies in five European countries (Finland, France, Germany, Ireland and the UK) in search of a "social inclusion" model of higher education', but found 'In each report, references to the primacy of the economy and the responsibility of the individual abound' (p. 9). The following pages examine the economic motivations driving the expansion of post-compulsory education.

Industrial decline and the growth of structural unemployment
Most countries in Europe (and the rest of the so-called 'developed' world) except countries, such as Norway, that have bypassed the industrial revolution of the last two centuries (OECD, 1999a, p. 113), have experienced severe structural unemployment in the latter part of the twentieth century. This is demonstrated in the unemployment figures for OECD countries (Table 2.1). The unemployment rate in the UK in 1997 was 7.1 per cent, which was above the OECD average of 6.9 per cent, but was similar to that of other European countries. Indeed the European Union average (based on 15 member states) was 10.6 per cent in 1997.

The justification for the expansion of participation in post-compulsory education, premised on 'industrial decline', can be demonstrated by reference to the UK. The expansion in student numbers *may* include greater diversity, but this is not an essential requirement for modernizers; indeed, it may be of secondary or no importance.

In the last two decades of the twentieth century, 7.5 million

Table 2.1: Unemployment[1] in OECD countries

	Both sexes % of total labour force		Women % of total female labour force		Men % of total male labour force	
	1997	1987	1997	1987	1997	1987
Australia	8.6	7.8	8.3	8.3	8.7	7.4
Austria	4.2	3.8	4.7	4.1	3.9	3.6
Belgium	12.7[a]	11.3	16.6[a]	16.4	9.6[a]	7.8
Canada	9.2	8.8	9.1	9.3	9.2	8.5
Czech Republic	4.6	...	5.7	...	3.8	...
Denmark	6.1	5.4	7.5	6.1	4.9	4.8
Finland	14.3	5.0	15.0	4.3	13.7	5.7
France	12.4	10.5	14.3	13.6	10.9	8.3
Germany	9.8	7.6[b]	10.9	8.8[b]	8.9	6.8[b]
Greece	10.3[a]	7.4	16.6[a]	11.3	6.3[a]	5.1
Hungary	8.7	...	7.8	...	9.5	...
Iceland	4.1	0.5	4.3	...	3.8	...
Ireland	10.3	17.6	13.5	10.4	19.4	
Italy	12.2	11.8	16.9	18.5	9.4	8.0
Japan	3.4	2.8	3.4	2.8	3.4	2.8
Korea	2.6	3.1	2.3	...	2.8	...
Luxembourg	2.7	1.6	2.8	2.0	2.7	1.3
Mexico	3.5	...	4.7	...	2.9	...
Netherlands	5.5	9.6	7.0	13.6	4.4	7.2
New Zealand	6.5	4.0	6.6	4.2	6.5	3.9
Norway	4.1	2.1	4.3	2.6	4.0	1.7
Poland	11.1	...	13.2	...	9.4	...
Portugal	6.7	7.0	7.6	9.4	6.0	5.2
Spain	20.6	20.1	28.1	27.2	15.8	16.7
Sweden	8.0	1.9	7.6	1.9	8.4	1.9
Switzerland	4.2	0.7	4.3	0.9	4.1	0.6
Turkey	6.2	8.1	7.4	...	5.8	...
United Kingdom	7.1	10.4	5.8	7.6	8.1	12.4
United States	4.9	6.1	5.0	6.2	4.8	6.0
G7[2]	6.6	6.9	7.1	7.5	6.3	6.5
EU – 15[2]	10.6	10.2	12.4	12.1	9.3	9.0
OECD total [2]	6.9	...	7.7	...	6.3	...

... not available
1. national definitions
2. Only data shown in this table are included in these totals.
a. 1996
b. former West Germany only

Source: *Labour Force Statistics: 1977–1997*, OECD, Paris 1999 and *Employment Outlook*, OECD, Paris, June 1998. Reprinted from OECD, 1999b, p. 20.

unskilled jobs disappeared in the UK. Coal mining alone employed 250,000 workers and supported 6 million people – but by the mid-1990s all mining and quarrying activities, combined, accounted for just 0.5 per cent of the workforce. A recent OECD publication noted that now 'coal mines and factories are part of a national heritage; miners and weavers now serve as tourist guides' (OECD, 1999a, p. 155). These somewhat flippant comments do serve to reinforce the severity of the situation.

It can be seen, by referring to Table 2.2, that unemployment in developed countries has tended to affect young people to a greater extent than the entire workforce, although these figures do hide trends in other age cohorts.

High levels of youth unemployment tend to encourage more young people to enter post-compulsory education, as well as encouraging governments to direct young people towards education and training – either with a 'carrot' or a 'stick' approach. This has been witnessed in the UK by the expansion of youth employment and training schemes at times when there is particularly high unemployment. For example, the introduction of Youth Training Schemes (YTS) in the 1980s (see Banks *et al.*, 1992) and the New Deal initiative in the late 1990s. Both of these programmes encouraged or even compelled young people into low-paid jobs with a training element, at times when reducing youth unemployment was a political expedient (see Chapter 8).

The 1990s saw an increase in youth unemployment, and an increase in participation in all forms of education and training. In the UK and Europe there has been growth in the introduction of schemes to capture the bottom 10–20 per cent of each age cohort who leave school without any qualifications, and the expansion of work-based training and day-release schemes to service the next level of school leavers who enter employment. The trend throughout Europe has been to increase participation in post-16 education, so that for the majority of young people the end of compulsory schooling does not mark the end of formal education and training (Leney, 1999, p. 42). Hence, it can be argued that education and training are short-term antidotes to structural changes in the economy and associated unemployment.

Towards an information and knowledge society

The post-industrial economy, or the information and knowledge society, is characterized by a declining dependence on manufacturing and heavy industry, the rise of new service industries (especially those based on new technology) and the increasing importance of 'knowl-

Table 2.2: Youth unemployment[1] in OECD countries

	Women		Men		Labour force	
	1997	1987	1997	1987	1997	1987
Australia	14.5	14.3	17.1	14.8	8.6	7.8
Austria	7.6	...	5.5	...	4.2	3.8
Belgium	25.7	28.6	17.6	14.7	12.7	11.3
Canada	15.7	12.3	17.6	14.6	9.2	8.8
Czech Republic	10.0	...	7.3	...	4.6	...
Denmark	9.9	10.0	6.6	8.0	6.1	5.4
Finland	25.0	8.1	22.0	9.7	14.3	5.0
France	32.8	28.5	24.6	18.3	12.4	10.5
Germany	9.6	9.0[b]	10.3	8.0[b]	9.8	7.6[b]
Greece	40.6	33.8	22.2	17.5	10.3	7.4
Hungary	14.5	...	16.9	...	8.7	...
Iceland	7.1	...	8.3	...	4.1	0.5
Ireland	15.2	21.4	16.9	27.2	10.3	17.6
Italy	39.3	42.2	29.1	29.8	12.2	11.8
Japan	6.3	5.0	6.9	5.4	3.4	2.8
Korea	6.6	6.0	9.4	10.0	2.6	3.1
Luxembourg	9.2	6.2	5.6	3.8	2.7	1.6
Mexico	7.8	...	5.4	...	3.5	...
Netherlands	10.0	16.9	9.1	12.9	5.5	9.6
New Zealand	13.0	7.6	13.2	8.4	6.5	4.0
Norway	11.1	6.6	10.1	4.2	4.1	2.1
Poland	28.0	...	22	...	11.1	...
Portugal	18.0	22.0	11.0	14.0	6.7	7.0
Spain	46.1	49.3	30.3	33.7	20.6	20.1
Sweden	21.9	5.4	23.0	5.3	8.0	1.9
Switzerland	3.8	...	8.0	...	4.2	0.7
Turkey	15.0	...	14.0	...	6.2	8.1
United Kingdom	11.0	14.7	15.6	16.7	7.1	10.4
United States	10.7	11.7	11.8	12.6	4.9	6.1
G7[2]	12.8	14.3	13.3	13.5	6.6	6.9
EU – 15[2]	22.3	23.7	18.6	18.5	10.6	10.2
OECD total[2]	13.9	15.6	12.9	14.4	6.9	...

... not available
1. national definitions
2. Only data shown in this table are included in these totals.
a. 1996
b. former West Germany only

Source: Labour Force Statistics: 1977–1997, OECD, Paris, 1999, and Employment Outlook, OECD, Paris, June 1998. Reprinted from OECD, 1999b, p. 20.

edge' in production and consumption. These societies are focused on knowledge (or information – see Coffield and Williamson, 1997a), and the production of new knowledge. An examination of employment patterns by sector in OECD countries, many of which may be described as post-industrial or knowledge economies, shows a decline away from both primary (agriculture, forestry and fishing) and manufacturing industries towards the provision of services (Table 1.3). The USA, Canada, Australia, the UK and some European counterparts can be seen to have had more than 70 per cent of the labour force employed in service industries in 1997, and the trend is towards further increases.

A consequence of the knowledge or information society is greater emphasis on further and higher education. Bell (1974) proposed that in the post-industrial society knowledge is the primary source of innovation and the basis of social organization, so knowledge-based professional occupational groups achieve dominance in the class structure. Galbraith (1967) predicted that the technical and bureaucratic class – technocrats – would replace the previously dominant capitalist class, creating a technostructure. It can be argued that there is evidence of these changes occurring in society now.

This functionalist approach can be summarized briefly as comprising the following stages (for discussion see Brown and Scase, 1994 and Coffield and Williamson, 1997b): rapid technological change, including new methods of production and the globalization of world trade lead to a perceived need for a more skilled workforce. Consequently, employers demand increasing skill levels (via both compulsory and post-compulsory education), and further and higher education expand accordingly, to provide an increased number of qualified personnel. Finally, this model advocates that technostructures should be 'learning societies' to ensure continual improvement, because 'competitiveness is dynamic' (HMSO, 1994). In this 'dangerously oversimplified account' (Coffield and Williamson, 1997b, p. 9) 'the key to sustainable economic prosperity is considered to be highly skilled workers who are also lifelong, flexible learners' (p. 10).

Internationally, and at governmental level, the concepts of a 'knowledge society' and a learning society have undoubtedly become attractive. Economic competition is a key motivating factor, as governments are keen to attain the benefits that education potentially yields. In a climate of globalization and post-industrialization, governments seem to believe that the main economic benefits will be gained by those countries that acquire the most knowledge, and achieve the most learning of the appropriate kind, to support the new

Table 2.3: Employment by sector in OECD countries

	% agriculture forestry and fishing		% industry		% services	
	1997	1987	1997	1987	1997	1987
Australia	5.2	5.7	22.1	26.2	72.7	68.1
Austria	6.8	8.6	30.3	37.7	63.8	53.7
Belgium	2.3	3.0	26.0	28.8	71.4	68.2
Canada	3.9	4.7	23.2	25.3	73.0	70.0
Czech Republic	5.8	12	41.6	47.5	52.5	40.5
Denmark	3.7	5.7	26.8	28.2	69.5	66.0
Finland	7.1	10.4	27.5	31.2	65.5	58.4
France	4.5	7	25.6	30.8	69.9	62.2
Germany	3.2	4.2^b	36.5	40.4^b	60.2	55.4^b
Greece	20.3	27.0	22.9	28.0	56.9	45.0
Hungary	8.0	...	33.4	...	57.0	...
Iceland	8.5	10.6	25.4	31.8	665.5	57.6
Ireland	10.4	15.3	28.4	27.9	61.7	57.0
Italy	6.8	10.5	32	32.6	61.2	56.8
Japan	5.3	8.3	33.1	33.8	61.6	57.9
Korea	11.0	21.9	31.3	32.6	57.7	45.5
Luxembourg	2.6	4.1	25.6	33.1	71.8	62.7
Mexico	23.2	...	22.7	...	54.1	...
Netherlands	3.7	4.9	22.2	26.8	74.1	68.3
New Zealand	8.5	10.3	23.8	27.4	67.6	62.2
Norway	4.8	6.7	23.7	27.0	71.6	66.3
Poland	20.6	...	31.9	...	47.5	...
Portugal	13.7	22.2	31.5	34.9	54.8	42.9
Spain	8.4	15.1	30.0	32.3	61.7	52.5
Sweden	2.8	3.9	26.0	29.7	71.3	66.3
Switzerland	4.7	5.7	26.8	34.6	68.6	57.5
Turkey	41.9	47.1	23.4	21.9	34.7	31.0
United Kingdom	1.9	2.3	26.9	32.9	71.3	64.8
United States	2.7	3.0	23.9	27.1	73.4	69.9
G7^1	3.7	5.1	28.1	30.9	68.2	63.9
EU – 15^1	5.0	7.7	29.8	33.4	65.2	59.0
OECD Total^1	8.2	...	27.7	...	64.1	...

... not available
1. Only data shown in this table are included in these totals.
a. 1996
b. former West Germany only

Source: *Labour Force Statistics: 1977–1997*, OECD, Paris, 1999. Reprinted from OECD,1999b, p. 16.

industrial service economy. The limits to this argument – primarily the existence of 'credentialism' (i.e. that recruitment decisions are made on the basis of qualifications, which are taken as a proxy for relevant knowledge and skills) and the lack of demand for highly educated employees – are discussed below.

A flexible workforce

In addition to the acquisition of specific learning for employment, the workforce (or, at least, sections of it) needs to become ever more flexible to cope with the rapid cycles of change. The information revolution caused significant changes to UK employment patterns, and most of the new jobs that have been created have been in the service sectors (Table 2.3). Much of this new employment has, however, been in the form of part-time employment and fixed-term contracts, affording employers much greater flexibility but reducing the security of employees. There has also been a growth in self-employment and very small firms, again increasing insecurity. The growth in part-time employment and self-employment has occurred throughout Europe and the OECD countries. For example, with the exception only of the Netherlands, male part-time employment has increased between 1987 and 1997 in every OECD country. The growth of part-time and self-employment is shown in Table 2.4.

OECD figures show that in the ten years from 1986 to 1996, the number of men in part-time jobs almost doubled from 4.6% to 8.1% of the male workforce. In the same period male unemployment rates fell from 13.5% to 9.7%, while female rates fell from 8.9% to 6.3%.

These structural changes in the economy require increased flexibility. Greater job insecurity requires actual or potential members of the labour force to update skills and re-train as necessary, and to acquire new skills such as self-management, administrative skills, negotiation skills, financial management skills and self-directed learning. Tony Watts and Brian Stevens (1999) have discussed the new imperative for workers to manage both their long-term careers and financial affairs. Responsibility for ongoing learning and career management is now that of the individual, and it is in this context that the conception of lifelong *earning* gives way to the conception of the necessity for lifelong *learning* (Jary and Thomas, 1999). This has been described by Ulrich Beck (1992) as an aspect of the 'risk society', and involves the removal of traditional employment patterns and associated securities, being replaced by pluralistic and more fluid patterns of work, and personal responsibility.

From the perspective of a modernizer it can be argued that an

Table 2.4: Part-time[1] and self-employment in OECD countries

	Part-time employment (% of total employment)						Self-employment (%) of total employment	
	Both sexes		Women		Men			
	1997	1987	1997	1987	1997	1987	1997	1987
Australia	25.6a	20.8	40.0a	35.9	14.2a	10.2	14.3	15.4
Austria	10.8	...	22.0	...	2.1	...	13.5	10.4
Belgium	17.4	14.1	34.3	30.1	5.0	4.9	15.2b	14.4
Canada	17.8	15.7	27.5	25.7	9.6	7.9	11.4	9.0
Czech Republic	3.3	...	5.3	...	1.7	...	12.0	...
Denmark	17.9	20.6	24.7	32.5	11.9	9.8	8.0	9.3
Finland	8.5	7.0	11.7	10.2	5.3	3.6	14.1	14.3
France	15.5	12.5	25.6	21.9	6.3	5.1	11.1	15.6
Germany	15.0b	10.5c	29.8b	25.0c	3.3b	1.1c	9.6	8.9c
Greece	8.7	7.1	14.2	12.9	5.3	4.4	33.7b	35.4
Hungary	3.3	...	5.0	...	1.8	...	11.0	...
Iceland	23.0	...	36.7	...	9.6		17.6	15.3
Ireland	16.7	9.2	27.1	17.1	8.0	4.1	19.5	21.8
Italy	12.4	8.5	24	17.8	5.1	3.6	24.6	24.6
Japan	23.2a	16.5	38.3a	30.4	12.9a	7.3	11.8	15.5
Korea	5.1a	...	7.8a	...	3.3a	...	28.3	30.5
Luxembourg	10.7	8.3	25.3	21.2	2.1	1.5	7.3	10.8
Mexico	10.4	...	19.5	...	5.9	...	29.0	...
Netherlands	29.1	25.4	54.6	49.7	10.6	12.1	11.5	9.9
New Zealand	22.7	17.6	37.4	32.6	10.9	6.7	19.3	17.5
Norway	21.5	...	36.8	...	7.8	...	7.8	9.0
Poland	4.5a	...	5.5a	...	3.7a	...	23.1	...
Portugal	7.9	6.6	14.1	13.8	2.7	1.9	27.4	32.2
Spain	7.9	4.2	16.6	11.3	2.8	1.3	20.8	23.1
Sweden	15.7	18.5	24.5	31.5	6.7	5.5	10.4	8.7
Switzerland	24.4	...	45.7	...	6.6	...	11.0	...
Turkey	5.8b	...	12.7b	...	2.9b	...	31.8	...
United Kingdom	23.1	21.4	40.1	41.5	7.6	4.9	12.6	12.4
United States	13.6	14.4	19.5	21.0	8.3	8.6	8.1	8.6
G7[2]	15.7	14.2	25.2	24.2	7.4	6.4	10.8	12.2
EU − 15[2]	16.6	13.4	30.6	27.5	5.5	3.9	14.8	15.9
OECD Total[2]	14.2	14.2	23.4	24.7	6.7	6.3	15.1	...

... not available
1 defined by a common definition based on 30 hours or less worked per week
2 Only data shown in this table are included in these totals.
a. based on 35 hours or less worked per week
b. 1996
c. former West Germany only

Source: *Labour Force Statistics: 1977–1997*, OECD, Paris 1999, and *Employment Outlook*, OECD, Paris, June 1998. Reprinted from OECD, 1999b, p. 18.

expansion in participation in post-compulsory education is a necessary consequence of late capitalism. The labour market is clearly undergoing almost unparalleled vicissitudes, and those seeking access to the labour market may, more than ever before, require specific and relevant training. Consequently, the role of post-compulsory education appears crucial (though what forms provision takes, and precisely what is taught will remain contested). Succinctly, learning may have become essential just to 'keep up', and in order for individuals to avoid becoming excluded from the labour market and, in many ways, wider society. Furthermore, extended participation in full-time education and training may not only equip potential employees with the qualifications and skills demanded by employers but may also reduce unemployment statistics and associated welfare costs.

There is not, however, a simple, direct correlation between industrial decline, increases in structural unemployment and the emergence of a post-industrial economy, and the expansion in participation in post-compulsory education. This can be demonstrated by an examination of the differential impact of unemployment and socio-economic change on men and women and their respective participation rates in all forms of learning. In the UK men have experienced greater unemployment than women, and there have been greater increases in male part-time employment and self-employment (although far more women than men currently work part-time). Growth in participation in higher education by women, however, has been faster than amongst men. Coffield and Vignoles (1997) note that an 'enormously significant development is that there are now equal proportions of women and men studying for a first degree' (p. 9) (Coffield and Vignoles cite UCAS, 1995 and Ramsden, 1997). It is therefore necessary to look beyond the needs of the economy in order to appreciate the range of sometimes competing explanations for the expansion of post-compulsory education.

'Imperfections' in the labour market: qualification inflation and discrimination

A second economic explanation for the expansion of post-compulsory education may be attributed not to a genuine demand for a more highly educated and skilled workforce; it may be caused by 'qualification inflation' in the labour market and discrimination by employers. The economic arguments outlined above assume that investing in human capital is comparable to any other investment. In other words, enhanced investment in education and training subsequently increases the financial returns received. This reasoning can be applied both to the economy as a whole and to the individuals concerned. The existence of qualification inflation and employer discrimination, however, denies the simple correlation between education and training, and success in the labour market.

Qualification inflation

The notion of 'qualification inflation' contends that potential employees are expected to hold higher qualifications than were previously needed in order to gain jobs that previously required lower or no qualifications. There are many such examples of this phenomenon, an obvious example being qualified teacher status. The prerequisite for this was two years' teacher training, until the late 1960s, when a three-year degree plus a one-year post-graduate teacher-training course was introduced as the professional standard. Similarly, nurses and other medical staff now require higher-level qualifications and more frequent professional development training than in the past. The growth in National Vocational Qualifications (NVQs) and undergraduate degree courses in health-related studies evince these changes.

Enhanced qualification requirements may be caused by 'vertical substitution' in the labour market. This implies that employers engage in upward substitution and employ people with higher qualifications for a particular job than were necessary in the past, while downward substitution is affecting graduates – previously a degree would probably have enabled them to secure employment at a higher level than it does today. The value of educational credentials subsequently declines as a larger number and proportion of each age cohort attains more and higher qualifications, if this is not accompanied by an expansion of elite employment opportunities. There is, therefore, a real danger that expanding education to an ever-increasing proportion of the population will not challenge existing discrimination on the basis of class, gender, ethnicity and so on, but will reinforce social divisions. Coffield and Williamson note this point:

> Additional public investment in higher and further education may only result in disappointment and frustration for future cohorts of graduates unless a means is found of increasing the demand for skills across the British economy. (Coffield and Williamson, 1997b, p. 11)

Recognition of this phenomenon is not new. In 1970, Ivar Berg referred to the situation as 'the great training robbery' and described the spiralling educational requirements as 'a race in which all run harder and nobody gains'. And in 1976, Dore called the same phenomenon 'the diploma disease', and noted the paradox that: 'the worse the educated unemployment situation gets and the more useless educational certificates become, the *stronger* grows the pressure for an expansion of educational facilities' (Dore, 1976, p. 4, quoted in Coffield and Williamson, 1997b, p. 13, original emphasis).

Coffield and Williamson argue that the direct link between economic change and the expansion of post-compulsory education is 'too one-sided' (*ibid.*, p. 10). The relationship between physical and human capital is complex, and one consequence of late capitalism is continued industrial automation, reducing, rather than increasing, dependence on skilled labour (see Parsons and Marshall, 1995). So while there is growing demand for highly skilled employees with specific attributes, there is also expansion of 'marginal' employment (Atkinson, 1998). Characteristically, these are temporary, low-wage and low-skill jobs. Such employment is the proverbial 'McJob', undertaken by members of Douglas Coupland's Generation X (Coupland, 1996, p. 5). Conversely, regular jobs have the expectation of continuing employment, offer training and prospects of internal promotion, and are covered by employment protection. Hence the polarization of employment opportunities may more accurately describe the post-industrial labour market: 'the result may be a highly skilled elite and a growing army of the (at best) semi-skilled and expendable' (Coffield and Williamson, 1997b, p. 10).

Coffield and Williamson (1997b, pp. 10–11) note that what commentators such as Reich (1993) in the USA and Ball (1995) in the UK have overlooked is the relatively limited demand for highly educated and -skilled employees. Consequently, those social groups who already have relatively high levels of education and skill can consolidate and improve their position, while the unskilled and semi-skilled do not experience a commensurate improvement in their skills or, concomitantly, their social position. Indeed, research carried out by the Joseph Rowntree Foundation, in 1995, found that the wages of the bottom 10 per cent of UK society hardly changed in real terms between 1979 and 1992, while those of the top 10 per cent rose by 50 per cent. Furthermore, Arulampalam and Booth (1998) report that workers on short-term employment contracts, or who are not covered by a union collective agreement, are significantly less likely to be involved in any work-related training to improve or increase their skills (p. 65). Gallie attributes 'skills stagnation' to class and gender discrimination in skill formation and development (Gallie, 1994 and Gallie and White, 1993). And Arulampalam and Booth comment that there seems to be a trade-off between expanding more marginal forms of employment, and expanding the proportion of the workforce getting work-related training (*op. cit.*, p. 65).

Growth in postgraduate education has allowed those with access to sufficient funds to further improve their advantage in the labour market. People from higher socio-economic classes (who are generally the more affluent) are likely to wish to preserve their status in the labour market and to send out appropriate signals to employers. Consequently, those who can afford to do so will not only graduate but will also study at postgraduate level (see Hirsch, 1977). This can readily be seen to be occurring in the UK. Bob Burgess reports that 'since 1979, the number of postgraduate students in the UK has risen from around 100,000 to 335,325' (Burgess, 1997, p. 5). This represents over a 300 per cent increase in postgraduate numbers, which reinforces qualification inflation, as Dore's paradox suggests.

Labour market discrimination
Increased participation in post-compulsory education and training has resulted in an expansion in the number and level of qualifications held by those seeking employment. Consequently, employers may undertake 'screening'. Screening can be defined as the use of qualifications as a means of selecting among candidates for employment, where it is the general level of qualification that is decisive rather than the particular contents of the education or training received. Employers may use educational qualifications, or sometimes also the type of institution attended, as a proxy for attributes such as social class, rather than the direct benefits of the education received, and the knowledge and skills required for the job in question (see Chapter 9). According to the 'screening hypothesis', it is the screening process itself, rather than any direct economic return on education, which helps to explain the correlation between level of education and income. Furthermore, the prioritizing of qualifications by employers continues to fuel the expansion of certification and, consequently, post-compulsory education. This, however, does not translate into increased productivity or competitiveness for the national economy; thus, this position is opposed to the human capital argument outlined previously.

The lack of demand for graduates (or the limited supply of 'elite' jobs), and the intensification of screening, fosters differentiation in the post-compulsory education sector on the basis of institution, subject and qualification level and grade (or degree classification). In the UK there is evidence of screening by employers in relation to the HE institution attended (see Brennan and McGeevor, 1988), although this in itself is nothing new – Oxford and Cambridge graduates have always commanded higher salaries (see Halsey, 1995, p. 31). The creation of a unitary higher education system has not altered this reality, as Coffield and Williamson note:

> Britain's blue chip companies are not, of course, even-handed in the universities they are prepared to recruit graduates from, with the result that more than 20 per cent of graduates from some of the 'new' universities are still unemployed six months after graduation. The unemployment rate for new graduates in the system as a whole was 11 per cent in 1993. (Coffield and Williamson, 1997b, p. 14)

In the UK the current proposals from the Russell Group of universities for elite institutions to charge massively higher fees threatens to reinforce differentiation between institutions and challenge the single notion of generic 'graduateness' further. In 1999–2000, UK university fees for home and European students were capped at £1025 per year and top-up fees are illegal, but: 'some of the country's most prestigious universities are considering charging up to £60,000 for a degree' (Grimston and Waterhouse, 2000). This would create a UK 'ivy league' of about twenty universities, below which would be 'regional' universities that would remain in the state system.

The Russell Group report (by Sir Colin Campbell, Vice-chancellor of Nottingham University) suggests that scholarships would be available for poorer students who cannot afford the fees, and as a result they are not contravening the government's aim of widening participation in higher education. There are, however, serious questions regarding the feasibility of this; in the USA (on which these proposals are modelled) elite institutions have very large endowment funds that are drawn on to support approximately half of their undergraduates through scholarships, low-interest loans and other forms of financial assistance. Even the wealthiest UK institutions do not have these financial assets. If these proposals are progressed, differentiation in the graduate labour market will be formalized and, for example, HE graduates from further education colleges may find that their degree is significantly devalued (Robertson, 1994).

Not only is the institution attended a factor affecting employment prospects; subject, level and type of qualification attained are also important. A survey for *The Sunday Times* revealed that 'science graduates earn the best salaries' (Waterhouse, 2000), but they are not necessarily employed in scientific posts. Conversely, a UK university was derided by the media for offering degree courses in Indian cookery, but there is no logical reason why the process of studying this subject equips a graduate less well for participation in the general labour market than a degree in many other subjects. However, Abigail McKnight found that 'employment in a non-graduate occupation is associated with particular degree subjects, gender, low entry qualifications and degree class' (DfEE et al., 1999, p. 6).

There is further discrimination in the labour market on the basis of class, ethnicity and gender, which again calls into question the reasons for expanding participation in post-compulsory education if traditional hierarchies are not challenged and allowed to remain intact. Research carried out in the UK by the Institute for Employment Research (Purcell et al., 1999) and published by the Council for Industry and Higher Education (CIHE) found 'extensive social class discrimination in graduate employment' (Taylor, 1999, p. 15). George Taylor, the CIHE adviser on widening participation said 'the general message is that those from a socially disadvantaged environment are less likely to win through, even if their achievements are comparable with those from more traditional backgrounds' (ibid.).

A similar picture exists for black graduates in the UK: 'graduates from Pakistani or Black African communities are more than three times as likely to be unemployed as white graduates' (HEFCE, 2000, p. 1). Research carried out by the Policy Studies Institute found that minority respondents reported widespread evidence of discrimination in job applications and promotion. For example, in a study of ethnic-minority staff working in higher education in the UK, approximately 20 per cent of respondents said that they had personally experienced discrimination in job applications or in promotion and had experienced racial harassment. This percentage increases for different groups: 30 per cent of non-British minorities reported that they had been discriminated against in job applications and a quarter of minority women said they had experienced racial harassment (Carter et al., 1999; see also Taylor, 2000). Thus, it must be concluded that if such discrimination exists in employment in higher education, the situation must be at least as bad, if not worse in other employment sectors.

Conclusions

Government policy advocates the expansion of third-level education to meet the needs of the economy, but evidence of credentialism and discrimination in the labour market is opposed to the human capital view of education. A more highly educated workforce may contribute to the prosperity of the economy and the individuals concerned.

Conversely, post-compulsory education may contribute to a 'zero-sum' situation, as increased qualifications do not correlate to increased returns to the economy or individuals. The latter view questions the extent to which education directly serves the needs of the economy, as qualifications are used to facilitate a screening process to select employees, rather than to prepare people with knowledge and skills to assist them to perform better. If there is not sufficient demand for a more highly educated and skilled labour force, those who embark on further and higher education with the intention of improving their employment status may be frustrated, as the number of appropriate jobs has not expanded. It is highly likely that traditionally disadvantaged social groups continue to lose out as a result of persistent inequalities in the labour market.

From the individual perspective, however, it may be necessary to obtain qualifications in post-compulsory education in order to *maintain* one's position in society – hence Berg's notion of a 'race in which all run harder but nobody wins'. For example, although graduates may experience some difficulty securing employment, in most countries they are less likely to be unemployed than non-graduates (Teichler, 1988, p. 29; see also Institute for Employment Research, 1999). Furthermore, as Adnett and Coates (1999) note 'graduate status is one of the most important ways in which women can protect themselves against the negative labour market consequences of family formation in later life' (p. 13; see also Sommerland and Sanderson, 1997).

The economic drivers of expansion are complex and disputed. To understand the expansion in post-compulsory education more fully it is necessary to move beyond the agenda of the modernizers and examine the non-economic drivers, such as self-fulfilment, personal development and to contribute to overcoming 'social exclusion'. These issues are discussed in the next chapter.

CHAPTER 3

Progressives and the Personal and Social Benefits of Post-compulsory Education

Introduction

It was noted in Chapter 1 that three broad attitudes towards widening participation in post-compulsory education to non-traditional students can be identified: those of modernizers; progressives; and traditionalists, or cultural restorationists. The previous chapter examined and critiqued the agenda of the modernizers which, simply stated, focuses on expanding education and training for economic purposes. This chapter considers the progressive or liberal perspective which, in summary, contends that education has personal, social and cultural benefits which add to or even supersede instrumental gains. These can be described as the 'non-economic' benefits of education.

First, this chapter contemplates the notion of 'education for its own sake', which rests on the premise that knowledge has an intrinsic value. Extending this argument, the chapter considers how education is of benefit to individuals personally, and, in particular, draws on the work of Paulo Freire.

Once one has established that education has non-economic benefits to individuals and, subsequently, everyone has the potential to benefit from learning (irrespective of their potential contribution to the economy), this raises issues relating to people's rights of access to all forms of knowledge acquisition. Hence the chapter turns to examine notions of citizenship, in particular rights and equality. Building on the concept of citizens' rights, and particularly citizens' responsibilities, the discussion moves on to the benefits of education to society, and examines the role of learning in overcoming social exclusion and developing social capital.

'Education for its own sake'

The liberal or progressive view of education proposes that people should acquire knowledge (and, in some formulations, skills) for its own sake, in contrast to an extrinsic purpose, such as for employment. For example, Paul Hirst has written influentially about the intrinsic value of knowledge (although not skills) (Hirst, 1974). Similarly, educational reformers, including those at governmental level, have supported progressive arguments. The report of the Russell Committee on adult education (DES, 1973), presented to the UK government, propounded the intrinsic values of education:

> [Adult] education is concerned with developing the ability of individuals to understand and articulate, to reason and to make judgements; and to develop sensitivity and creativity [and provide] opportunities for men and women to continue to develop their knowledge, skills, judgement and creativity throughout adult life. (para. 8)

Adoption of this recommendation would entitle people to access formal and informal learning opportunities throughout their lives, without having to demonstrate that they have the necessary qualifications or other credentials to deserve access on the basis of merit. These recommendations were made over a quarter of a century ago but they were not translated into legislation, and so did not become a reality.

The Learning Age (DfEE, 1998a) tries to reassert these ideals in the UK. It refers to the contribution of learning to individual development, spirituality, appreciation of the arts, the family and community, active citizenship, social cohesion and independent living. Professor Bob Fryer (Chair of the National Advisory Group for Continuing Education and Lifelong Learning) described this as 'Blunkett's lyrical vision of the purposes of learning' (Fryer, 1999b). There is, however, a danger that, despite the rhetoric, these ideals will again not be realized (Davies, D., 2000).

The argument in favour of 'education for its own sake' has always faced difficulties. There are clearly issues pertaining to what knowledge is and, hence, what the form and content of liberal education should be. More generally, however, there are difficulties emanating from the assertion that the central aim of education should be the pursuit of knowledge for its own sake – certainly, some Marxists have criticized this aspiration, as it is a luxury suitable only for a privileged elite with leisure time available for such activities.

Education and personal development

Liberal educational ideals are bolstered by the notion of 'personal autonomy'. It can be asserted that everyone should be equipped with knowledge and skills to determine his or her major aims or goals in life, and not to have these imposed paternalistically by parents, tradition and culture, compulsory schooling, politicians, religion and so on. To be fully prepared to be autonomous one needs a good understanding of the options available and an appreciation of the social world in which one makes decisions.

Such an assertion suggests a role for education that is not about reproducing social patterns and reinforcing existing relations (see Bourdieu and Passeron, 1977, and Chapter 9), but is about facilitating learners to establish control over their own lives. Paulo Freire (his most influential book *Pedagogy of the Oppressed* was published in English in 1972) criticized traditional education for keeping learners passive and accepting of their situations. Instead he argued that education is for liberation and 'empowerment'. He postulates links between knowing, learning and action. Freire sees the primary function of education and educative processes to be the dynamic development of critical consciousness, which involves critical thought and action. This leads to 'critical transitivity of the group' and a 'critical transitive individual'. This status is defined by Shor: 'A critical transitive thinker feels empowered to think and act on the conditions around him or her, and relates those conditions to the larger contexts of power in society' (Shor, cited in De Koning, K. and Martin, M. (eds) 1993, p. 32).

Although Freire's work is focused primarily on less developed countries, particularly his native Brazil, his work is readily applied to education in the 'developed' world. For example, in the UK, adult educators have been strongly influenced by Freire's approach (cf. Lovett, 1975; Allman, 1987 and Grant, 1989). Indeed, the distinctions between 'developing countries' and the 'developed world' are far too simplistic (Macedo, 1994). Freire's approach is, therefore, equally valid in post-compulsory education in the UK, and other so-called developed countries, as anywhere else.

Freire advocates learning to foster reflection and critical under-standing, which directly encourages or incites political action to challenge existing oppressive structures. De Koning and Martin (1996), for instance, argue that a critical understanding of society and the social, political and economic structures that have subjugated it, enables marginalized and disempowered groups and individuals to work towards change (*ibid.*, p. 6).

Thus, Freire's philosophy, which has significantly influenced adult educators, emphasizes the personal development and autonomy functions of education. This approach shifts the liberal argument for education away from Hirst's pure notion of the pursuit of knowledge for its own sake, towards education being sought for the benefit of the individual, but not necessarily with reference to economic gains.

Citizenship and equality

If it is accepted that learning is theoretically of value to all individuals and groups (irrespective of their ability to contribute to the economy), and is potentially of greater value to the more marginalized and disadvantaged, it is necessary to consider people's rights of access to education. This is closely related to the ideas of citizenship, which embrace both the notions of citizens' rights and responsibilities. Much post-war writing on citizenship draws from the seminal work of T. H. Marshall (1950) (see, for example, Bulmer and Rees, 1996), who divided citizenship rights into civil, political and social rights:

> The civil element is composed of the rights necessary for individual freedom ... By the political element I mean the right to participate in the exercise of political power ... By the social element I mean the whole range from the right to a modicum of economic welfare and security to the right to share to the full in the social heritage and to live the life of a civilised being according to the standards prevailing in the society. The institutions most closely connected with it are the educational system and the social services. (Marshall, 1950, p. 10, reproduced in Finch, 1984, p. 237)

Social rights complement civil and political rights, and enable people to exercise them fully; thus, together, they constitute 'a kind of basic equality associated with full membership of a community' (Marshall, 1950, p. 8).

The post-war social policy reforms were based largely on the rights of individuals to access public services according to need and irrespective of the ability to pay, or of economic power. For example, the UK Education Act 1944 strongly expressed the rights of the individual. The emphasis, however, was on the rights of the individual to be educated to the limit of his or her ability. Paradoxically, this effectively means that everyone has the equal right to be recognized as unequal, and so policies based on this premise reinforce existing inequalities and disadvantage. Consequently, the principle of citizenship rights that are implicit in the 1944 Education Act accommodate, rather than challenge, underlying inequalities.

Citizens' rights must therefore be conceptualized in terms of 'equality of results' rather than of a more limited interpretation of equality in order to overcome the biases of cumulative disadvantage. Patricia Callaghan argues forcibly that it is necessary to unpack the different 'layers of meaning that can be ascribed to the moral and legal concept of equality' (Callaghan, 2000, p. 24), and to differentiate between 'formal equality', 'equality of opportunity' and 'equality of results' (idem.). It is the latter that must inform government and institutional policy-making in order to create an inclusive post-compulsory education system and society.

Formal equality simply requires everyone to be treated alike, irrespective of gender, class, ethnicity, age, physical ability and so forth. But this approach, as discussed above, may exacerbate inequality. Equality of opportunity, however, moves a step further and advocates positive discrimination for disadvantaged or under-represented groups. This strategy, however, can be rejected for a number of reasons. It reinforces prejudiced attitudes, rather than promoting equality, and may simply call into question the achieve-ments of members of these groups. Furthermore, it promotes tokenism rather than change, and once targets have been met, discrimination can continue. Positive discrimination locates the 'problem' with the individual, rather than the system and structures, and is likely to result in 'special' initiatives and the 'ghettoization' of the target groups. This has been described as 'perverse access', and raises serious questions regarding 'access to what?' (see Jary and Thomas, 1999, p. 4). It seems indefensible to many to provide access only to second-, or even third-class educational experiences for disadvantaged and under-represented groups. Hence it is appropriate to consider a third form of equality: equality of results or equality of outcomes:

> Equality of results is centred on the notion of equalising end results regardless of a person's ability to perform socially, politically, culturally or economically ... It is not surprising that this conceptualisation of equality has been the least advanced in our modern societies as it goes against the grain of market values and economic rights. (Callaghan, 2000, p. 25)

Access to education, drawing on the equality of results or outcomes approach, is not premised on the experiences and successes of an individual so far (for example, indicated by school performance and exam scores). Instead, opportunities and supporting mechanisms should be provided to enable people to enter and *succeed* in further and higher education. This, therefore, expands the notion of formal equality, and moves away from equality of opportunity based on positive discrimination towards providing appropriate educational opportunities and support mechanisms to meet the different needs of a diverse student population.

Patricia Callaghan's final comment may point to the key reason for the failure of 'equality of results' to underpin citizenship rights in general and educational policy in particular – they go 'against the grain of market values and economic rights' (*ibid.*). Indeed, a central criticism of the further education sector made by Helena Kennedy is that the increased 'marketisation' of education renders it 'uneconomic' for colleges to serve the needs of non-traditional students (see Kennedy, 1997, p. 3).

The notions of citizenship rights and responsibilities were revived during the 1980s and 1990s as a counter to the excesses of consumerism (see Lister, 1990, p. 1). Much of the emphasis, however, has been on the obligations of citizens, rather than their rights. The Conservative government in the UK in the 1980s and 1990s promoted citizenship and the notion of the 'active citizen', who gives money and time to the community, to contrast with the images of Thatcherism as harsh and uncaring (e.g. Patten, 1988; Rogaly, 1988 and Hurd, 1989). Ruth Lister, however, notes that 'the Government's emphasis on the *duties* of the *active* stands in stark contrast to its neglect of the *rights* of the *citizen*, creating a potential contradiction in terms of the notion in the "active citizen"' (p. 15).

Citizenship has also been attractive to, and revived by, Britain's Centre and Left political thinkers, potentially providing an alternative to Thatcherism. The *New Statesman and Society* (1988) argued that citizenship 'offers the best hopes of reconciling individualism and social justice' (cited in Lister, 1990, p. 22). One aspect of the concerns of the Centre and Left relate to the perceived emergence of an underclass (see Dahrendorf, 1987), and, consequently, the assertion that, effectively, only some citizens have rights. This value-laden language and the images associated with 'underclass' allows this section of society (however it is defined) to be written off and exempt of citizens' rights, including rights to education. Critical social policy criticizes the liberal assumptions underpinning citizenship, as they are largely blind to gender, race and disability issues, and the associated power relations that have subjugated these groups (see, for example, Hall and Held, 1989; Williams, 1989). It is therefore necessary to move beyond simplistic notions of citizenship to ensure equality of outcomes for all individuals and groups in society.

Some notions of citizenship indicate that individuals have a right to access post-compulsory educational opportunities. Citizenship premised on formal equality or even equality of opportunity does not, however, produce fundamental social change, or radically alter patterns of participation (including in post-compulsory education). It is necessary to take into consideration the cumulative disadvantages of class, and also to consider the negative impacts of patriarchy, racism and discrimination towards people with disabilities, and so adopt an equality of outcomes approach. The value of citizenship rights can be further undermined by the notion of 'citizen duties' (that grew in significance and emphasis in the 1980s). For example, citizens' duties include the obligation of the poor to work as a means to combat the 'dependency culture' (Lister, 1990, p. 20). This type of duty is still evident in the UK under the New Labour government, which has introduced a series of measures that link social security benefits (citizens' rights) to citizens' responsibilities to work. For example, the Benefits Agency and the Employment Service are to be integrated, so reinforcing the link between rights to benefits and obligations to work. If citizens have societal duties, then education may be advocated not to benefit individuals, but for the good of the wider society and even the economy.

Education for society: overcoming social exclusion

It may be that some non-economic benefits of education are advocated not to benefit individuals, but for the benefit of society, or particular groups within it. This is noted in national and international policies. David Blunkett, the former UK Secretary of State for Education, wrote, in the foreword of *The Learning Age*: 'As well as securing our economic future, learning has a wider contribution. It helps make ours a civilised society, develops the spiritual side of our lives and promotes active citizenship' (DfEE, 1998a, p. 7).

The Irish Green Paper *Adult Education in an Era of Lifelong Learning* (Department of Education, 1998) presents 'sustained government commitment to combating social exclusion through lifelong learning' (Woodrow et al., 2000, p. 8). The aim of the UNESCO World Conference on Higher Education (UNESCO, 1998) sought to guide higher education to meet its tasks for the next century, 'to help humankind, society and the community of nations to stride out towards a better future, towards a world more just, more humane, more caring and more peaceful' (Mayor, 1998, p. 1).

In the past decade or more there have been growing concerns in many so-called developed countries about 'social exclusion'. Although these countries can be seen to have experienced increases in material affluence, this growth has not been shared equally among all citizens. This reflects the situation in the UK: society as a whole has become more affluent, but the relative position of the poorest has worsened. Researchers at Oxford University, in 1997, studied how much family income remains after housing costs are deducted; in 1971 just 7 per cent of homes fell below the poverty line, but by 1990 a quarter did so. Social exclusion is a topic in European Union policy debates (see Room, 1995b; Duffy, 1995 and Berghman, 1995) and in individual states. In the UK, in August 1997, Peter Mandelson, then Minister without Portfolio, announced that there would be a campaign against social exclusion as a prominent plank in government policy. In December of the same year a new Social Exclusion Unit was established in the Cabinet Office, reporting directly to the Prime Minister. The Prime Minister cited this as 'the defining difference between ourselves and the previous government' (Blair, 1997).

Although there is a lack of consensus surrounding the definition of social exclusion (cf. OECD, 1999a; Atkinson and Hills, 1998 and Hayton, 1999a), most conceptualizations link together a number of issues, such as material deprivation, the agency that individuals and groups have to effect changes in their lives and the social support or participation that they have. The UK Social Exclusion Unit uses the term in an attempt to recognize the impact of multiple disadvantages:

> Social exclusion is a shorthand label for what can happen when individuals or areas suffer from a combination of linked problems, such as unemployment, poor skills, low incomes, poor housing, high crime environments, bad health and family breakdown. (Social Exclusion Unit, 1998)

The OECD highlights the importance of social relations and social integration in its definition of social exclusion: 'Exclusion involves a lack of social belonging and the absence of a sense of community. There are grounds for concern that lives are becoming more fragmented and less inclusive' (OECD, 1999a, p. 9).

Berghman (1995) notes the emphasis given by the European 'Poverty 3' (the Third European Poverty Programme) researchers to what they cited as two key aspects of social exclusion, these being its 'comprehensive' and 'dynamic' characteristics. And from these it is concluded that the term should be defined in relation to the following:

1. the democratic and legal system, which promotes civic integration;

2. the labour market, which promotes economic integration;
3. the welfare state system, promoting what may be called social integration; and
4. the community system, which promotes interpersonal integration.

Thus, social exclusion incorporates the denial or non-realization of citizenship rights, or lack of access to the major institutions that give rise to these rights. This conceptualization takes account of the multidimensional aspects of people lives, beyond material deprivation. (For a more in-depth analysis of the term 'social exclusion' see Thomas and Jones, 2000.)

In response to the awareness of the phenomenon of social exclusion, education is often implicitly or explicitly expected to contribute to creating pathways from exclusion to inclusion. Indeed, it is not new for education to be utilized to help achieve social objectives, although the emphasis may change (Halsey, 1997; Smith and Noble, 1995). In the UK, the New Labour government sees education as a major tool for tackling social exclusion (Hayton, 1999a, p. vii), and within the member states of the European Union the educational sector has been targeted at all levels (Leney, 1999). This is not to suggest, however, that education is a panacea, but that it has a role to play as part of the much vaunted 'joined-up thinking':

Policies to address social exclusion involve, at least, access to employment that can be sustained, access to education, training and skills, changes in the housing sector, improved standards of living – including those locked outside the labour market – and an enhancement of social capital through improved social networks. (Leney, 1999, p. 36)

The OECD (1999a) identifies three ways in which learning can help to counteract social exclusion: learning to meet basic needs; learning for labour market participation; and learning to foster social action and participation.

There are significant numbers of people who lack basic skills, even in developed countries. For example, the Moser (1999) Report outlines the scale of literacy and numeracy basic skill deficits in the UK: it suggests that 1 in 5 adults aged over 19 years have problems with literacy and numeracy (see Figures 3.1 and 3.2). Basic skills are crucial to learning, employment and social participation. At least minimal levels of literacy are required for everyday life, for example to gain information about housing, health, welfare, benefits and

One in sixteen people cannot say where the concert is being held. This is 6.25%, or approximately 2.2 million adults.

One in four people cannot calculate the change out of £2 when they buy the goods above. This is 25%, or approximately 8.8 million adults.

Figures 3.1 and 3.2   *Example of poor literacy and numeracy cited in the Moser Report*

education. Improving literacy and basic skills is also likely to have a positive effect on self-confidence, and, subsequently, may contribute to greater community participation and activity. Basic skills are a necessary first step towards closing the gap between the 'education-rich' and 'education-poor', and the 'work-rich' and the 'work-poor'. Facilitating the acquisition of basic skills is a role that further education must, at least partially, embrace if serious attempts to reduce polarization in society are to be made.

The Delors White Paper and the Flynn White Paper (European Commission, 1993 and 1994, cited in OECD, 1999a) both envisage a key role for employment in combating social exclusion, which may be dependent on acquiring qualifications and skills. The OECD notes that: 'credentials are increasingly necessary and decreasingly sufficient for successful labour market participation' (OECD, 1999a, p. 22). In a culture of credentialism, qualifications are likely to increase employment prospects, although this may be impeded by labour market discrimination. Unemployment, especially involuntary unemployment, undoubtedly contributes to social exclusion, but it must not be assumed that a return to work will necessarily foster social inclusion. The impact of employment is likely to depend on pay, job security and the intrinsic level of satisfaction (Atkinson, 1998).

Learning may also be thought to contribute to alleviating social exclusion by helping to create social cohesion and fostering 'a sense of belonging, responsibility and identity' (DfEE, 1998a). Such outcomes are usually reliant upon the notion of 'social capital', the development of which is said to be important for overcoming social exclusion and disadvantage. The term 'social capital' is used to signify the extent to which people have access to networks, their levels of political and civic engagement and membership of associations. It can be argued that those people most vulnerable to exclusion are increasingly less able to call upon networks that yield some form of support. The OECD prescribes social participation and citizenship as contributory factors to overcoming social exclusion:

> Measures to combat exclusion should be broadened still further beyond economic activity to include a greater array of social activities related to citizenship, voluntary action and culture. This is not as an alternative to employment but because inclusion takes many forms. Successful participation in different social, community and cultural activities can also prove an effective bridge in building the skills, confidence and social capital that lead to labour market participation. Adult learning offers both preparation for such social participation and an element of it since education is a form of social inclusion itself. (OECD, 1999a, p. 23)

Like social exclusion, the idea of 'social capital' has a range of meanings, some of which are at variance with others. Preece (1999b) argues that disadvantaged people do have access to networks and support, but that these are not recognized or acknowledged by dominant groups. Similarly, Putnam et al. (1993) argue that social capital is subjectively interpreted, but, simultaneously, not all social networks are productive. Coleman (1988) believes that social capital is 'context-specific', and what functions as social capital in one situation may not work in another. Gamarnikow and Green (1999, pp. 49–50) recognize the tensions between different conceptualizations of the term, and identify a 'continuum of social capital manifestations':

> At one end of the continuum, social capital embraces progressive, liberal and civic notions of co-operation, empow- erment, participation and community action in the construction of needs and priorities .... . At the other extreme social capital

may be realised in a normative order of traditional institutional forms, for instance, favouring two-parent nuclear families; locating the 'parenting deficit' in women's increased labour market activity; and arguing for a collective non-relativist moral regime of duties and responsibilities to which all are expected to conform, particularly those least well placed in the system . . . . At this end of the continuum traditional forms of power relations, although invisible in the accounts, appear to form an essential feature of social capital, rendering citizenship ambiguous in relation to subjecthood.

There is a danger that the process of widening participation in post-compulsory education is not about allowing people to develop the former liberal, empowering conceptualization of social capital, but is more about covertly 'normalizing' people. If post-compulsory education is to provide routes out of social exclusion by aiding the acquisition of social capital, it must operate at the former end of Garmarnikow and Green's continuum, and not impose and reinforce traditional, white, male and patriarchal, middle-class norms.

Combating social exclusion requires both economic and cultural change – economic redistribution and cultural recognition. Education therefore is well placed to span this dual role, potentially offering economic and cultural advancement. Employment brings income and status, and facilitates participation in other activities. Furthermore, participation in education tends to help foster a habit of lifelong learning. Thus education may operate at a number of levels to help reduce social exclusion.

Conclusion

This chapter has rehearsed some of the arguments, difficulties and counter-positions regarding the non-economic benefits of education. If education and lifelong learning are to have a more far-reaching impact than simply to train more people to meet the needs of industry, it is up to us to influence policies and practices now. For, as David Davies recognizes, there is currently a new opportunity to ensure that education and lifelong learning is inclusive and progressive, and does not reinforce traditional elite patterns of learning and employment. This opportunity must be acted upon, to ensure that post-compulsory education retains at least a liberal element, and that it is not captured by the modernizing agenda solely to serve the needs of the economy, thus reinforcing divisions in society. He writes:

> Lifelong learning must … include[s] **all** the arenas of learning, including work, community, family, identity and the formal and informal structures and institutions which shape a life … We need to recognize that there exists a **process** of learning as well as a product and that learners will increasingly want to speak for themselves as part of gaining control over their own lives … They, the learners, are not just a 'product portfolio' or the pathological victims of a marketised culture … Lifelong learning is now everyone's business and … [it] may still be located in the emancipatory domain. (Davies, 2000, p. 48 original emphasis)

We must not be captured by the discourse of the market; instead we should critically assess the value of education and, concomitantly, what is taught. The OECD notes the international tendency for expansion of learning to focus on the needs of the economy rather than personal development and social cohesion: 'By the mid-1990s, lifetime learning was viewed as something which promoted individual advancement and corporate and national competitivity; its role in respect of social inclusion was limited and largely remedial action' (OECD, 1999a, p. 160).

In summary, post-compulsory education and training in general, and higher education in particular, have expanded rapidly, internationally, in recent years. This expansion is driven partly by economic arguments and national competitiveness within a context of globalization. In addition to economic returns, education offers people intrinsic benefits, including the potential for greater social participation. It is for these two reasons that education is valued in the drive to reduce social exclusion. These agendas, which sometimes come into conflict, are largely driven by government policies, but an analysis of these suggests that economic rather than social motivations dominate.

CHAPTER 4

Access to Post-compulsory Education by 'Non-traditional' students

Introduction

The various drivers of expansion in the post-compulsory education sectors have undoubtedly led to a greater number of students accessing learning. But this expansion in participation does not necessarily imply that there is now greater diversity among the student population. This chapter disaggregates participation rates, paying particular attention to the *level* and *forms* of participation by non-traditional students. The chapter considers participation in relation to socio-economic class, ethnicity, disability, gender, age and entry qualifications, using examples from further and higher education in the UK, and higher education in Australia and Ireland.

Despite the expansion in post-compulsory education that was discussed in Chapter 1, it is important to analyse *who* is accessing formal learning. Although there are currently about 5 million post-16 learners in England (see Chapter 1), there are many more who are not participating. The Moser Report (1999) suggests that there are severe basic skills deficits in the UK (see Chapter 3). This clearly inhibits participation in most traditional forms of learning, and indicates that these people have not so far benefited from basic skills courses offered by the further education sector, which may be a necessary requirement for additional participation in learning.

Participation in post-compulsory education in many 'developed' countries has grown exponentially during the last 10–15 years. In Australia, enrolment statistics for higher education demonstrate that the number of students increased by 67 per cent between 1987 and 1997 (DETYA, 1997). In the UK the API (age participation index) is 33 per cent. The API measures the percentage of the population aged between 18 and 21 that participates in higher education, but it masks many different participation rates between social groups. Similarly, in Australia the student population in higher education in particular does not reflect the composition of the overall population (Postle *et al.*, 1995); it is, in short, stratified according to class, gender, ethnicity and culture. And, although according to Marginson (1999) higher education is becoming more accessible and increasingly representative of the population as a whole in Australia, it is acknowledged that 'pockets of advantage' persist, particularly in the most prestigious institutions and courses. Ferrier and Heagney (2000), in their study regarding disadvantage in higher education in Australia, report that class, educational establishment, family responsibilities and rural and isolated locations all influence participation rates. They cite evidence that patterns of participation in higher education by people from lower socio-economic groups and from rural and isolated areas have changed the least, while students from elite private schools dominate in the law and medicine faculties of the older universities in each state.

In order to address issues of under-representation and inequity, the Australian government-funded *Unified National System* (UNS) of higher education identified six broad categories of groups to be targeted in equity programmes at the national and institutional levels. These are: Aboriginal and Torres Strait Islanders; people with disabilities; people from low socio-economic backgrounds; people from rural and isolated areas; people from non-English-speaking backgrounds; and women in non-traditional subject areas. The Australian government adopted these categories, and HEIs report annually on their progress in relation to improving access, participation, success and retention for each group (see Ferrier and Heagney, 2000). Ferrier and Heagney report that not only are these categories insufficient, but also that many people may be members of more than one 'equity group', and that this compounds their disadvantage.

The expansion in post-compulsory education has been restricted to certain social groups, particularly those who were already well-represented. These groups have been able to capitalize on their social and cultural positions and this expansion may have exacerbated the gaps between rich and poor included and excluded. (This issue is central to the work of Bourdieu and Passeron (1977) and is considered in Chapter 9. Ball (1993) discusses this in relation to the marketization of compulsory education.) To illustrate these points, empirical data relating to instances of involvement in post-compulsory education (especially in higher education) in England, Ireland and Australia are reviewed. Comparisons are, however, difficult; internationally, data, if it is collected at all (see Woodrow *et al.*, 2000), uses different criteria and methods. In the UK alone a range of providers deliver further education with the result that information is often not standardized, as Table 4.1 shows.

Prior to 1994 there were few national statistics relating to participation in the non-higher education sector of post-compulsory education. Furthermore, the Kennedy Committee found that 'schools, colleges and private training providers have different systems for collecting data' (Kennedy, 1997, p. 19) and 'there is little detailed information on the training carried out by employers' (*ibid.*). Consequently, Kennedy *et al.* commissioned FEFC research and analysis into participation differentials in further education in the UK (FEFC, 1997a). They also recommended that 'the government should accelerate its activities to harmonise systems for measuring participation and achievement in post-16 learning and publish an annual report on progress in participation and achievement' (p. 16). The only statistics regarding participation in further education are those produced by the FEFC and relate solely to FEFE-funded providers, excluding school sixth forms and other external providers including those in the private sector. The difficulties indicated by Kennedy *et al.* with respect to acquiring data on the attributes of learners in further education are even greater in contexts beyond one country.

In the UK, in the context of higher education, the situation is somewhat less difficult. For instance, centralized agencies – UCAS (Universities and Colleges Admissions Service) and HESA (Higher Education Statistics Agency) – facilitate in-depth analysis of participation rates in higher education by different social and cultural groups. This information relates only to full-time students, however, and thus precludes analysis of participation by their part-time colleagues. Participation by different social groups is now discussed.

Socio-economic dimensions of participation

Although an increasing number of people enter post-compulsory education, the gap between the participation rates of students from different social classes is extremely wide. Such patterns have historical precedents (e.g. Robbins, 1963 and Kelsall *et al.*, 1972), and are, to varying extents, reproduced in other countries (Anderson, 1990; Halsey, 1993; Skilbeck and Connell, 2000). Indeed, so entrenched is this aspect of participation that the Committee of Vice-chancellors and Principals of the Universities of the United Kingdom (CVCP, now Universities UK) has been moved to speak of class as the 'last frontier' in the battle to create an inclusive higher education. It asserts that: 'The failure to achieve a significant increase in the number of students

Table 4.1: Availability of data on further education students and providers (UK)

Provider	Location of provision	Students' location	Age	Sex	Ethnic group	Qualification aim	Other student data	Data source
Further education colleges	Postcode of main college site	Student postcode	✓	✓	✓	✓	Disability, fee remission, retention, achievement destination	Individualized student record (ISR)
School sixth forms	Postcode of main school site		✓	✓	–	✓ Broad group only (*)	Achievements (GCSE, GCE, A/S level) destination of Year 11 pupils	Form 7 data, GCSE and A-level performance tables, careers service data
Higher education institutions	Postcode of main institution site	Student postcode	✓	✓	✓	✓	Disability, retention, achievement destination	Higher Education Statistical Agency (HESA) return
External institutions (Council-funded provision)	Postcode of institution (a)	Student postcode (from 1995–6)	✓	✓	✓	✓	Disability, fee remission, retention, achievement destination	Individualized student record (ISR)
External institutions (other provision)	Locations of LEA only, not point of delivery		✓ Broad group only	✓	–	✓ Broad group only		AEI return
Private providers	Not available – limited information only							DfEE training statistics

(*) The broad groups are GNVQ advanced, GNVQ intermediate, GNVQ foundation, GNVQ advanced precursor, GNVQ intermediate precursor, NVQ3, NVQ2, NVQ1, GCE A/S LEVEL, GCSE and Other.
(a) An external institution funded by the Council may be a consortium of several institutions.

Source: FEFC, 1997a, p. 4.

from less affluent backgrounds is the single greatest challenge to higher education' (CVCP, 1999).

This problem is also endemic in the higher levels of post-compulsory education in other OECD countries (Skilbeck and Connell, 2000, p. 25) and member states of the European Union (Green *et al.*, 1999); students come disproportionately from the upper-socio-economic groups (see, for example, France: French Ministry of National Education, Research and Technology, 1999; Germany: Schnitzer *et al.*, 1999; Belgium (Flanders): Hostens, 1999 and Denmark: Nexelmann, 1999).

Participation and socio-economic group: higher education in the UK

In 1997, 31 per cent of young people (aged 18–21) entered higher education in the UK, but, predictably, the proportions from different socio-economic groups varied significantly. In the upper-socio-economic groups – that is social classes 1, 2 and 3 (non-manual) – 49 per cent of young people took up higher education places, while only 18.4 per cent entered higher education from the lower socio-economic groups, i.e. 3 (manual), 4 and 5. Even these figures, however, disguise significant differences between the rates of participation among those in the highest strata and those from the lowest income groups. Over 80 per cent of young people in social class 1 entered higher education in 1997, while only 14 per cent of the same age group entered from group 5 (all statistics from CVCP, 1999). These figures can be compared with entry rates in 1990. In this year 36.7 per cent of young people from the top three social classes entered higher education, and 10.3 per cent entered from the lowest social classes, while only 6 per cent entered from socio-economic group 5 (see also Robertson and Hillman, 1997, p. 40). Although participation rates among the least affluent did increase during the 1990s, this group continues to be significantly under-represented in higher education because participation by *all* social groups has expanded (see 'credentialism' in Chapter 2).

International comparisons of participation in higher education and socio-economic group

In Australia, participation in higher education by the lowest socio-economic group (defined as the lowest 25% of the population in a given region) was 14.5% in 1997, but this varies according to institution, from 5.4% to 40%. This represents a slight proportional decline from 15% to 14.5% between 1991 and 1997 (DETYA, 1999). In

Ireland, steps have been taken to overcome poor access by students from lower socio-economic groups following the publication of the government White Paper *Charting Our Education Future* (Department of Education, 1995). But despite these special initiatives Dooney (in Skilbeck and Connell, 2000, p. 29) notes that the rate of increase in the number of disadvantaged school students entering higher education is accelerating rather slowly.

Participation and socio-economic group: further education in the UK

Information collected regarding participation in further education in the UK does not contain explicit details about social class. The postcode of each entrant is recorded, and this is used to identify social characteristics of groups in specific geographical locations, which in commercial applications are known as geodemographics, (Tonks, 1999 and Batey *et al.*, 1998, discuss the use of geodemographics in higher education in the UK). The only direct indicator of low income selected by the FEFC in their 1997 report was with regard to those students receiving state benefits (FEFC, 1997a, p. 11). Benefits recorded include unemployment benefit, income support and other means-tested benefits. More significantly, however, the figures only relate to adult students (i.e. those over the age of 19). Overall, in 1994–5 and 1995–6 18 per cent of adult students had their tuition fees waived because they, or whoever they were dependent upon, were in receipt of benefits. A cursory glance might therefore suggest that UK further education is more 'inclusive' (i.e. has a wider socio-economic base of involvement) than higher education. But there are some provisos that must be made before this conclusion can be asserted.

First, this figure refers to the number of people in further education in receipt of benefits, as a proportion of all adults who are participating in further education. This can be contrasted with an alternative measure, based on the number of people in further education on benefits calculated as a proportion of the total number of people in receipt of benefits in the population. As the former measure is used, rather than the latter, a direct comparison cannot be attempted with higher education. The participation rate in higher education for socio-economic group 5, cited above, is derived by calculating the number of students from class 5 as a proportion of the population of socio-economic group 5, rather than as a proportion of the higher education population. Succinctly, the further education participation figures relate only to the further education population, whereas the higher education figures relate to population as a whole.

Second, these further education statistics refer to adults only (aged over 19). It can be surmised that many 'traditional' students will already be in higher education, or have passed through it, therefore further education *should* have more adults who have not taken the traditional educational route. In other words, they have taken one or more years above the minimum time required to progress from compulsory schooling to higher education.

Finally, the figures relating to participation in further education exclude people participating in other sectors, such as school sixth forms and private providers, which are utilized more by people from higher socio-economic groups. This point is acknowledged, albeit somewhat implicitly, by the FEFC when it notes that 'the profile of young people recruited by sixth form colleges is significantly different from other colleges' (FEFC, 1997a, p. 10). It can be concluded that FEFC-funded further education may be more equitable regarding provision for people from low-income groups than other providers, such as sixth forms and higher education institutions, but participation by students from lower socio-economic groups in post-compulsory education as a whole is far less inclusive.

Conclusions about socio-economic dimensions of participation
Less than proportional participation in post-compulsory education by students from lower socio-economic groups is an international feature, the implications of which are exacerbated by examining where students are participating, and at what level. It must be stated, though, that data collection is not comprehensive or uniform. For example, in the UK there is insufficient information about students studying part-time, which may in fact be a more feasible option for students from low-income families, enabling them to combine studying with some form of paid employment.

Students from ethnic and minority groups
Skilbeck and Connell (2000, p. 39) identify three main ethnic and minority groups who are under-represented, excluded or discriminated against. First, *indigenous populations* (e.g. the Inuit from the north of Europe, Asia and Canada, native Americans, and Australian Aboriginals). Second, *migrant groups* in societies where they constitute a *minority* of the overall population (e.g. Turkish community in Germany, Portuguese and North Africans in France, Surinam and Antillean communities in the Netherlands and West Indians and Asians in the UK). Finally, *minority populations* who have elected a *different way of life* from the majority (e.g. travellers in Ireland and the

UK and the Amish in the USA).

Reliable and comparable international statistics concerning ethnic and minority participation in post-compulsory education are difficult to acquire. Nevertheless, as Skilbeck and Connell (*ibid.*) note, 'many countries report that particular ethnic minorities are seriously under-represented at the tertiary level' (p. 40. See also Papadopoulos, 1994). In Australia, Aboriginal and Torres Strait Islander people, and people from non-English-speaking backgrounds have been identified by the government as under-represented groups in higher education (DEET, 1990). Furthermore, students from ethnic and minority groups often experience disadvantage that is 'complex, compounding and dynamic' (Ferrier and Heagney, 2000). An individual or group might not only be categorized as an ethnic or minority group, but also come from a low socio-economic class, live in a rural and isolated or poor urban location, experience language difficulties, lack traditional entry qualifications and enter as a mature student. The next sections review participation rates by ethnic and minority groups in higher education in the UK and Australia, and in further education in the UK.

Participation by ethnic and minority groups in higher education in the UK

In the UK the National Committee of Inquiry into Higher Education (NCIHE, 1997) found that, overall, minority ethnic groups are more than proportionately represented in higher education. In 1994, 12.2 per cent of young people in higher education were from minority ethnic groups and in 1997 ethnic minorities constituted 13 per cent of all first-year undergraduate admissions. The same ethnic groups represented approximately 7.3 per cent of the 18–20-year-old population as a whole (Coffield and Vignoles, 1997, p. 6). Yet, as Coffield and Vignoles go on to note, these ostensibly positive figures disguise the complex nature of ethnicity and the ways in which it is cross-cut by other factors such as gender and class. Hence, Bangladeshi women and Afro-Caribbean men are particularly prone to experiencing lower rates of participation. There are also important variations between institutions and disciplinary fields.

Research demonstrates that ethnic minority students are more likely to be accepted into post-1992 institutions, and within this category they are concentrated in particular institutions (Modood, 1993). A number of reasons can be identified for the predominance of certain ethnic minority students in post-1992 institutions. Modood (*ibid.*) identifies a preference for institutions that are close to home, where family and support networks can be retained, and for those institutions that demonstrate themselves as 'friendly' towards ethnic minorities. Particular post-1992 institutions have tended to fall into this category; for example, West Hill University College in Birmingham is attractive to members of the local Muslim community; evidence of its 'friendliness' is the provision of a prayer room and the opportunity to study for a degree in Islamic Studies. Taylor (1992) has identified the acceptance of students with non-standard entry qualifications as a reason for greater participation by ethnic and minority groups in post-1992 universities as a greater proportion of these students do not hold traditional A-level qualifications (Hogarth et al., 1997). Ethnic and minority groups are, subsequently, more likely to enter higher education as mature students through alternative entry routes (Singh, 1990), while pre-1992 universities tend to prefer entry to degree programmes on the basis of A-level points score. Commentators are, however, agreed that racial discrimination is occurring (cf. Coffield and Vignoles, 1997; Taylor, 1992; Modood and Shiner, 1994).

Participation by ethnic and minority groups in higher education in Australia

A similar overall picture can be found in Australia, which is now one of the world's most culturally diverse societies (Ronanye, 2000, p. 142). Students from non-English speaking backgrounds (NESB) are over-represented in the sense that they account for 5.2 per cent of new enrolments and only 4.8 per cent of the total population. But, as the Department of Education, Training and Youth Affairs (DETYA) is aware, the situation is more complex. Some ethnic and minority groups, particularly students from parts of Asia and eastern Europe, are more than proportionately represented in higher education, but this again masks lower participation by other groups, especially those originating from the Middle East and southern Europe and indigenous Australians (DETYA, 1999). A further dimension to participation by different ethnic and minority groups is not just access, but also retention. Access to higher education by indigenous Australians, including Aboriginals and Torres Strait Islanders is now almost equivalent to their population share, but retention and completion is poor (Skilbeck and Connell, 2000, p. 41).

Participation by ethnic and minority groups in further education in the UK

In further education in the UK, ethnic and minority groups as a whole are, again, well represented. The FEFC report states that 'the ethnicity profile of students shows that nationally, further education colleges are recruiting a higher proportion of students from ethnic minorities than the percentage in the population generally' (FEFC, 1997a, p. 9). Interestingly, and unlike higher education in the UK, the report states that *all* ethnic minority groups are more than equally represented in further education than in the population as a whole (see Table 4.2).

Table 4.2: Students' ethnicity profile (%) compared to the population

Ethnicity	1994–5	1995–6	Population
Bangladeshi	1.1	0.7	0.3
Black African	1.5	1.5	0.4
Black Caribbean	2.2	2.0	1.1
Black Other	0.7	0.6	0.4
Chinese	0.5	0.5	0.3
Indian	2.4	2.4	1.8
Pakistani	2.3	2.0	1.0
White	86.4	87.6	93.8
Other – Asian	0.6	0.8	0.4
Other	2.2	1.8	0.6
Total	**100**	**100**	**100**

Source: FEFC, 1997a, p. 28

But, yet again, it is instructive to move beyond mere participation statistics, and to examine differences between ethnic groups with regard to level of study. Table 4.3 demonstrates the level of qualifications that students are registered to study for (where specified on individualized student records); this enables a comparison between the percentage of ethnic minority students studying at different levels and the average percentage of all students.

In 1995–6 the group 'Other Asian' had a higher than average percentage of students studying at lower levels ('entry and level 1' and 'level 2'), while there was a below-average percentage of this ethnic group studying at higher levels (level 3 and levels 4 and 5). Similarly, the categories labelled 'Black Other', 'Pakistani' and 'Other' all had a more-than-average percentage of students studying level 2 qualifications and a below-average percentage of students studying level 4 and 5 qualifications. Thus, some ethnic and minority groups are over-represented in lower-level qualifications, and under-represented in higher-level qualifications.

A contrary picture is revealed with regard to 'white' students studying in further education in the UK in the same academic year. There was a below-average and average percentage of 'White' students

Table 4.3: Distribution of students by ethnic group (%) by notional level of qualification, 1995–6

Ethnicity	Entry and level 1	Level 2	Level 3	Levels 4 and 5
Bangladeshi	21	27	49	3
Black African	28	28	38	5
Black Caribbean	24	32	36	7
Black Other	21	34	40	5
Chinese	24	27	43	6
Indian	20	27	48	5
Pakistani	21	31	44	4
White	29	28	36	7
Other – Asian	31	30	34	6
Other	29	29	36	5
All Students	30	28	36	7

Source: FEFC, 1997a, p. 30

studying lower-level qualifications ('entry and level 1'), and average percentages studying higher-level qualifications ('level 3' and 'levels 4 and 5'). It can be concluded that some ethnic minority groups are studying at lower levels than white and other ethnic groups, and this pattern of participation is reproduced in higher education.

Conclusions regarding ethnic and minority groups

A cursory glance at participation in post-compulsory education by ethnic and minority groups might suggest that there are no particular problems. But, what the above discussion reveals is that the broad category 'ethnic and minority groups' is not sufficiently sophisticated. It does not identify the differential participation by different sectors of the community. Both Ferrier and Heagney (2000) and Skilbeck and Connell (2000) suggest that the classification 'ethnic and minority groups' needs redefining to enable 'useful' information to be generated – and acted upon. There are certain ethnic and minority groups who are under-represented, especially in higher education. These specific groups should be identified and targeted as part of a systematic approach to widening participation and promoting equality.

A second conclusion about participation by students from these groups is with regard to the type of institution at which they are studying and the level they are studying at (particularly in further education). Perhaps the exemplar of the 'ghettoization' of ethnic and minority students is the US system. Access to US universities has involved what has been described as a 'perverse access' since the opening of entry to previously excluded categories of students has been, disproportionately, to lower status or special category institutions. While an emphasis on educational 'diversity' can be valuable as a way of opening access to new students, there is an ever-attendant risk that it leads to a marginalization of students and credentials.

Participation by students classified as having a disability

This section examines the participation of students who are classified as having a disability. Of particular significance, with regard to this category is not only measurement and data collection, but also labelling. There is not an agreed international definition of disability. For monitoring purposes within education, 'disability' may be self-defined and identified by students. The Americans Disabilities Act 1990 and the Australian Disability Discrimination Act 1992 both define 'disability' very broadly and include physical, intellectual, psychiatric, sensory, neurological and learning disabilities (Skilbeck and Connell, 2000, p. 42). Similarly, the UK Code of Practice embraces physical and mobility difficulties, hearing impairments, visual impairments, specific learning difficulties including dyslexia, medical conditions and mental health problems (Waters, 2000). As Shaw has shown, society's responses to people with disabilities helps to determine the number who identify themselves in this way (Shaw, 1999a). For example, the number of students registering themselves with a learning disability in Australia is very low – only 2 per cent in higher education – as there have been negative funding implications; whilst in the USA, 50 per cent of all students are registering a disability (Shaw, 1999b). For these, and related reasons, calculating and comparing the numbers of students with disabilities is a formidable task.

Despite these difficulties, people with disabilities have been identified as an under-represented group by the Australian government (DEET, 1990). Students with disabilities have been targeted by the Higher Education Funding Agency in England (HEFCE); financial incentives have been offered to institutions that recruit more students with disabilities (HEFCE Circular letter 7/00). But, as Skilbeck and Connell (2000, p. 43) point out, there are two important features that differentiate students with disabilities from other under-represented groups. First, disability can affect people of either gender, of any ethnicity, at any time in their life and from across the social class stratum. And, second, the 'disabled' are not generally an easily identifiable group or a close-knit community; only the deaf have, at least to some extent, developed their own identity and culture based on their common use of sign language (see Danermark, 1999). It may be that 'other' socio-cultural attributes are more important than 'disability' in defining whether or not, and how, a person participates in post-compulsory education.

In the UK population as a whole, about 12.5 per cent of people have a disability, and in higher education about 4 per cent of students have identified themselves as having a disability (CVCP, 1999). This figure is confirmed by Skill – the National Bureau for Students with Disabilities – who reported that 3.8 per cent of HE students had a disability in 1997/8 (Waters, 2000). HEFCE (1996) estimates that 2 per cent of the total student body report that they have a disability, which can be compared with the 7 per cent of the 18–30 age group identifying a longstanding disability, according to the Labour Force Survey. But this includes 'learning disabilities', which makes comparisons with the HEFCE figures more difficult, and, once again, illustrates the differences and problems with regard to definitions.

There is, of course, the issue of institutional variations. Perhaps not surprisingly, the Open University is particularly significant as a provider of accessible higher education to students with physical disabilities. It should be noted that, currently, in the UK, higher education institutions are exempt from the disability discrimination legislation, although the National Committee of Inquiry into Higher Education recommended that they should seek to adhere to it (Robertson and Hillman, 1997, pp. 74–5). By contrast, colleges funded by the FEFC in the UK are required to meet a statutory obligation to provide for students with learning difficulties and other disabilities (*ibid.*; see also FEFC, 1996). UK legislation in this context compares less favourably with Australia and the United States, where strict disability laws apply to education, and so people with disabilities are more than proportionately represented in higher education.

It is almost impossible to reach any conclusions with regard to participation by students with disabilities in post-compulsory education, as the definitions are either fluid or incompatible. There are two indicators that students with disabilities are under-represented. First, the acknowledgement by governments (e.g. in Australia) and quasi-governmental bodies (e.g. HEFCE) that students with disabilities should be targeted as they are under-represented groups. The second is the proportion of staff with disabilities employed by HEIs in the UK. An interesting survey in the *Times Higher Education Supplement* showed that HEIs, in general, employ fewer staff with disabilities than the proportion in the population (THES, 2000). These data must be treated with caution as it is contingent with all the problems discussed above, but these findings may be indicative of the attitudes of institutions, and irrespective of this point, this precedence does not provide positive role models for people (staff and students) with disabilities.

Women

Until comparatively recently, women were under-represented in post-compulsory education. Feminists have campaigned for the educational rights of girls and women since the nineteenth century, and yet, in the UK at least, it was not until the 1944 Education Act that some measure of gender equality in compulsory education was realized. The 1960s saw feminists continue to struggle against discrimination towards women in education and society generally. Eventually, in 1975, the Sex Discrimination Act was passed in the UK, which sought to address discrimination against women in all spheres of society, including education. This period saw similar changes in many other countries, and helps to explain marked gender differences in educational attainment among older people. This is evident by an examination of OECD countries, where the proportion of women with only primary or lower-secondary education is much greater amongst 55–64-year-old women than among 25–34-year-old women (OECD, 1998b).

Today, there is no significant difference between the proportion of women and men completing secondary school in OECD countries (OECD, 1998a), and this has had a knock-on effect in the context of post-compulsory education. In most OECD countries the majority of first-generation higher education entrants are women, and in many countries more than 50 per cent of higher education students are women. For example, in the UK in 1980/81, 41 per cent of full-time higher education students were women, but by 1997/98 the proportion of women had risen to 52 per cent, which is approximately in line with women's demographic representation (CVCP, 1999 and Dugdale, 1997; cf. Coates and Adnett, 2000). In further education colleges in the UK more women (55%) are enrolled than men (45%), and they are 'over-represented' compared to the population as a whole (which is composed of 51% women and 49% men). Although among young students there is not a significant gender difference, women dominate in older age groups (FEFC, 1997a, p. 9); this may reflect the restricted educational opportunities previously available to women, and/or a greater reluctance on the part of men to return to education. In Denmark, women's participation in tertiary education has risen to 60 per cent (OECD). But these positive participation rates by women conceal significant differences.

In particular, women are unevenly distributed across subjects (Williams, 1997). This distribution may not be caused directly by gender discrimination by post-compulsory institutions, but may emerge as a result of direct and indirect discrimination in society and the compulsory education system. The CVCP reports that in the UK women are significantly under-represented in engineering and technology and are over-represented in the arts, humanities and natural sciences. Adminicle evidence is provided by the OECD (1997a). In OECD countries women were found to be more likely to enrol in the generic fields of health, education and social and behavioural sciences, and less likely to participate in the natural sciences and industrial and engineering fields (OECD, 1997a; see also Kosuch, 2000). Such gendered patterns of participation can be explained, in part, as resulting from education at the compulsory level, as Coffield and Vignoles (1997) note:

> These choices [in higher education] can be traced back to gender specialisation in early schooling, linked to the general expectation that girls do not do well at more advanced levels in some subjects, and to the lack of female role models in those subjects. (p. 9)

This position is supported by the work of others (cf. Edwards, 1993; Pascall and Cox, 1993), and the author's own research with school pupils aged from 5 to 14 years (Thomas and Slack, 2000a). The latter research demonstrated that from the early years children had gendered expectations regarding subject preferences and career choices.

But, despite the existence of apparent discriminatory tendencies prior to entry, once women gain access to non-traditional subject areas their success and retention rates are high (Skilbeck and Connell, 2000, p. 34). Consequently, it is important to consider what women study, and at what level, rather than just their rates of participation.

Unless, that is, one is examining postgraduate study. In this context women continue to be under-represented in postgraduate studies (although the expansion in postgraduate education as a whole has kept pace with the expansion of undergraduate study). Skilbeck and Connell (*ibid.*, p. 33) note that men outnumber women in four out of five OECD countries, and in the Czech Republic and Korea less than one third of postgraduate students are women. This received corroboration from CVCP data, reports that women are particularly poorly represented in research degrees: in the UK only 38 per cent of postgraduate research students are women (CVCP, 1999). Australia also features comparable participatory patterns. As a result of access and equity initiatives women have significantly increased their participation in taught postgraduate courses, but not research degrees. An Australian study 'Improving women's participation in research degrees' (Monash Postgraduate Association, 1996, cited in Poole and Spear, 1997) found that although women's participation had improved, it was significantly lower than the female participation rate at undergraduate level 'even in those faculties in which women have high participation rates at the undergraduate level'. It is clear therefore that gender imbalances and stereotypes persist in higher education with regard to both choice of subjects and postgraduate study.

Mature students

Mature entry can refer to circumstances where 'after a prolonged absence from the formal education system, students embark as adults on tertiary-level studies, often through special entry schemes' (Skilbeck and Connell, 2000, p. 37). This is a useful summary, but different definitions prevail both within one country (cf. Parry, 1997) and internationally: indeed, the problem is heightened when comparisons are sought. In UK higher education, students are generally classified as 'mature' if they are aged over 21 when they start their undergraduate study, or over 25 at the commencement of postgraduate work.

In a number of countries there has been an expansion in adult participation in post-compulsory education. In New Zealand, Sweden, Norway and Denmark, more than 20 per cent of first-generation entrants are aged 28 or older; although in France, Ireland and Greece, less than 5 per cent of first-time entrants are over 25 (OECD, 1997b). Adults are likely to continue to be targeted as the concept of 'lifelong learning' takes hold, which it is set to do: 'lifelong learning has become a European and indeed a world-wide dynamic' (Woodrow, 1999a, p. 9; see also Woodrow *et al.* 2000).

Mature students now account for 54 per cent of entrants to higher education in the UK (CVCP, 1999). Mature students, however, tend to favour part-time or evening courses, rather than full-time study. In 1998–9, only 22 per cent of first-year students on full-time undergraduate courses were mature, but 94 per cent of first-year, part-time students were mature (statistics from HESA, in CVCP, 1999). Mature students tend to cluster in a relatively small number of institutions, rather than being distributed throughout the sector, and are concentrated in post-1992 universities (see Table 4.4 below and Wakeford, 1993); as may be expected, the Open University is an important institution for mature students.

Table 4.4: Age of students by university sector, 1996

University sector	19 years of age and under (%)	20–25 years of age (%)	26 years of age and over (%)
'Old'	68	37	35
'New'	32	63	65
TOTAL	100	100	100

Source: Coffield and Vignoles, 1997, p. 12

Furthermore, mature students study a narrower range of courses, are more likely to be self-financing and are more likely to interrupt their course of study. Although more likely to intermit, those that complete are more likely to attain a first-class degree than their young, traditional-entry contemporaries. The expansion in the number of mature students has been a successful feature of the UK higher education system, and this growth has helped to alert HEIs to the need for flexibility, including alternative admission routes, different locations and times for learning and developing appropriate curricula (discussed in Chapter 7). Mature students (over 25) also account for a highly significant proportion of postgraduate-level study in the UK: 46 per cent of first-year, full-time postgraduates are mature, as are 90 per cent of part-time, postgraduate students.

Rates of participation decline when 'older' learners are considered (see Marshall 1999). For example, in 1997, 6909 students over the age of 40 entered as undergraduates into higher education in the UK, which represents 2.1 per cent of all undergraduates entering higher education (UCAS, 1997). As with mature students in general, differences between institutions and subjects are apparent. The national average rate of entry is 2.1 per cent; in the West Midlands the regional rate is 1.8 per cent, but within this region there are significant institutional differences (see Table 4.5). Worcester College and the University of Wolverhampton, which are both post-1992 universities, recruit more than the national average of over-40-year-olds, whereas Aston University and the University of Birmingham accept a far lower percentage of over-40s. Both are pre-1992 universities.

Table 4.5: Entry of over 40s to West Midlands Universities (undergraduate degree programmes), 1997

HEI	Percentage of students over 40 (accepted in 1997)
Aston	0.5
Birmingham	0.5
Keele	1.4
Staffordshire	1.9
University of Central England	1.7
Wolverhampton	2.4
Worcester College	4.0
Regional Average	1.8
National Average	2.1

Source: UCAS Statistics, 1997

The average age of entry to HE in the UK is 20.6 years; with the oldest average age of entry being 22.3 for general and combined studies, and the youngest average age being 18.7 for medicine and dentistry. Table 4.6 shows the average age of students entering higher

Table 4.6: Average age of accepted applicants by subject (1997 entry)

Subject	Average age
Medicine and dentistry	18.7
Biological sciences	20.9
Agriculture	21.0
Physical sciences	19.4
Mathematics	20.4
Engineering	20.2
Architecture	20.5
Social studies	21.1
Business	19.9
Communications	20.5
Languages	20.2
Humanities	21.4
Creative arts	21.4
Education	21.7
Combined sciences	20.2
Combined social studies	19.9
Combined arts	21.3
Social studies/arts	20.2
General and combined	22.3
AVERAGE	**20.6**

Source: UCAS Statistics, 1997

education, by subject. From this, it can be surmised that some subjects are either more desirable for older students, or that age discrimination is occurring (cf. Woodrow, forthcoming). The analysis of students by age, however, does not indicate the importance of other social factors, such as class. The categories 'mature student' and 'older learner' can include both 'second helpings' and 'second chances', i.e. those people who are already well-educated and can access more learning, against those who have missed out the first time around, and who seek a second opportunity to participate in tertiary education. Data from the Higher Education Funding Council for England (HEFCE, 1997) show that 'the pattern of participation by social group for mature entrants is not very different from young entrants' (see also Metcalfe, 1993). Similarly, in Germany there is a direct relationship between participation in adult education and previous educational attainment (Kommer, 1998). Kivinen and Rinne (1996) document similar findings and conclude that participation by mature students is a 'mode of cumulative cultural capital' (p. 126). Maggie Woodrow concludes:

> Overall it appears that adult education is more useful for integrating into the system those who are most similar to traditional entrants, than for encouraging participation by new groups from different socio-economic or cultural backgrounds. (Woodrow, 1999, p. 10)

Mature students form an important sub-group when examining participation, but age is far less likely to be a barrier to participation than other social factors. Measures targeted at specific equity groups are required, in addition to expanding the number of mature students (see Gallagher et al., 1993).

Students with non-traditional entrance qualifications

An indication of diversity in participation in post-compulsory education is the *level* and *type* of qualifications with which students enter. For example, students from lower socio-economic groups, ethnic minorities and mature students often have 'poorer' qualifications than their younger, white, middle-class contemporaries. Skilbeck and Connell (2000, p. 38) note the fact that mature students have often fared badly at school, and thus need a 'second chance' and are less likely to have traditional entry qualifications.

The FEFC note Black and Pakistani students entering further education have the 'lowest qualifications on entry. Only 27 per cent of Black Caribbean 16 year olds have achieved foundation target 1 when they enter further education or tertiary college' (FEFC, 1997a, p. 11). Traditionally, in the UK, all (young) students have entered higher education on the basis of their A-level subjects and grades, usually taken at the age of eighteen. Students who have experienced disadvantages that have affected their educational achievement, and older students who have left school without A-levels are, potentially, debarred from higher education and will face restricted educational opportunities. In 1997–8 about 67 per cent of students entered higher education with A-levels (UCAS, 1998). Alternative entry routes facilitate entry for people who have either not studied A-levels (for example older students) or for those who have not achieved the grades. Such routes include BTEC/SCOTEC, Advanced General National Vocational Qualification (AGNVQ), the International Baccalaureate, Access courses, foundation years, accreditation of prior (experiential) learning (AP(E)L), remedial skills courses and entrance interviews.

In 1998/99, 33.4 per cent of higher education applicants who were offered a place had non-traditional qualifications (UCAS, 1998), but Coffield and Vignoles (1997) note that 'entering HE without A Levels remains a difficult task' (p. 12). Of course, international differences exist, and something of a continuum opens up between New Zealand, where an 'open admissions' route for adults is present, and Ireland, where there are very limited opportunities for mature students to participate in adult education.

In the UK the distribution of students with alternative entry qualifications between institutions is marked. In 1992 traditional universities admitted only 16 per cent of students without A-level qualifications, whereas modern universities admitted 41 per cent without A-level qualifications (Coffield and Vignoles, 1997, p. 12). Many traditional, pre-1992 universities are reluctant to alter their entry requirements, and the issue of quality often emerges in this context. Important differences also exist at the institutional level, however, and admissions tutors are able to exercise considerable discretionary power here. Smith, Scott and Bargh (1995) and Hogarth et al. (1997) report that such staff tend to 'view students without A levels as problematic and resource intensive in terms of recruitment and teaching' (Coffield and Vignoles, 1997, p. 12). There is evidence to suggest, however, that the performance of students without traditional A-level qualifications exceeds that of their peers, especially when compared to those with low A-level scores (Hogarth et al., 1997 and Robertson, 1997). Furthermore, Bull (2000) reports that in Australia, non-traditional students entering higher education via an 'enabling programme' (i.e. without traditional entrance qualifications) perform better than their peers.

In further education in the UK, students were categorized according to whether or not they had reached the foundation target 1, which is five GCSEs at grades A–C, or equivalent. A points score was calculated for other students, with seven points awarded for a grade A, down to one point for a grade G. The entry qualifications from a sample of 176 colleges (of which 82 were sixth-form colleges) were analysed by the FEFC for 1995–6. At the national level, about 45 per cent of young people were found to have obtained the foundation target 1 when they completed school, but a significant difference was found between entrants to sixth-form colleges and young people entering further education colleges. Seventy-two per cent of 16-year-olds in sixth-form colleges had reached foundation target 1 when they were recruited, compared with 44 per cent entering further education colleges (FEFC, 1997a). This is shown in Table 4.7.

Table 4.7: Percentage of students with foundation target 1

	Sixth-form colleges (SFCs)		FE colleges (except SFCs)	
	16-year-olds	17-year-olds	16-year-olds	17-year-olds
Female (%)	75	83	48	59
Male (%)	69	81	39	53
All (%)	72	82	44	56

Source: FEFC (1997a), individualised student record (ISR) 1995–6, from 178 colleges

The FEFC has examined the impact of 'additional support' on student retention. Additional support is defined as 'an activity which provides direct support for learning to individual students which is over and above that normally provided in a standard learning programme which leads to the primary learning goal' (FEFC, 1997a, p. 12). The findings are that 'in all age groups students receiving additional support have higher retention rates than those not receiving support. This is particularly noticeable for full-time adult students aged 25 and over receiving support where the retention rate is 93 per cent, compared to 86 per cent for those not receiving support' (FEFC, 1997a, p. 12). This again demonstrates that entrance qualifications are not necessarily a good indicator of ability or performance, and perhaps of equal importance, or more important, is the level of support that students receive once they have entered post-compulsory education.

Conclusion

At the international macro level, participation rates in post-compulsory education are encouraging. A more in-depth analysis of participation using a range of equity categories reveals a more patchy picture. In particular, non-traditional student groups tend to be concentrated in particular subjects and types of institutions. For example, the UK scene demonstrates that further education is more representative than higher education; and modern, post-1992 universities are more inclusive than traditional universities. Similarly, in the USA, wider participation in post-compulsory education has seen non-traditional students being over-represented in lower-status or special-category institutions (see Jary *et al.*, 1998), and a comparable trend can be witnessed in Japan (Kaneko, 1997). This can lead to the marginalization of these students and the qualifications gained from institutions that are *perceived* to be 'second rate' or worse. This situation is reinforced and exacerbated when education that is nominally the same receives differential unit funding (per student) on the basis of the status of the institution. This phenomenon is likely to grow in the UK, particularly as the 'Russell Group' of traditional universities argues to be allowed to charge higher tuition fees. This seems at odds with the needs of the students, as it is widely agreed that 'non-standard students are more resource intensive in terms of recruitment and teaching' (Coffield and Vignoles, 1997, p. 13).

The examination of participation rates by under-represented social groups in a number of so-called 'developed' countries demonstrates that an *increase* in access is insufficient to overcome entrenched patterns of disproportionate participation. To provide equality of opportunity (and this in itself does not guarantee equality of outcomes) it is necessary to *widen* participation in further and higher education, rather than to simply expand it, a distinction discussed in Chapter 1. Furthermore, access rates do not translate directly into successful completion and progression rates, and without these it is impossible to judge equality of outcomes.

CHAPTER 5

Identifying Assumptions and Barriers to Participation

Introduction

The previous chapter illustrated that although there have been major increases in the number of students participating in post-compulsory education during the last decade, there are still significant variations between the participation rates of different sectors of society, and the institutions and fields in which non-traditional student groups participate. The remainder of the book considers the different types or categories of 'barriers' that contribute to low participation rates by individuals and groups, and starts to indicate solutions to them. In particular, the focus is on students from low socio-economic groups.

This chapter outlines the categorization of barriers that is employed. It then, briefly, justifies the use of the equity group 'low socio-economic status' to explore the different barriers discussed. Finally, it turns to the 'assumptions' that underpin our conceptualization of barriers.

Barriers to participation in post-compulsory education

The term 'barrier' is used to refer to factors that discourage or prevent participation in post-compulsory education. The modalities of barriers will vary, and could include factors such as distances between communities and colleges or minimum entry-qualification requirements. They also relate to perceptions regarding who 'should' undertake post-compulsory education, and how difficult this may be. Indeed, barriers are culturally constructed; there are, for example, significant differences between the 'barriers' created by geographical distance in Canada and the UK, but they are equally inhibiting (Thomas *et al.*, 1999/2000, p. 56). Hence: 'Measured then as time, cost, or even perceived/social distance, the concept of "a long way" can be very fluid' (p. 57).

Four categories of barriers are considered. First, those that pertain to features of the compulsory and post-compulsory education systems; Second, those related to the economy, particularly the impacts of the labour market and unemployment; and third, the influence of social and cultural factors on participation in post-compulsory education. Finally, the notion that individual 'deficits' are to blame for non-participation is examined.

These four categories of barriers interact to limit participation, as is illustrated in Figure 5.1. In reality, it can be difficult to disentangle the impacts of the education system, the labour market, social and cultural norms, and individual issues, but for the sake of clarity of explanation these distinctions are drawn and some key consequences are discussed. Hodgson (1999, pp. 18–20) identifies the broad factors that are cited in the literature as the underlying causes of disaffection, non-participation and social exclusion from education and training for children and adults, and proposes a similar framework for analysing problems and policy solutions in that field.

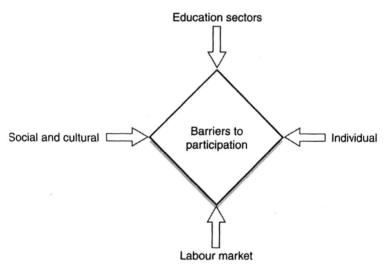

Figure 5.1 *Categories of barriers to participation*

A central argument is that acknowledging only one category (especially just one particular barrier) is unlikely to be the most effective way of addressing the complex issues surrounding low participation by some sectors of society. Only recognizing and remedying one of the barriers to access may even be counter-productive, as non-traditional students may enter education but be unable to complete as other obstacles remain in place. For example, providing education in a more accessible location, without offering appropriate personal and academic support services, may be insufficient and may result in withdrawal. This experience, which could be perceived as 'failure' (whether by students or institutions), may discourage or prohibit future involvement in formal learning. It is, therefore, suggested that an effective *strategy* to widen participation among under-represented groups of students should take account of the differing categories of barriers that exist, and seek to develop an approach that engages with as wide a range of factors as possible.

Low socio-economic status

The following chapters tend to focus on the target or equity group described as 'low economic status'. This is supplemented by examples and issues relating to other groups that were identified in Chapter 4 as under-represented in post-compulsory education. It is widely acknowledged (Kennedy, 1997; CVCP, 1999; Woodrow, 1999b; and Bekhradnia, 2000a, b) that lower rates of participation by students from lower socio-economic groups, i.e. by those with low incomes, is the most persistent failing of the post-compulsory education system in the UK. It is also a significant problem in many other countries, especially in those where education is not free. For example, 'people from low socio-economic backgrounds' are recognized as an under-represented group in Australia (DEET, 1990) at both the national and the institutional level. The focus on socio-economic status is not meant to underestimate the gravitas of factors confronting other groups, but to draw on the author's experience and empirical research. Many of the comments and arguments are intended to be applicable to other under-represented groups.

Assumptions

In the formal and informal literature, in policy circles, in practice and in discussions at various levels, there are implicit or explicit assumptions relating to the nature of the barriers that inhibit participation and progression by certain groups. These assumptions not only underpin people's perceptions of the barriers to access, but also the extent to which they need to be removed, and the best way to do this (if at all).

An example can be used to illustrate these points. Think about the perennial question: Why are students from low socio-economic groups less likely to go to college than their middle-class peers? The way one starts to answer this question will strongly influence the way the issue is tackled, if indeed it is. Does the situation arise from 'ability', inclination or lack of opportunity? If the 'cause' is attributed to a perceived 'lack of ability' this raises a further set of questions: Is ability innate, and therefore unalterable? How is ability measured? Does quantification rely on past performance and qualification achievements as a proxy for potential ability, and, if so, how significant are the school system, home culture and individual motivation in accounting for prior attainment? Is past performance an effective and satisfactory indicator of future capacity? The responses to these and similar questions will inevitably rest on a range of assumptions. Exploring the answers to these and related questions helps to expose the assumptions that underpin thinking about widening participation in post-compulsory education. Assumptions such as these shape the policy and practices that are intended to reduce inequality, and if the assumptions are ill-founded, then the ensuing policies and practices are highly likely to be of limited effectiveness, and may fail or even do more harm than good.

Box 5.1 Examples of assumptions underpinning widening participation initiatives

'This situation is exacerbated by relatively poor aspiration and poor educational achievement.'

'Students' backgrounds and cultures need to be clearly acknowledged ... Wider cultural issues need to be addressed.'

'The scheme focuses upon those students who are judged to have high ability ... but whose family and educational background is such that they might not consider applying for higher education ... The objective is to encourage these students to raise their aspirations.'

The project aims 'to involve and educate policy-makers ... to develop together new approaches within mainstream training and education agencies which facilitate the particular needs of women.'

Box 5.1 includes some examples of statements from literature produced by initiatives intended to widen participation in further and higher education. These (admittedly selective) comments indicate some of the assumptions that the authors of the documents have made, and that have shaped the nature and contents of the project or policy that has been developed and implemented. But to what extent do these assumptions correspond to the perceptions and experiences of the particular target groups? To what extent have these assumptions been explored and investigated with the intended beneficiaries?

Any assumption that underpins a social programme needs to be explicit – partly so that it can be examined. An assumption is not *necessarily* right or wrong, but perceptions differ between individuals or 'stakeholders', and so the position and experiences of the person or group making the assumptions must not be ignored. For example, one would probably receive different answers to the questions in Box 5.2, from students, a college principal, teaching staff, local employers and the funding body. Furthermore, different students may have different perceptions depending on income, past experience of education, whether they have their own transport, whether they have children (either requiring childcare or needing collecting from school), whether they are employed, seeking work, wanting to meet people etc.

Box 5.2 Questions that would probably receive different answers from different stakeholders

---

Is the college too far away?

Is childcare available and affordable?

Are courses timetabled conveniently?

Does the college meet the needs of the local people?

Should the college prioritize academic, vocational or leisure courses?

By their very nature, assumptions are not recognized, unless a conscious effort is made to do so. Project organizers and policy-makers often assume the causes of low participation – and then seek to redress them – without comparing their assumptions with those of other people – particularly the group the initiative seeks to support. It is valuable to reflect on, and identify, underlying assumptions and to make them explicit. This helps to avoid 'killer assumptions'; assumptions that, if they do not hold 'true' (for example, in the eyes of the intended beneficiaries), the whole scheme will be undermined and will fail. An example of a killer assumption is discussed in Box 5.3.

Box 5.3 An example of a killer assumption

> It was assumed by project organizers that members of a 'community' living on a particular housing estate were homogeneous; and did not participate in college courses because the college was too far away.
>
> Members of the community were consulted about what type of courses they would like to attend, with a view to these being provided in a local venue. But divisions in the community meant that they would not all be willing to attend a course at the same location in the community. Fortunately, this barrier was made explicit by working closely with different community members, but if the issue had not been clarified this scheme would have been less effective.

The reasons for non-participation are complex and not always obvious. Making assumptions about the causes and solutions is potentially unproductive. Research, consultation and participation in planning and implementation are required.

Once assumptions are identified, they can be investigated critically and analysed, and, if necessary, re-conceptualized. Assumptions can perhaps best be challenged through participatory planning and implementation processes which involve a range of stakeholders, particularly those who are expected to benefit from the new policy or practice that is being developed. An examination of community development in both the UK and developing countries shows support for moving away from 'top-down' initiatives that are planned and implemented by the government (or an institution), to participatory processes involving a range of actors (see Mackintosh, 1992). Maureen Mackintosh sees policy not as prescription but as a process, which involves different stakeholders having different interests. The role of intervention is not to plan and implement change, but to facilitate coherence, and, ideally, to build consensus (although it may involve deciding whose views are prioritized).

The process of examining assumptions, and involving others in the planning process, can seem daunting, as it appears to expose 'those in control' – assumptions may be 'wrong' and power and control may be relinquished. The well-known 'prisoners' dilemma', however, illustrates how decisions taken independently can lead to an inferior outcome compared with the situation where the decision is taken jointly (see Box 5.4).

Box 5.4 The prisoners' dilemma

Two prisoners, kept in separate cells, are accused of jointly carrying out a crime. The objective of each prisoner is to minimize the individual period of imprisonment. Each one knows that, if both confess, each will receive four years' imprisonment, but if they both deny, each will receive only two years. They also know that if one confesses and the other denies, then the confessing prisoner receives one year and the denying prisoner receives five years.

Prisoner B

		Not confess	Confess
Prisoner A	Not confess	2 years each	5 years for A and 1 year for B
	Confess	1 year for A and 5 years for B	4 years each

For prisoner A the best strategy is to confess: if B confesses, it is better for A to confess (4 years rather than 5), and if B denies, it is better for A to confess (1 year rather than 2). Similarly, B's best strategy is to confess. Consequently, both confess and receive 4 years each, but if they had both denied they would have each received only 2 years. This demonstrates that the best option is the collective decision, but such an action is ruled out when the decision is taken individually.

This book, therefore, aims to explore the different types of barriers that exist in some sectors of society and which may impede participation in post-compulsory education and more importantly, to stimulate thinking about these. The book rests upon a number of assumptions: for example, that formal learning is of value to people; that post-compulsory education should be available to everyone; and that certain groups face more severe barriers to access than the average. It does not claim to provide all the answers, but to encourage policy-makers, practitioners, researchers and other 'interested parties' to engage in the process of thinking about assumptions and barriers – and to involve other stakeholders in this process.

The rest of the book

The next five chapters explore barriers that may limit participation in post-compulsory education, using the schema outlined above. Chapter 11 then discusses the importance of developing a strategic approach to widening participation. In order to help promote awareness of a broad range of barriers facing potential entrants, and to assist with strategic thinking, at the end of each chapter (5–11) some 'key questions' are posed. These are not intended to act as a checklist, but to stimulate thinking, and, in particular, they could be used in participative planning processes to initiate discussions. They are used to examine the case studies presented in Chapters 12, 13 and 14. This is not to evaluate each initiative, and then pronounce its utility and effectiveness, but rather to seek to illustrate the different assumptions that can underpin outreach work, and the potential benefits of moving towards strategic thinking, involving a range of stakeholders. To assist the thinking process each case study ends with a table listing some key questions, and a 'score' of how well I think the scheme rates in relation to each issue. This is *not* an objective score, and, as such, is of no value. Instead, the *process* of completing the grid is perceived to be of value, particularly when it is undertaken as a group activity and is used to stimulate reflection and debate between stakeholders. The scores indicated in the grids relate to my perceptions of the projects.

Conclusions

This chapter has outlined the schema that is used to discuss barriers to participation, and has noted the focus on students from low socio-economic groups. It has highlighted that assumptions underpin conceptualizations of 'barriers' to participation. To avoid dependence on assumptions that are not shared by others, such as intended beneficiaries, a participative approach is recommended. The arena in which widening participation policy and practice occurs is not uniform, static or unchanging, so there cannot be a prescription or formula for widening participation. In consequence, the remainder of the book raises issues for reflection and debate, but is not intended to offer a blueprint for thinking or action.

Key questions to ask about assumptions:

- What are the underlying assumptions?
- Who is making the assumptions?
- Have these assumptions been investigated?
- Are there likely to be any killer assumptions?

CHAPTER 6

Schools and Progression: Barriers Created by the Compulsory Education System

Introduction

The next two chapters examine some of the impacts of the education system on participation in further and higher education and on lifelong learning. This chapter focuses on the compulsory sector, while the following one examines the post-compulsory sector.

Schools help to determine the future participation of pupils in further and higher education and other forms of lifelong learning. This is achieved partly through educational achievement, as this facilitates progression to the next educational level. But also, and perhaps more importantly, schools contribute to the ways in which education is perceived by learners. For example, is learning seen as enjoyable or difficult or even humiliating? The experience and process of education contribute to the image pupils have of themselves; how they relate to education, and whether or not they perceive themselves as learners. Consequently, it is important that schools enable pupils to maximize their achievements, build their confidence and encourage them to progress in education, not necessarily immediately, but at some future point. This chapter looks first at qualifications and achievement, and second at attitudes towards learning, and hence the barriers that may be attributable to the compulsory education system.

Qualifications and achievement

Pupils who do not achieve the required qualifications in compulsory schooling are often prohibited from progressing into other forms of education and training, or, as a consequence, find their options limited (although there is often provision for re-studying, and, in some instances, alternative entry routes exist). In the UK, the national target is for pupils to achieve five GCSEs at grade A–C at the end of compulsory schooling, at age sixteen. 78 per cent of seventeen-year-olds in sixth forms and 44 per cent in further education colleges have reached this target. In the UK, 49.2 per cent of pupils achieve this target (DfEE, 2000), so many school leavers may face limited educational opportunities, and they might either not continue in education, or study a subject (or enter an institution) that is not their first preference. In the UK, to enter both nursing studies and teacher training, a GCSE (grade C or above) or equivalent qualification in maths is a prerequisite. But without this qualification (which is usually gained in school), students wishing to pursue these educational and career pathways will be prevented from doing so. For this reason, a maths summer school, recently organized by Staffordshire and Keele universities, proved popular with students who wanted to enter these professions.

Peter Mortimore and Geoff Whitty state: 'there is longstanding – and continuing – evidence that students from disadvantaged social backgrounds fare relatively badly within formal education systems' (1999, p. 80). In support of this they cite the work of Douglas, 1964; Davie *et al.* 1972; Essen and Wedge 1982; Mortimore and Mortimore, 1986; Osborne and Millbank, 1987; Gorman and Fernandes, 1992; and OECD, 1995. Likewise, Glennerster (1998) emphasizes that, whatever the causal relationship, poverty and deprivation in children's families and the neighbourhood in which they grow up tends to correlate with their school performance, and that there is a clear correlation between poor educational achievement and unemployment or low income. In a similar vein, Machin notes that educational disadvantage is highly likely to span generations (Machin, 1998; Gregg and Machin, 1997).

Although it is beyond the scope of this book to examine these claims, it can be stated confidently that social class, at least in part, influences school achievement, and this in turn impedes or enhances progression into post-compulsory education. This latter assertion is further supported by the low participation rates, particularly in higher education, by students from lower socio-economic groups, and the predominance of A-levels as the main entry qualification in the UK (as discussed in Chapter 4).

It follows that, as George Papadopoulos (formerly Deputy Director for Education in the OECD) argues, to democratize post-compulsory education and to ensure equality of outcomes, the school sector needs to be reformed. He notes that: 'despite the moral and economic arguments for the democratisation of higher education [and further education], governments have so far largely failed to achieve this goal' (Papadopoulos, 2000, p. 33).

This, he asserts, is because: 'educational disadvantage is strongly rooted in socio-economic disadvantage', and, therefore, 'those who benefit from post-compulsory education, in whatever setting, are those who are already well-educated' (p. 35).

Thus a key element of his prescription is to 'seek to imbue in pupils both a capacity and an interest in learning to learn' (p. 36) in the early stages of the education system, including pre-school provision 'to bring all pupils, irrespective of class or family background, to the same starting point at the end of compulsory schooling' (*ibid.*). He continues:

> Radical conclusions must be reached. Higher education must be considered as an organic part of the total education system, with a corresponding need of a downwards shift, refocusing resources to attack the problem at its roots, namely: combating failure at school and improving post-school pathways to further and higher education and/or work. (*ibid.*)

It should not, however, be assumed or implied that teachers and schools are to be blamed for the 'failure' of some pupils to achieve sufficient qualifications (furthermore, there is a debate to be engaged in regarding whether or not certification is the primary aim of education). There are multiple reasons for underachievement, and these must be considered as constituent parts of the problem, rather than in isolation (cf. Whitty *et al.*, 1999; Mortimore and Whitty, 1999).

Mortimore and Whitty note three ways in which social disadvantage works against educational achievement. Poverty and material disadvantage is frequently accompanied by poorer health (Holtermann, 1997); consequently children tend to have more time away from school with illness, and they have less energy than their peers, both of which have negative impacts on their school work. These children are also more likely to experience tension, stress and emotional upset in their lives; concomitantly, they are also less likely to be able to study at home or out of school hours, and have less access to educational help and support from home. So it can be concluded that social and economic disadvantage tend to manifest themselves as educational disadvantage at an early stage, and this is perpetuated throughout a child's educational career.

The following will use a framework drawn from elements of the work of Mortimore and Whitty (1999) to illustrate different approaches to improving educational opportunities and outcomes in school of children from poorer backgrounds. This analysis demonstrates that the task has only ever been, at best, partially successful. Post-compulsory education, and particularly higher education, should not, therefore, rely solely on qualifications to determine admission, as these are indicators of past performance only, not of potential capacity. Furthermore, the following discussion highlights the limitations of trying to solve multi-dimensional problems through a single approach.

One approach to overcoming disadvantage in schools is meritocracy. The meritocratic principle – that those with the greatest ability are rewarded – informs all public examinations. This philosophy underpinned the 11-plus exam in the UK. All pupils were entitled to enter the examination, and all successful candidates were offered a grammar school place, irrespective of social class. But this strategy did not ensure equality of outcomes; instead, it reinforced privilege and disadvantage respectively.

Meritocracy largely fails to deliver equality in education, because it does not take account of the underlying causes of educational success and underachievement. Research has shown a meritocratic approach helps a few individuals with 'outstanding talents' to overcome the limitations of social disadvantage, but it overlooks many more, and does not improve the educational experience for the majority who are 'left behind' (Mortimore and Whitty, 1999, p. 82; see also Brown et al., 1997).

Despite the limitations of meritocracy, this approach is still used to offer scholarships and 'assisted places' to elite schools for a limited number of pupils who perform well in pre-entry examinations. Indeed, providing more state-supported scholarships to private schools is one solution proposed by the Sutton Trust to increase participation in elite universities by students from low socio-economic groups (Sutton Trust, 2000; cf. Jary and Thomas, 2000).

In recognition of the failure of the UK dual education system (based on the 11-plus exam and differentiation between grammar and secondary modern schools) to deliver educational equality of outcomes, comprehensive schools were introduced. Comprehensive schools were intended to expand the principle of meritocracy by offering all pupils an equal opportunity (i.e. the 'same' school experience), irrespective of their performance in an exam at the age of 11. But, as Chapter 4 demonstrated, this approach has not led to representative participation by social class in post-compulsory education. Entry to higher education, in particular, is still largely dependent on examination in many countries including the UK, Ireland, Australia and Sweden. Hence, pupils from disadvantaged backgrounds may be unfairly excluded if they have underachieved at school.

Differentiating the various components of the post-compulsory education sector, Halsey (1986) cites universities as the pinnacle and the most sought-after form of education beyond school, and the form of post-compulsory education to which disadvantaged pupils are the least likely to gain access:

> The evidence is that comprehensive reform of the secondary schools has contributed heavily to the output of entrants to higher and further education but without changing the correlation between social origin and educational attainment. (p. 143)

This observation was made fifteen years ago, before the reform of the higher education sector in 1992. It is still true, to a large extent, today, however, as the breakdown of participation in higher education by social class (discussed in Chapter 4) demonstrates. This class bias is further exaggerated in the UK, when the ostensibly unitary higher education system is disaggregated into traditional universities (pre-1992) and modern universities (formerly polytechnics), revealing a stratified, hierarchical structure. The HEFCE performance indicators relating to social class (published in *The Times* on 6 October 2000, see Charter, 2000) indicate that modern universities out-perform traditional universities in terms of recruiting students from state schools, the lowest social classes and from the poorest postcode areas. It can be concluded that a meritocratic compulsory education sector that offers all children an 'equal chance', does not overcome social disadvantage, and class, ethnicity and other biases continue into the post-compulsory sector.

As social disadvantage continues to be translated into educational disadvantage, with implications for access to post-compulsory education, various 'compensatory mechanisms' and 'specific inter-ventions' have been introduced into schools. These types of strategy involve identifying and targeting those pupils thought to be disadvantaged and providing additional support to compensate them. Such initiatives may be targeted at individuals or, as is frequently the case in compulsory education, at particular schools. Individual benefits include free school meals, uniform grants and other measures for low-income families. Smith and Noble (1995, cited in Mortimore and Whitty, 1999) argue that individual benefits tend to involve low funding levels, and have been unable to compensate for the significant differences in children's lives, and so have been largely ineffective.

In the UK, in the 1960s and 1970s, Educational Priority Area programmes sought to target schools with high levels of disadvantaged pupils, and to make additional payments to them (Smith, 1987). These can be compared with contemporary Education Action Zones (EAZs) that also focus on areas of deprivation. A limitation of this approach is its inaccuracy in targeting the pupils in need, as advantaged pupils in selected schools will benefit from additional resources, while disadvantaged pupils in other schools will not be supported. Research conducted by the Institute for Access Studies (Thomas and Slack, 1999a) into a project focusing on a whole year group demonstrates that this approach to reaching disadvantaged pupils is potentially flawed and ineffective. Some pupils are better able to utilize the experience than others, and this tends to coincide with existing advantages. For example, those who participated in the programme of activities were described as 'keenos' and 'swots' by their peers who had either not chosen to participate or who had not been selected by the school staff (this is discussed further in Chapter 10). Thus, the benefits of this, and similar interventions, is limited.

Some compensatory mechanisms, or special intervention projects, target disadvantaged pupils with the explicit intention of accelerating their educational development. A significant number of schemes have been implemented in many countries, and have been shown to have positive impacts on disadvantaged children. Mortimore and Whitty note the following initiatives: schemes in the USA include the High/Scope programme for pre-school children (Schweinhart and Weikart, 1997) and Success for All (Madden et al., 1993; Herman and Stringfield, 1995). In New Zealand, the Reading Recovery Programme has helped to overcome reading difficulties (Clay, 1982; Rowe, 1995). In the UK there have been a range of projects (see for example Athey, 1990; Tizard et al., 1982; MacBeath and Turner, 1990) which have been welcomed and endorsed by teachers, but which have not been implemented widely, as government support (especially financial support) has been restricted.

Compensatory and intervention initiatives have proved costly, and when they are less resource-intensive they tend to be less effective. Furthermore, poor targeting can result in no comparative improvement by pupils from disadvantaged backgrounds, and interventions can actually exacerbate the problem. Mortimore and Whitty (1999) conclude that educational success, like poverty, appears to be *relative*. They say: 'One of the depressing findings is that the relative performance of the disadvantaged has remained similar even when the absolute performance of such groups has improved (p. 86; see also

Mortimore *et al.*, 1988; Thomas *et al.*, 1997).

This lack of success, and the inherent costs involved, have led UK governments towards the notion of 'school improvement' to overcome disadvantage. This strategy is based on the belief that responsibility for change lies with schools (Stoll and Fink, 1996, cited in Mortimore and Whitty, 1999). The emphasis is on each school developing and implementing its own policy for improvement, which is not prescriptive, but which draws on the expertise of the head teacher, teaching staff and the governing body. This approach often relies upon good leadership and teamwork – and extraordinary effort on the part of all staff. It can, therefore, be argued that it is, generally, an unsustainable solution, and cannot be applied universally. Mortimore and Whitty warn:

> whilst it might be possible, for example, for the ethos of a particular school to help transform the aspirations of a particular group of students within it, it seems highly unlikely that all schools could do this in the absence of more substantial social changes. (p. 86)

These various school-focused approaches to overcoming the social and economic disadvantages of young people, manifested in educational underachievement, have proved to be either ineffective or only to reach some of those who could and should benefit. Success in school can be a key factor facilitating progression into further and higher education for students from lower socio-economic groups, and helps to ensure that these young people are not funnelled into lower-level qualifications, to become marginalized, or even ghettoized, in lower-status institutions. This is what has tended to happen in the USA through the development of two-year programmes in community colleges (Jary, *et al.*, 1998).

Schools alone cannot be expected to compensate for social and economic divisions and disadvantage in society; the causes of underachievement are multiple, and so the solutions need to be multifaceted too (see also Whitty, *et al.*, 1999). Post-compulsory education must play its part. It is important that institutions recognize that an admissions policy based on the premise of either formal equality or equality of opportunity will not ensure greater participation by currently under-represented, groups as there are significant differences in performance and achievement in the compulsory sector between different social groups. Despite the best efforts of committed educationalists, this is likely to continue to be the case. Institutions in the post-compulsory sector will only perpetuate disadvantage if past performance continues to be the only passport to entry to further study. This will tend to create greater social division, rather than overcome disparities. Neither should it be assumed that lacking the relevant entry qualifications is an indicator of low ability; an apparent lack of interest or poor motivation may be related to a wide range of other factors, some of which are embedded in the school system. Some of these issues are discussed in the next section.

Perceptions of self and attitudes to learning

The school environment contributes not just to the qualifications with which pupils emerge but also the expectations and self-images that they hold in relation to education and, concomitantly, jobs, careers and lifelong learning. Linda Clarke comments on the importance of 'opportunity structures' that shape the thinking of young people in relation to jobs and careers, and the way that education can reinforce social expectations and stereotypes:

> Careers can be regarded as developing into patterns dictated by the opportunity structures to which individuals are exposed, first in education and subsequently in employment. Individuals' ambitions in turn can be treated as reflecting the influence of the structures through which they pass. (Clarke, 1980)

Julia Preece (1999a, b) undertook research with adults who had been excluded from the educational system for a range of reasons, including gender, class, ethnicity and physical ability. Using a life-history approach the participants 'constructed their identities in relation to work, family and schooling' (1999b, p. 21). She reports findings similar to those of Clarke. Preece found that people's perceptions of themselves were constructed in relation to the 'dominant discourses of their time' and that 'people's sense of self proved fluid and malleable' (ibid.). She concludes that experiences in school help to determine participants' perceptions of education and their own position in relation to this dominant discourse – one of the respondents described herself as a 'dunderbrain' as she failed to secure a place at grammar school. Preece reports that people reconstructed their personal ambitions to coincide with the dominant view of themselves as women, disabled persons or whatever (op. cit., p. 19).

Val Millman explored the impact of 'opportunity structures' or the 'dominant discourse' on the decisions that girls made about their education and employment. She found that the 'hidden curriculum of the school had clearly influenced their aspirations and their expectations of their future' (Millman, 1985, p. 99). The term 'hidden curriculum' has been widely used to refer to the idea that many things learnt in school are not actually taught. There are values, attitudes and knowledge frames entrenched in the school system and the schooling process, which are implicitly conveyed to pupils. Both Marxists and structural-functionists agree, although for different reasons, that the role of the hidden curriculum is to promote social control of young people, and an acceptance of the dominant authority structure. Thus, through the school experience and the hidden curriculum, attitudes to learning, expectations relating to gender, class, ethnicity, disability and so on, and self-perceptions are formed. So influential is this informal learning that it can be argued that the hidden curriculum is more important than the official curriculum (see, for example, Parsons, 1959; Jackson and Marsden, 1968; Bowles and Gintis, 1976).

A good example of the influence of the hidden curriculum, or the 'dominant discourse' in Preece's conceptual framework, is provided in relation to education and physical disability (Preece, 1999b). Her study sees a disabled tutor note that people assume that people with disabilities are unable to succeed in education: 'you begin to realise actually how many people patronise you and how many people think you are not quite up to scratch ... I mean you get used to that and you get to think well it must be true' (p. 19). In turn, a research participant with cerebral palsy describes how she was steered away from education because of her disability. She had worked hard and secured a place at grammar school, but was persuaded, or forced, to leave school before taking her exams. She wanted to be a nurse, but accepted the fact that her disability would make this difficult (or impossible), but she was not encouraged to take her exams and try for a similar status career; instead, she was talked into accepting a job working in a shop.

From these examples (and there are many more), it can be concluded that school equips people not only with qualifications to progress to other educational opportunities, but also helps them to form a set of ideas about themselves in terms of whether or not they are 'good' learners, and the sort of aspirations they should have. Indeed, there appears to be a direct relationship between participation in post-compulsory education and previous educational *experiences* and *qualifications*. This claim is supported by German research by Kommer (1998), who found that not only do earlier educational, social or vocational disadvantages inhibit progression, but they also become reinforced by post-compulsory education. This, it can be argued, is because earlier advantages enable people to benefit more from subsequent opportunities (this is discussed in Chapter 9 in relation to 'cultural capital'). Social divisions are, at best, maintained and, at worst, broadened. Those of us in the post-compulsory sector *must* be aware that inequalities are not overcome by the compulsory education sector itself.

Conclusion

This chapter has sought to demonstrate that experiences of schooling have direct effects on participation in post-compulsory education. The achievement of 'good' qualifications provides a passport to further study. But, perhaps more importantly, compulsory education develops dispositions towards learning, and negative attitudes are difficult to challenge and reverse. The school system can reinforce and perpetuate the effects of social and economic disadvantage, allowing them to continue to impinge on people throughout their lives. The post-compulsory sector must, therefore, continue to seek to find more and better ways to overcome the negative and limiting impacts of the compulsory education sector on some students, and not simply blame individuals, their families or the communities they inhabit.

Key questions to ask in relation to overcoming barriers created by compulsory education:

- What steps have been taken to avoid using past achievements as an indicator of potential in further learning?
- How are stereotypes about 'good learners' and 'bad learners' challenged at the institutional and individual level?

CHAPTER 7

Barriers and Opportunities created by the Post-compulsory Education System

Introduction

This chapter examines ways in which the structure of the post-compulsory education system inhibits and limits participation in further study by some students, and considers certain attempts to overcome these barriers. The UNESCO World Conference on Higher Education noted the importance of changing higher education in order to promote greater equity through wider access:

> It is now clear that, to fulfil its mission, **higher education must change** radically, by becoming organically flexible, and at the same time more diverse in its institutions, its structures, its curricula, and the nature and forms of its programmes and delivery systems. (Mayor, Foreword, UNESCO World Conference on Higher Education, 1998, p. 2 original emphasis)

The structure and operation of the post-compulsory education sector may be determined by the state and/or individual institutions. The degree of autonomy that institutions have will usually be a political decision (cf. Salter and Tapper, 1994). In the UK, institutions can help to structure and create access and progression routes, the existence and degree of flexible learning opportunities, and welfare and support services, but the state determines fee levels and thus has significant control over the income of institutions. In other countries, institutions have less agency, and the state has more.

This chapter considers the role of the state and institutions in the post-compulsory sector in promoting or curtailing learning opportunities for under-represented groups. First, it demonstrates that government policy can be extremely influential in promoting and providing learning opportunities, but also that governments can erect barriers and create obstacles to participation. Second, it considers the impediments caused by the cost of participation, including direct costs such as course fees, and also living costs. The discussion then turns to examine constraints associated with entry qualification requirements and the role of alternative admission routes. The need for appropriate and flexible learning opportunities is then assessed, as are the potential strengths of support services and institutional cultures that engage with and appreciate difference (such as diversity with regard to the backgrounds of those who enter and work in post-compulsory education institutions (see Skilbeck and Connell, 2000)).

Government policy: creating or restricting learning opportunities

Promoting wider participation in education and training for students of all ages is a concern for many governments, especially in economically developed countries (see Chapter 2). This has generated a range of discussions and policies at the international, national and institutional level. There are, however, contradictions and competing political agendas that mean that widening participation is not necessarily a priority, either for the state or for any one institution.

Government and institutional policy both have the potential to help extend educational opportunities to a wider cohort of students and, conversely, to construct barriers to participation. Using the UK as an example, the next section illustrates both positive and negative impacts of national education policy on participation in post-compulsory education. The following sections consider the impacts of institutional policy on access and retention.

In 1997, two reports relating to widening participation were published in the UK that indicate the political climate within which post-compulsory education is situated. There are, however, many contradictions within this policy climate. *Learning Works: Widening Participation in Further Education* (Kennedy, 1997) is the report of a committee established in December 1994 by the Further Education Funding Council. The aim was to advise the funding council on the identification of under-represented groups in the sector, and how funding arrangements should be developed to facilitate wider participation in further education in particular, and in post-compulsory education in general. The government reacted positively and sympathetically to the report and produced a formal response to the Kennedy Report: *Further Education for the New Millennium: Response to the Kennedy Report*. It can, however, be argued that the government failed to address, and thus implement, a very significant and potentially radical recommendation of the Report, involving changing the governance of further education institutions in favour of greater representation from the community (Jones, 2000; cf. Parry and Fry, 1999). Ostensibly, the UK government is supportive of strategies to widen participation. This must, though, be contextualized against the contemporary policy climate of the further education sector. The challenge for further education, as Kennedy notes, is to widen participation to non-traditional students within a *marketized* sector. Following the 1988 Education Reform Act (ERA) and, particularly, the 1992 Further and Higher Education Act, structural changes occurred in the further education sector. Section 152 of ERA sought to dictate the composition of colleges' governing bodies, giving far greater emphasis to business representatives and reducing the role for local education authorities (LEAs), with the expressed intention of enabling colleges to manage their own affairs. This process of removing control from local authorities and vesting it in college governing bodies (or corporations) was furthered by the 1992 Act, as colleges (i.e. staff, including management) were subjugate to these newly formed governing bodies – a process known as 'incorporation'. In keeping with other social policy changes that occurred at a similar time, accountability to central government was extended. The Act also changed funding mechanisms, including a decrease in the amount paid per student by the FEFC of approximately 3.5 per cent per annum (Ainley, 1999). In the years following the implementation of the 1992 Act, many further education colleges experienced severe financial difficulties, including institutions being declared bankrupt (see Goddard-Patel and Whitehead, 2000a and 2000b). In the 1997/98 Annual Report the FEFC described the further education sector as being 'in weak financial health' (FEFC, 1998, p. 17).

The result of incorporation was a sector that was forced to act in an increasingly business-like manner, in order to make up shortfalls in FEFC funding and to avoid financial disaster and further penalties. Kennedy notes that colleges were encouraged to 'not just be businesslike but to perform as if they were businesses' (*ibid.*, p. 3). Consequently, during the 1990s, the FE sector expanded by approximately one third (FEFC, 1998, p. 9). However, greater participation does not necessarily equate to wider participation (as discussed in Chapter 4). Much of the expansion took the form of franchises with business, where, at worst, colleges validated company training schemes primarily in order to draw down unit funding for each student enrolled. This nominally increased the number of students in further education colleges, without actually expanding the number of people participating in training in the UK, and without providing new learning opportunities to marginalized groups and non-traditional students.

To widen participation in terms of class, gender, ethnicity and previous educational attainment is costly or 'financially unrewarding' (Kennedy, 1997, p. 3), and thus goes against the ethos of the business approach that now characterizes the further education sector. Non-traditional students are likely to require extra support to help them succeed and thus colleges incur additional costs, both to recruit them initially and to support them through their learning. It is, therefore, questionable whether or not FE colleges are currently able to widen participation given the restrictive financial climate.

The Kennedy Report therefore recommended Widening Participation Strategic Partnerships that brought together 'key local agencies in their region to plan and deliver programmes which seek to widen participation among disadvantaged groups' (FEDA, 1998). One of the main intentions was to reduce the negative effects of competition by promoting co-operation and collaboration to widen participation. The case study examined in Chapter 13 is an example of a Strategic Partnership.

A second influential document, published in the UK in 1997, was *The Report of the National Committee of Inquiry into Higher Education*, a government committee chaired by Ron Dearing (NCIHE, 1997). Although widening participation was not the primary focus of the Committee, two sections of the report address these issues (reports 5 and 6). These two sub-reports (Coffield and Vignoles, 1997; Robertson and Hillman, 1997) presented evidence regarding the representation of different groups in higher education (and are utilized in Chapter 4 of this book). The Dearing Report recommended that, particularly in the light of the expansion of higher education, costs should, in part, be borne by those who benefit, hence a contribution to higher education fees was recommended. The Committee was concerned to ensure that students from poorer families should not experience a reduction in public support, and so did not recommend the complete abolition of maintenance grants and the move to a 100 per cent loans system. The incoming labour government had, however, already made a pledge to replace grants with loans in their manifesto, and thus they adopted the recommendation to introduce a student contribution to the cost of higher education. The impact of the introduction of tuition fees and student loans and the abolition of maintenance grants is discussed below. Suffice to say, then, government policy in the post-Dearing era created financial barriers to participation in higher education, especially by low-income groups – despite the fact that the Dearing Report located under-representation of particular social and cultural groups, especially those from lower socio-economic groups, as a pertinent issue.

In addition, there have been attempts to influence positively participation in post-compulsory education through the education funding bodies. The Further Education Funding Council funded 'Strategic Partnerships' (after Kennedy, 1997). The Welsh Higher Education and Further Education Funding Councils will introduce a Partnership Fund in the financial year 2000/1 to encourage higher and further education institutions to work together and widen participation in learning. The Higher Education Funding Council for England (HEFCE) has introduced a combination of funding approaches to widen participation. This includes additional funding weightings for institutions that can demonstrate increased levels of involvement by students from low-income backgrounds (identified by school attended, parental employment and postcode), and students with disabilities. The introduction of this supplement recognizes, in part, the additional costs of recruiting and retaining such students. There is also a special funding programme, through which HEFCE has allocated funding for widening participation to regional partnerships between higher education institutions and other organizations. For the first time, in 1999–2000 institutions were required by the HEFCE to provide an Initial Statement regarding facilitating access and wider participation. Thus, the funding councils are using financial incentives to encourage educational institutions to widen participation.

In December 1999, HEFCE created performance indicators to measure the extent to which each higher education institution was performing in relation to access and overcoming social exclusion (HEFCE 99/66), which may appear to be a step in the right direction. However, the use of 'benchmarks' for each institution, based on its 'profile', can be understood to let traditional institutions 'off the hook'. As Roper et al. note:

> This amounts to saying that if an institution only takes students with very high A level grades, then it can't be expected to take on many students from the lower socio-economic classes, or students from ethnic minority backgrounds. The HEFCE tables for the participation of under-represented groups are simply an acceptance of the status quo, and are being used to justify inaction. (Roper et al., 2000, p. 10)

Institutions can either perform better or worse than their benchmark. These differ significantly, according to the profile of each university, and are intended to enable comparisons to be made between institutions of a similar ranking only. Thus, traditional universities (drawing students from non-state schools, from social classes I to IIIn and from more affluent neighbourhoods) are able to review their performance in relation to institutions of a similar 'rank' only. There is thus a danger that the incentive for such universities to make positive efforts to extend access to their institutions is significantly reduced, enabling them to remain as elite institutions. Conversely, a modern university in the same geographical area may be admitting significantly more 'non-traditional' students, yet this success may go unrecognized if they are below their benchmark.

A further area of concern is the use of the 'drop out' rate as a performance indicator. It is argued by critics that as the number and diversity of students participating in higher education increases, so, too, will the number of students who either are unable to complete or who take longer to achieve their qualification. Brian Roper, the vice-chancellor of North London University commented:

> The University of North London is proud of its long-standing commitment to widening participation and proud of every student who graduates, no matter how long it takes. The overwhelming reason for people dropping out is financial hardship. (Roper, cited in Charter, 2000)

Martha Casazza (2000) remarked that it is useful to differentiate students who 'stop out' from those who drop out, the former being those who take time out from their studies for personal, financial and family reasons, but who intend to resume their studying when circumstances permit. In addition, it should be acknowledged that if the drop-out rate is used as a performance indicator there is a danger that institutions will be less willing to 'take a risk' on students from non-traditional backgrounds who may not be able to complete their course of study for a wide range of reasons.

These selective examples from the UK demonstrate that government policies are able to influence participation in further and higher education, both in terms of how many and also, more importantly, who participate. This can be a positive influence on participation by under-represented groups or, conversely, policy can contribute to the construction of barriers to participation. Maggie Woodrow (2000) strongly criticizes the UK government, for, on the one hand, identifying widening participation as a 'key priority', and on the other for not providing sufficient resources to undertake this work, and indeed reducing the financial support available to less well-off students through the abolition of maintenance grants. There are conflicting political agendas at all levels – but for widening participation to be successful it needs to be top priority.

Barriers created by the cost of education

The direct and indirect costs of education can provide a major barrier to students from low-income groups. Kennedy reported that in further education the 'confusion and uncertainty which surround financial support for students create significant barriers to entering and staying in learning for those whose need is greatest' (1997, p. 72). Statistical research commissioned by the Kennedy Committee corroborated this claim, revealing that 'student withdrawal rates in further education colleges were higher for those qualifying for income-related fee remission than for others' (*ibid.*).

In the UK fees for higher education were introduced in 1997. This was accompanied by the complete abolition of maintenance grants for students, thus effectively raising the cost of higher education and, inevitably, penalizing students from poorer backgrounds. In the light of these recent changes to the cost of higher education, incurred by students and their families, the UK is a good example to use to examine the barriers to participation imposed by the direct and indirect costs of education. (This issue is also returned to in Chapter 8 in relation to the labour market.)

Summarily, students whose parents' residual income is less than £17,370 (or their own income if they are classified as independent) do not have to pay course fees, but, above this threshold, students' families (or, indeed, students themselves) are expected to contribute to fees. These rose proportionately with income, up to a maximum of £1025 in the academic year 1999–2000. Students are entitled to student loans to fund their living costs, although students from high-income families are only eligible to borrow up to 75 per cent of the maximum student loan. Repayments are made on student loans after the completion of studies, and only when graduates enter a job in which they earn more than £10,000 per year. A sliding scale then applies, which is linked to income. These repayments are deducted at source by employers. (All figures apply to the year 1999–2000.)

Both the government and the Committee of Vice Chancellors and Principals (CVCP, now Universities UK) assert that the introduction of student tuition fees and loans will not pose barriers to students from low-income groups. Kim Howells, Education and Employment

Minister, said: 'I find it very odd that some people assume that because poorer students will get access to larger subsidised loans than those from better off families, we're somehow penalising the poor' (Howell, 1997, quoted in Knowles, 2000, p. 15).

The CVCP not only claimed that the new funding arrangements would not be detrimental to poorer students, but would actually prove auspicious: 'In terms of widening access to higher education, the new funding scheme benefits students from poorer backgrounds in two ways. The state will pay their tuition fees in full; and they will have access to larger subsidised loans for living costs' (CVCP, 1999, p. 3).

But many others reject these prognoses, especially in relation to the impact of loans on the participation by students from low-income groups and non-traditional student groups. in 1999 John Knowles (2000) conducted group interviews and survey research with Year 12 pupils, and interviews with senior staff from a range of institutions, in order to investigate attitudes to higher education and the likely impact of loans and fees. The research identifies a number of trends that suggest that the financial changes have had negative impacts on the attitudes towards higher education of students in general and, particularly, among students in the lower income groups. These findings are supported by other studies, including research in Scotland undertaken by Helen Sinclair and Lorna Dale (2000) and evidence supplied by Maggie Woodrow to the Independent Committee of Inquiry into Student Finance in Scotland (Woodrow, 1999b).

Knowles's research found that as a result of the introduction of tuition fees and maintenance loans, students, particularly from more disadvantaged backgrounds, are reconsidering their intention to participate in higher education. Knowles's research found that in the further education college which 'is situated near the outskirts of a major city, and serves a wide range of communities, from relatively advantaged to severely disadvantaged' (*ibid.*, p. 17) there was a strong disinclination to participate in higher education. When they first entered post-compulsory education 69 per cent of the college students said they were likely to apply to higher education, but after they had found out more about HE, particularly financial issues, 59 per cent of these students were less likely to apply (*ibid.*, Table 2, p. 20). Sixty-two per cent of college pupils also agreed with the statement: 'The thought of owing a lot of money makes it difficult for my family to consider higher education' (*ibid.*, Table 4, p. 20). Thirty-four per cent of college students said that 'Having to take out a loan is likely to stop me going to university' (*ibid.*, Table 6, p. 20).

The students also worried about the longer-term impacts of loans (*ibid.*, p. 18). Knowles quotes one student's comments thus: 'You probably need a degree to get a decent job, and it really, really scares me to be looking for a job having all that debt. It's really scary, it's going to be hanging over you' (Knowles, 2000, p. 18).

Fears regarding personal finance amongst would-be students were also identified by Thomas and Slack (1999b). They found that sixth-formers and FE students intending to go to university felt they had little or no information about student finance (although this varied between institutions), and many sought details of how to qualify for and repay student loans. Group discussions revealed that students had heard of friends or acquaintances who had entered higher education and who had accrued 'thousands of pounds of debt at the end of the first year' (*ibid.*, p. 5). Anecdotes of this nature worried students and, overall, they felt anxious about being responsible for their own financial welfare in such potentially debt-laden situations.

In addition, research by Knowles and by Sinclair and Dale shows that students are also thinking far more carefully about the location and duration of their course. Knowles reports that students are ruling out more expensive locations (i.e. London); also that they are less likely to embark on longer courses, such as 'sandwich courses', that involve a year in industry or overseas, and courses at Scottish institutions that are four years (compared to three in the rest of the UK). This finding is substantiated by research from one Scottish university (Sinclair and Dale, 2000) which found that between1996/7 and 1999/2000 there was a 6 per cent fall in the number of students from other parts of the UK (*ibid.*, p. 9). Knowles found that in institutions with higher percentages of students from severely disadvantaged backgrounds, more considered applying to local or regional institutions in order to reduce costs (see Knowles, 2000, Table 3, p. 20). Similarly, Sinclair and Dale (2000, pp. 13–14) found a 6 per cent increase in the number of students who chose an institution on the basis of it being 'convenient to home'.

Knowles also found that eight in every ten students involved in the research (irrespective of the institution at which they were studying) 'felt that they would need to work part-time to help with the costs of HE' (Knowles, 2000, p. 22). This figure is only slightly higher than other research findings, indicating strongly that the general trend is towards part-time employment by higher education students. Connor *et al.* (1999) found that 75 per cent of Scottish students anticipated working part-time while at university. Sinclair and Dale found that 68 per cent of students were working part-time in 1999–2000, compared with 43 per cent three years earlier in 1996/7 (p. 10). Furthermore, their research showed that almost a quarter of first-year students in 1999/2000 were working more than sixteen hours per week.

These, and related points, led Knowles to conclude that: 'Far from improving access to higher education, these funding changes may have the effect of reversing the trends of the last decades, and returning higher education to its former role of being only for relatively affluent and educated family backgrounds' (op. cit., p. 23).

Maggie Woodrow reported to the 'Cubie Committee' – the Independent Committee of Inquiry into Student Finance, established by the Scottish parliament and chaired by Sir Andrew Cubie – that responses to the study *From Elitism to Inclusion* (Woodrow, 1998) 'identified the cost of student subsistence as being the major financial barrier to participation by lower socio-economic groups' (Woodrow, 1999b, p. 7).

To reiterate, then, a growing corpus of evidence suggests that the abolition of student maintenance grants, and the increased reliance on student loans and part-time employment have all had a major impact on the ability and willingness of students from lower socio-economic groups to participate in higher education.

In recognition of these issues, the Cubie Committee recommended a radical alternative funding mechanism for higher education in Scotland. This is based on 'a revised means test arrangement ... whereby the parental or spousal contribution reflects the financial pressure on those on low to middle incomes, while deriving a greater contribution from higher income groups' (quoted in Woodrow, 1999c, p. 9). The Cubie Committee proposed that students pay nothing when they go to university, but that graduates should contribute to the cost of their education through some sort of deferred payment scheme, once their salaries exceed a certain level. In May 2000 it was confirmed by the Scottish Executive that 'from this autumn, there will be no tuition fees for eligible full-time Scottish and EU students studying in Scotland' (Scottish Executive, 2000). Thus, in Scotland, there has been recognition of the barriers to participation created by increasing the costs of higher education that are borne by the students and their families, especially to low-income groups.

One way to further illustrate the importance of the cost of education can be seen in relation to the success of the pilot of Education Maintenance Allowances (EMA). The EMA is a new means-tested allowance for 16- to 18-year-olds (piloted in selected locations in the UK in 1999–2000) that is intended to act as an incentive to enter, and stay in, further education. The scheme includes a weekly payment direct to the student and includes bonuses for attendance and achievement. The total sum available is about £1500 per year. Stoke-on-Trent was one of the pilot cities in 1999–2000, as traditionally it has one of the country's lowest staying-on rates in post-compulsory education for 16- and 17-year-olds. By January 2000, 1227 young people had received an EMA, and by March 2000 only 54 students (4%) had withdrawn from the education sector (Staffordshire Careers, 2000a). In 1999–2000, when the scheme was piloted, the staying-on rate rose by almost nine percentage points, from 56.3 per cent in 1998–9 to 65.1 per cent (Staffordshire Careers, 2000c). Furthermore, based on the average level of payments, Staffordshire Careers (2000b) concluded that the EMA is reaching 'low income families'.

The evidence discussed above demonstrates that finance and the cost of education affects participation in both further and higher education. Furthermore, young people take account of the costs they will incur when they make decisions at the end of compulsory schooling about whether or not to continue in full-time education. In the context of older students, the importance of financial factors can be even greater, as is demonstrated in part by the decline in the number of applicants to university by mature students in the UK, which coincided with the abolition of grants and the introduction of tuition fees. The cost of post-compulsory education is examined further in relation to labour market opportunities in the next chapter.

Entry qualifications and alternative admissions routes

There is sufficient evidence to suggest that financial issues are related to participation in post-compulsory education, and the negative effects are felt more strongly by students from lower socio-economic groups. These barriers will often function in conjunction with other obstacles, such as those surrounding entry qualifications and alternative admissions routes. Entry qualification requirements tend to create greater barriers for access to higher education than to other forms of post-compulsory education for non-traditional students. Indeed, Coffield and Vignoles (1997) and Robertson and Hillman (1997) note that many groups of non-traditional students tend not to have the required entry qualifications for higher education. For example, 'the higher socio-economic groups (I–IIIn) dominate all qualifications routes into higher education. In particular, they overwhelmingly dominate in the A-level route (80% of all holders of the qualification)' (p. 47). As has been discussed above there is a wide range of reasons why pupils fail to achieve in schools, and thus admission based solely on past performance in examinations reduces opportunities for individuals, and society as a whole is likely to lose out.

One response to facilitate greater diversity in the composition of students participating in higher education has been to develop alternative entry routes and qualifications. In the UK, A-levels are often viewed as the 'gold standard' for entrance into higher education, and indeed the majority of students, about 67 per cent (UCAS, 1998), still enter university with these qualifications. To attract a wider diversity of students, however, alternative admissions procedures and the recognition of previous experience and other qualifications are necessary. In the UK, two alternatives to A-level qualifications of particular significance are the well-established Access courses and the more recently introduced Advanced General National Vocational Qualification (AGNVQ).

Access courses were introduced over twenty years ago and have been an officially recognized entry route into higher education since 1987. They were designed specifically to enable adults (21+) with insufficient formal qualifications to gain access to higher education (see Parry, 1996; Kirton, 1999). Access students currently constitute about 8 per cent of the UK's HE population (UCAS 1998), although recent statistics suggest this may be lower in the next few years, reflecting a general downturn in applications from mature students (THES, 1999). It should also be acknowledged that similar programmes exist, and have been successful, in other countries, such as the USA (Tripodi, 1994), New Zealand (James, 1994) and Australia (Postle et al., 1997).

The success of Access courses for mature students in the UK, and comparable courses elsewhere, has encouraged the growth of other special programmes for younger 'disadvantaged' students, such as the well-documented University of Dundee Access Summer School (Woodrow, 1998; Blicharski, 1998). The University of Dundee Summer School is designed for students who have had their educational development 'held back' (Blicharski, 1998, p. 31), and offers a chance to 'students who missed the traditional route to university', so that they 'can now redirect their potential and begin to catch up' (ibid.). Summer schools of this nature have been successful in helping (comparatively small) cohorts of students to access higher education who would not otherwise have been able to do so. At Dundee 277 students started the course between 1995 and 1998, and 262 completed it, with 231 proceeding to enter higher education (representing 88 per cent of the students who completed the Summer School), and 75 per cent of these students are likely to be awarded a degree (Blicharski, 2000, pp. 182–3).

Other initiatives have been developed to facilitate the progression of students into higher education. Some universities have developed 'compacts' to encourage and reassure local students to apply to enter higher education. A compact is an arrangement between a school or college and a university whereby students achieving specific qualifications and/or alternative targets will be guaranteed a place on a award. The Priority Application Scheme at Staffordshire (PASS) was launched in 1991 with the intention of encouraging students in the region to apply for higher education. Some of the uncertainty of the application process is removed, as they know that they will, at the very least, receive one offer from their local higher education institution. The PASS initiative (see Box 7.1) was commended by the Dearing Committee (NCIHE, 1997).

Box 7.1 Priority Application Scheme at Staffordshire (PASS)

PASS – Priority Application Scheme at Staffordshire – was launched in Staffordshire in 1991 to encourage students in the local region to apply for higher education in the knowledge that they would at the very least receive one offer from their local higher education institution. This removes some of the uncertainty from the UCAS (Universities and Colleges Admissions Service) application system of not knowing whether or not a place will be offered. In 1993 the scheme was broadened and it now applies to students who are under 21 years of age, who live in Staffordshire, Shropshire or Cheshire and who name Staffordshire University as one of their six UCAS choices. Applicants are guaranteed a conditional offer provided they meet the entry requirements for their chosen named award. The success of PASS can be measured by a significant percentage rise in local applications to Staffordshire University each year, from 26% in 1992/3 to 38% in 1997/8.

Applications to Staffordshire University from the PASS area:

Year	Total number of students admitted	Number on PASS	% PASS
1992/3	6982	1823	26
1993/4	7974	2395	30
1994/5	9882	3243	33
1995/6	10,618	3705	35
1996/7	10,993	4046	37
1997/8	11,685	4384	38

Again, there are international examples of similar initiatives. In Australia the 'Q-Step Programme' was developed and is organized by Queensland University of Technology. This scheme works in partnership with schools located in areas with low participation rates in higher education. It then identifies suitable school and college students, and offers them places at university on the basis of evidence of interest and motivation in learning and higher education, rather than examination grades only.

In the UK, Advanced GNVQs were developed to provide a vocational alternative to A-levels that would be valued by employers, but which would also have academic parity with A-levels and so be accepted as an entry route to higher education. AGNVQs were piloted in 1992 as part of a government initiative intended to enhance recruitment and retention in the post-compulsory sector (Shirtliff, 1996). AGNVQs have been moderately popular with students, as evinced by annual increases in student enrolments from their inception (UCAS, 1998). On average 32 per cent of AGNVQ students make an application to higher education, of which 66 per cent are offered a place; this is only 2 per cent less than offers made overall to all applicants (UCAS, 1998). Alternative entry qualifications, such as the AGNVQ, may be attractive to students who are more vocationally oriented, and who would not continue in post-compulsory education to study for A-level qualifications.

Another alternative entry procedure, which is not based on the gaining of a particular qualification, is the accreditation of prior (and experiential) learning, AP(E)L. These approaches award credit for previous educational or professional qualifications and relevant experience, and are likely to be of particular benefit to mature students, and for entry to postgraduate education. AP(E)L entry routes are being developed by many HE institutions; for example, Wailey and Simpson (1999) detail a programme being developed at the University of East London, and Carol Costley (2000) recounts a scheme at Middlesex University that enables students to gain credits for work-based learning. At Middlesex University, 'work' is defined very broadly, including, for example, unpaid and domestic work. This approach recognizes that learning can take place through a wide range of activities, not just through formal learning, and therefore enables students to gain maximum benefit from all their previous experiences.

The extensive range of alternative entry routes helps to demonstrate recognition of the barriers erected by rigid entry procedures. They also provide evidence of the commitment of some institutions to overcoming these types of barriers, to facilitate students who have not succeeded in compulsory education to continue their education. Universities and colleges must not penalize students for past performance, but find alternative approaches to selecting students who will benefit from further and higher education. There is, however, a danger that alternative entry routes are only available at some institutions and not others – and that these may be the less prestigious institutions – and only for less popular courses where there is a greater incentive for institutions to 'lower' the entry qualification requirements. This would further reinforce the hierarchical nature of higher education, and possibly lead to the 'ghettoization' of particular 'non-traditional' student groups in less eminent institutions (as discussed in Chapter 4).

A further concern is that currently 'flexible entry routes' are 'alternatives' rather than the norm. In other words, many of the initiatives mentioned above are comparatively small-scale projects, which only benefit a limited number of potential students. Rather, it would be desirable for all HEIs to recognize that past performance is not necessarily a good indicator, or the only indicator of the potential to gain from higher education, and thus develop far more flexibility within their entry systems. This, however, is unlikely to be achieved, unless it is state directed. In the UK at least, this is a step that the government seems unlikely to take, and thus a stratified system is likely to remain intact.

Appropriate and flexible learning opportunities

Non-traditional students not only require formal entry to post-compulsory education; a further way to facilitate involvement by under-represented groups involves developing a range of study options across the spectrum of environments and contexts. The idea of appropriate and flexible learning opportunities emphasizes the maxim that non-traditional students have non-traditional learning needs. This statement may be an over-simplification of reality, but

> There is still a tendency for efforts to widen participation in higher education to concentrate on the task of preparing 'non-traditional' entrants to conform – academically, socially and culturally – to accepted higher education norms. This *normalisation* process is often regarded as an essential pre-requisite both to their entry and their success in higher education. Pre-entry access programmes are frequently designed (as a conscious survival technique) to acclimatise potential entrants to an alien culture: post-entry programmes often involve mentoring or

guidance schemes to speed up this acclimatisation process and smooth out any remaining rough edges of cultural non-conformity. (Woodrow, in Thomas and Cooper, 2000, Preface)

Providing appropriate and flexible learning opportunities means that HEIs have to become responsible for the development and delivery of courses that have a relevant curriculum that empower learners, rather than seeking to control students as part of a 'normalization' process. It also includes making learning available in accessible locations, at convenient times, and attending to other organizational issues that can create barriers for some students. It should also involve being aware of such matters as different learning strategies, paces and other preferences that learners may have.

Providing a relevant and empowering curriculum requires flexibility, and is only possible if the definitions of what constitutes knowledge are not rigid and elitist. If education providers adhere to a closed and monopolistic model of knowledge, in which the elite (i.e. traditional academic disciplines) define knowledge, there is no room for other experience and knowledge to be validated. An open system of knowledge involves constructing knowledge from different perspectives, and challenging dominant forms of knowledge, in the way that feminism has succeeded, at least to some extent, in challenging traditional forms of 'legitimate knowledge'. Such an approach moves away from a traditional model of teaching that focuses on transferring information to students. Instead, the processes of learning are accorded more importance; learners participate in defining knowledge and there is greater recognition of learning that has taken place outside formal educational contexts (Bruffee, 1995).

Some modern universities in the UK have been criticized for offering 'Mickey Mouse' degree courses in subjects that are not traditional academic fields. This raises the question of whether the contents of the degree are of primary importance (i.e. the information learnt), or whether the process of studying and learning at this level is of greater value (i.e. the ability to study independently, to synthesize information and ideas, to apply concepts to different areas of interest and so forth). For example, employers often cite communication skills, ability in number, IT experience, problem-solving ability and team-working as important attributes of graduate employees – and these skills can be acquired through learning at an advanced level in a wide range of subjects, not only in traditional academic disciplines.

In order to avoid constructing or maintaining barriers to non-traditional students, universities and colleges should be aware of the impact of their curriculum on potential learners. At a recent conference of the British Educational Research Association practitioners working with deprived communities all stressed the need to provide learning opportunities that are of interest to learners (Feetham, 2000; Hargrave and Tudor, 2000; Spedding and Gregson, 2000), especially as learners take their first tentative steps into post-compulsory education. This idea is encapsulated in the title of Vivien Feetham's paper: 'Working From Where They Are At: Successful Approaches to Engaging the Excluded with Lifelong Learning'. This position is supported by writers such as Brookfield (1993) and Hager (1998) and is returned to in Chapter 9.

Institutions should be aware of the value of a 'dynamic curriculum' (Teare, Davies and Sandelands, 1998) that responds to learners' needs and interests. As noted above, this concept challenges the dominance of the 'academy' (educational institutions); it recognizes that valid learning takes place in a much broader range of contexts and about a much wider range of subjects. Currently, too few education providers seem to be willing to share the power they possess by only validating traditional and elite forms of knowledge.

In addition to providing a relevant curriculum, institutions need to overcome practical barriers to access, such as the location, timing and pace of courses. Kennedy (1997, p. 7) notes that learning does not just happen in colleges, and that there are many other potential sites for learning to take place: 'The trick is to bring learning to learners wherever they are, whether it be in family rooms in primary schools, libraries, betting shops, snooker halls, rooms above pubs, or shopping malls' (*ibid.*, p. 8).

Not only does the location have to be appropriate, but so, too, does the timetable. Non-traditional students are more likely to study part-time, and/or have a range of other responsibilities, such as employment and family commitments, so timing is important. This also extends to the opening times of other academic facilities and support services. Registration and similar activities should not only take place during the working week, and libraries and other services should be available at weekends and evenings if students are to flourish. The pace of the course is also important in order to allow students to keep up and fit learning in with the other elements of their lives. The requirements of timing, place and pace are becoming more widely acknowledged by education providers – although this does not, of course, mean that they are being addressed.

The requirement for flexibility will increase as more and more students, especially those from lower socio-economic groups, engage in paid employment as well as full or part-time studying. Greater flexibility also facilitates lifelong learning, as people move in and out of learning, between subjects, institutions and levels, and in conjunction with other major activities such as employment and family commitments. There is, again, a danger however, that flexibility is only available in certain institutions, or is extended only to certain subjects. Elite institutions offering flexible participation in competitive subjects, such as medicine and law, should be commended. The innovations and progress made by other institutions should not be undervalued. It is, however, difficult to envisage how 'non-traditional' students can achieve parity with their more advantaged peers, unless change takes place at the level of the sector, rather than the institution, discipline or the discretion of an admissions tutor.

Support services

Once students have negotiated the barriers to access post-compulsory education, it is widely reported that some non-traditional students require additional assistance. This however is a contentious claim – it is certainly true that some non-traditional students require support, but so, too, do other students (cf. Gutteridge, 2000). In preference, it should be recognized that support services can play a vital role to assist students to both engage in and remain in post-compulsory learning. Support services can include both academic and personal support. Academic support services may provide students with study skills and learning strategies, equip them with specific skills such as computing and word processing, offer educational and careers guidance and generally provide an encouraging environment. Personal support could include a range of services. Counselling services may be offered, as entering education and changing lifestyles can put a strain on personal and family life. Affordable childcare should be available, and not just during lectures, but the facility should allow for private study time as well; and facilities should also be available for school-age children after school and during the holidays. Disability support services may include assessment of need and provision of support. Emergency and ongoing financial support may also be offered, as should other services.

Without such assistance it is likely that many non-traditional students either will not be able to contemplate entering post-compulsory education, or will be unable to sustain their involvement. It is imperative, however, that institutions do not assume, or merely try to guess, what kinds of support different student groups would find useful. Research is required to understand the complex needs of all students, but especially those for whom lack of support services may bar their participation or inhibit progression.

An observation from my own research is that when institutions provide alternative learning sites, such as community locations, this is the only concession that is made to non-traditional learning needs. Institutions tend to fail to provide additional support services, such as those mentioned above, even when these are available at the main institutional site(s). The irony of this is that the students who may have the most to gain from such services are the least able to access them!

Institutional culture

A recurring theme in the discussion above relates to the willingness of particular institutions to embrace change and respond to the differing needs of student groups who are traditionally under-represented. Thus, an important factor in widening participation to non-traditional students is the 'institutional culture', as this is crucial in determining the flexibility of the institution, its willingness to change and the extent to which it embraces or suppresses diversity.

In the 1980s interest and concern developed around the notion of 'organizational culture' in business management in the UK and the USA. For example, in the UK, Charles Handy developed a comprehensive description of four cultural organizational types (Handy, 1985). Handy, and others, argue that each organization (including each educational institution) has its own culture, but that these can be categorized and used to understand how different types of institution react in particular circumstances. The mix of the four types of organizational culture constitutes the unique culture of a particular institution. Thus, colleges, universities and other learning providers in the post-compulsory education sector can be seen to possess their own cultures, which help determine their attitudes to diversity and change.

The notion of different organizational culture is reflected in the typology of universities, developed by Connor et al. (1996), which demonstrates how some institutions are much more flexible and are seeking to attract non-traditional students, while others wish to reinforce traditional elitism and exclusivity (see also Callaghan, 2000).

In research with eight further education colleges (see Thomas et al., 1999), different institutional cultures were witnessed. Each college was trying to widen participation via community outreach work. The research found that the attitudes of senior management in each college contributed to the status accorded to widening participation initiatives, and thus the extent to which other college staff supported

1. **Traditional elite:** a small number of elite, pre-1992, universities that have not significantly changed their recruitment profile. They are still recruiting mainly young, A-level or higher students directly from school, from a wide geographical catchment area. They expect to continue this recruitment pattern without lowering their current entry requirements, or making significant institutional changes. They have little vocational education (excluding professional areas such as law and medicine). Future growth is more likely to be at postgraduate level, especially in research.

2. **Quasi-old:** a much larger number of pre-1992 universities that have traditionally recruited school leavers; they are reluctantly introducing structural and policy changes to broaden their student profile, but they are facing internal tensions between traditional cultures and the need for change. Their catchment area is becoming increasingly regional, but they are less clear about their strategic direction and identity than group 1.

3. **Quasi-new:** former polytechnics and colleges that are developing a dual strategy to attract traditional and non-conventional students. They have traditionally recruited a diverse student cohort, and are introducing new kinds of provision to continue to attract these recruits. But they are simultaneously trying to emulate some of the older universities. Again, there is a lack of clarity about direction and identity.

4. **Real new:** former polytechnics and colleges that are prioritizing broadening their student profile. They are the most innovative of the universities, strengthening local identities and links, moving further towards vocationalism, developing more access arrangements and a flexible range of delivery mechanism. Their focus in the future is likely to be on teaching at various levels and modes.

Figure 7.1   *A typology of universities and their future recruitment strategies*

Source: Adapted from Connor *et al.*, (1996) in Callaghan, 2000

the work. For example, quick, flexible responses were required to meet the needs of the new students, and some colleges devised new systems to provide greater flexibility, while others retained traditional bureaucratic approaches that made it difficult to respond and thus these potential students were not recruited (this is discussed further in Chapter 13). This example demonstrates that 'leadership' and commitment at the senior level within institutions is essential if fundamental change is to occur. Too often, potential students constitute the only group which is expected to change. Institutions and staff attitudes need to change also.

This process of change can be described as 'organizational learning' and is considered in Chapter 11. It is salient to note the point that D. Davies (2000) makes, that 'the concept of organisational learning has gained credibility in recent years … whilst paradoxically within higher education itself organisational learning proceeds at an almost glacial pace' (p. 43).

An indicator of institutional attitudes and values or their culture is the composition of an institution's staff, both academic and non-academic. In relation to minority ethnic groups Paul Taylor (2000) contends that

> a major starting point should be the attempt to make the staff of higher education reflect the diversity that … is being aimed for, within the student body. It is therefore necessary to create an organisational culture within higher education institutions which recognises the value of cultural diversity … In this way potential students should be provided with an atmosphere and role models that may encourage them to become more engaged with higher education. (p. 197)

Taylor's analysis demonstrates that there are various mechanisms that exclude minority ethnic groups from employment and career progression in higher education in the UK, and as part of a reinforcing, cyclical process, this helps to explain the lack of engagement with local minority ethnic groups as students.

Similar staffing patterns can be observed in relation to other groups who are under-represented in post-compulsory education. Gender imbalance has been the subject of much research, demonstrating that women are more often in junior positions than men (Poole et al., 1997), and when they achieve senior positions they are often stereotyped into 'caring roles' with less power and influence (see Skilbeck and Connell, 2000, pp. 34–6; Eggins, 1997).

A recent survey in the UK, conducted by the Times Higher

Education Supplement (Hague, 2000), found that 'eleven percent of adults in work are disabled – but only 1.2 percent of professors in British universities are' (p. 20). In the same article, Sophie Corlett, the policy director for higher education at Skill, the national bureau for students with disabilities, is reported as saying: 'the absence of disabled staff militates against an atmosphere where disabled students feel welcome' (*ibid.*). These traditional employment patterns may be indicators of conservatism at a broader level, and they certainly do not encourage participation by 'non-traditional' students, but instead, reinforce the need for change.

Conclusions about the barriers and opportunities created by the education sectors

Education offers many opportunities to people, but it can also construct structural deterrents and barriers. The previous chapter sought to demonstrate that the compulsory education sector does not overcome the social, economic and cultural disadvantages that pupils experience – and it is highly unlikely to do so. The limitations of the school system require the post-compulsory education sector to take responsibility for facilitating access and progression for non-traditional students if participation is truly to be widened.

The distinction and boundaries between the role of government and education institutions is complex, and varies between countries, but taken as a whole there are structural barriers that are inherent in the post-compulsory education sector. Often 'lip service' is paid to the notion of widening participation and promoting access to particular groups in society, but there are competing political agendas at the state and institutional level, and thus widened participation is not necessarily prioritized (see Woodrow, 2000). This chapter has highlighted some of the barriers that exist, and indicated approaches to overcoming them.

Some of the types of barriers that can be seen to exist within the sector are the direct and indirect costs of education that are borne by students (and their families), rigid entry qualification requirements, inflexible and inappropriate learning opportunities, insufficient support services and the culture of institutions themselves. Moreover, the recurring theme is the need for institutional flexibility and change. Thus, perhaps the most important issue relating to educational institutions is their culture – do they want to find out about the perceptions and needs of alternative students – and change accordingly, or would they prefer to continue to be discriminatory and elitist? The answer to this question is an indicator of their culture, as reflected in the following questions:

Key questions to ask in relation to overcoming barriers created by the post-compulsory education sector:

- How does your work help to promote 'widening participation' issues at the policy level, nationally, locally and in your institution or organization?
- In what ways does your work help to reduce the cost of education to individuals?
- Have you developed a range of entry routes that meet the needs of all the potential students you are targeting?
- Is learning appropriate and flexible with regard to the curriculum, the location, the timing and the pace?
- Are personal and academic support services provided at all sites and at accessible times to meet the needs of your students?
- How is organizational learning and change (with respect to widening participation) encouraged?

CHAPTER 8

The Labour Market and Participation in Post-compulsory Education and Training

Introduction

In addition to the impacts of the education sector, the labour market can impinge upon participation in post-compulsory education and training in a number of ways. Of particular significance are the availability of jobs and the level of general wages, and, concomitantly, levels and extent of unemployment. This chapter considers the opportunity cost of post-compulsory education; the impact of the labour market on the ability to 'invest' in education and training; and financial returns to education that are determined by the labour market. A further important influence on participation in post-compulsory learning is employers' demand for education, training and qualifications. This topic is discussed in Chapter 2 in relation to the changing – and possibly expanding – economic demand for education, training and qualifications, so it is not revisited here.

First, this chapter considers the role of labour market opportunities that help to determine the other options available to 'potential students', in particular, what sort of job they can get if they choose not to go into full-time education or training. This can be termed as the 'opportunity cost' of post-compulsory education, and includes forgoing remuneration (e.g. wages) that may be involved in undertaking certain forms of post-compulsory education, especially full-time studying. The economic opportunity cost of post-compulsory education is highly influenced by unemployment levels.

Second, this chapter turns to the impact of labour market opportunities and job security that contribute significantly to the income available to 'invest' in education and training. Family income levels, and entitlement to benefits, will influence this for both dependent and independent students. The direct and indirect costs of education (i.e. tuition fees and living expenses, respectively, which were discussed in the previous chapter) largely determine the investment that is required to support a student participating in education. The ability of people to support themselves during post-compulsory education may be further influenced by the availability of part-time or flexible employment and opportunities for paid work during vacations.

Finally, this chapter considers the influence of rates of return from the labour market on participation in post-compulsory education, as this determines the economic rate of return on 'investments' in learning. This will be influenced by the nature of the 'certified labour market'. In other words, the demand for qualified labour, wages paid and whether or not employers discriminate against some sectors of society (e.g. graduates from working-class backgrounds, from minority ethnic groups, with disabilities or women).

The opportunity cost of post-compulsory education

The opportunity cost of any course of action refers to what is forgone. Hence, if a person opts to participate in either full- or part-time post-compulsory education, this will reduce his/her ability to take up opportunities in the labour market. Even if a person is unemployed, participation in education or training will limit that person's ability to seek work, and there may be financial penalties associated with this action, such as a reduction in entitlement to benefits. Consequently, the opportunities available in the labour market, and with regard to benefits, too, may influence some people's decisions about post-compulsory education. In other words, if there are employment opportunities that are well paid, provide good terms and conditions and offer long-term prospects (or whatever other characteristics are valued), the 'opportunity cost' of forgoing participation in the labour market is higher than when poor employment prospects prevail. Thus, in a buoyant labour market, the opportunity cost of education is higher. This section of the chapter notes the impact of unemployment on participation in training and education both for young people and for adults, and the influence of the graduate labour market on participation in postgraduate education. It can be surmised that the opportunity cost of the labour market influences participation in education and training at all levels.

In the UK, young people first have a choice regarding whether to continue in education or to enter the labour market at the age of 16. Young people in comparable countries are faced with this choice at a similar age. Education and training hold the possibility of enhanced career opportunities in later life, while labour market participation offers financial independence and greater autonomy in other respects, such as from parental and family strictures (see Banks *et al.*, 1992, p. 2). The positive impact in the UK of the pilot of Education Maintenance Allowances (EMAs) (an allowance paid to 16- and 17-year-olds who attend full-time education or training) was discussed in the previous chapter. This demonstrates that increasing the income available to young people while they participate in full-time education or training reduces the opportunity cost of pursuing this route, rather than employment, and so makes it more attractive.

Empirical research shows that the availability of opportunities in the labour market and in the education sector are both highly likely to influence people's decisions. This can be demonstrated with regard to young and mature students, and in relation to higher education as well as vocational training.

Michael Banks and colleagues report that while they were conducting research in the mid-1980s about young people growing up in the UK, two significant changes took place. First, in 1986 the government Youth Training Scheme (YTS) was extended from one to two years' duration, and from solely community to (some) employer-based provision. Second, legislation in 1988 prevented most young people under the age of 18 claiming social security benefits, and young adults under the age of 25 from receiving state benefits when living away from home. The expansion of the training scheme and the reduction in the entitlement to benefits affected the decisions made by the young people. The availability of 'training' increased (to compensate for the lack of employment opportunities) and for many young people there was a decrease in economic returns from the labour market (either wages or unemployment benefits). This encouraged more young people into YTS training programmes, rather than the labour market.

Similar trends can be seen amongst mature students during times of economic decline. In South Yorkshire the closure of coal mines and the loss of associated employment in the 1980s and 1990s gave rise to more mature students participating in full- and part-time further and higher education courses, with the primary aim of improving their position in the labour market. For example, a group of mature students in receipt of benefits, participating in a part-time community radio course, which could be viewed as an ostensibly leisure programme, all said they went on the course to improve their employment prospects and because they wanted to secure work (Thomas, E., 1996, p. 7). For mature students attending access courses the motivations were also strongly employment-related – they wanted to embark on a career that they enjoyed, rather than 'just a job' (*ibid.*, p. 16, 20).

A closely related issue for the mature students involved in this research was the availability of benefits. Many of the students involved in the research were studying part-time and were also in receipt of benefits, primarily because they were unemployed. These students reported obstructions to participation by the Department of Social Security (DSS) that administers welfare benefits. For some students there was direct opposition from the DSS to participate in education. This included being called to 'Restart Interviews' to prove they were searching for work, having to demonstrate that the education they were undertaking was 'training for work' and being informed that they should accept employment at much lower incomes than they had been earning previously, rather than study. Other students studying full-time, particularly those supporting a family, lamented the fact that on entering education their entitlement to benefits had largely ceased. For some potential mature students, forfeiting welfare benefits makes the opportunity cost of education too high and, consequently, they do not participate.

In general, it can be surmised that one impact of high unemployment is greater participation in post-compulsory education and training, although this may be offset to some extent by financial constraints. Greater participation in education and training during high unemployment may be encouraged by the state, for example, by the expansion of training schemes. In the UK, the YTS was introduced during a period of high unemployment in the 1980s (Banks *et al.*, 1996, pp. 4, 34). Similarly, the UK government's contemporary New Deal scheme was introduced as a measure to combat unemployment because there was a lack of employment opportunities for some sectors of the labour market. New Deal was originally aimed at combating youth unemployment and dependency on state benefits, and has now been extended to unemployed people over the age of 25. Throughout Europe similar policies can be seen, offering training to capture the 10 to 20 per cent of each age cohort who leave formal education with few or no qualifications (Leney, 1999, p. 42), for whom there are very limited labour market opportunities. Thus it can be argued that training schemes provide an alternative to employment, and because of high unemployment the opportunity cost of training is comparatively low (people have little to lose, and may gain something).

It is debatable, however, whether or not employment training schemes should be classified as 'training' (on a par with vocational education), or whether they should more accurately be described as a (poor) substitute for employment, and a means of gaining access to cheap labour by employers. Furthermore, such schemes have been criticized as being a means of social control (Edwards, 1983). But it is beyond the scope of this chapter to enter the debate surrounding the motivations behind employment training schemes. Suffice to say, when there are poor labour market opportunities, the opportunity cost of participation in such a scheme is low.

During periods of high unemployment both governments and students are not only attracted to training and vocationally orientated education, but also towards higher education. The expansion of higher education in the UK in the early 1990s coincided with an economic recession (Dugdale, 1997, p. 145). Similarly, Banks *et al.* (1992) note that the contraction in the youth labour market throughout Europe in the 1980s stimulated an expansion in both vocational training *and* higher education:

> Economic transformation affected all European countries, though the responses of young people to it varied. The most striking change in the countries of Western Europe was the virtual disappearance of a youth labour market, and its replacement up to the age of 18 (and beyond) with extended education and training, including a steady rise in the number entering higher education. (*ibid.*, 1992, p. 5)

Similar patterns can be seen with regard to entry into postgraduate education. Keith Dugdale (1997) demonstrates that the graduate labour market influences participation in postgraduate study and professional training. Higher levels of graduate unemployment result in greater participation in further learning, as there are fewer other opportunities; hence, the opportunity costs are lowered. Talking about the UK, he comments:

> It is noticeable that the increase of graduates moving directly on to further academic study, teacher training and other forms of training, all peaked at the height of the recession in 1992. This suggests that a major factor encouraging larger numbers of graduates to remain in higher education was the lack of opportunities in the job market. (*ibid.*, 1997, p. 145)

Economic and political factors can contribute strongly to increasing participation rates in post-compulsory education and training. The labour market alone, however, cannot explain participation rates.

Banks *et al.* (1996) note that 'in 1985, 43% of 18-year-olds were in full-time education in France compared with 17% in the UK (DES, 1990). By 1988, the gap had widened with 52% in full-time education in France and 20% in the UK' (p. 5). They conclude:

> over the whole decade, the staying-on rate in education only increased marginally: from 40% in 1978 to 47% in 1988. From 1981, unemployment remained fairly constant at around 10%, and YTS participation increased steadily, reaching 24% in 1988 (DES, 1988). (p. 6)

Thus, the high youth unemployment rate in the UK, was, on its own, insufficient to effect a significant shift towards full-time participation in education, especially in comparison to other European countries where greater value and status are accorded to vocational education, and transitions to work are longer (Bynner and Roberts, 1991). The economic value of education is discussed below, and the differing perceptions of the value of post-compulsory education between social groups is considered in the next chapter.

It can be concluded that the opportunity cost of education, which is determined, at least in part, by the labour market, influences decisions about participation in both education and training, although it is not the only factor influencing demand for education. A buoyant labour market may discourage people from post-compulsory education. This can be further manipulated by the provision of education and training places and the availability and terms of social security payments; if participation in education or training results in a decline in benefits, then this will impact negatively on participation in learning, and vice versa. Research suggests that the opportunity costs of the labour market influence participation in all forms of post-compulsory education from training schemes to postgraduate studies.

The labour market and the ability to 'invest' in education and training

Not only is the opportunity cost of education important, but so, too, is the actual cost of education, which includes tuition fees, living costs and associated expenses such as travel, books and equipment. Some of the impacts of the cost of education were discussed in the previous chapter, but it is pertinent to note the link between the costs incurred by participating in education and training, and concurrent employment prospects. When education is not free, and students are not in receipt of a maintenance allowance or other financial benefits, participating in education is equivalent to making an investment.

This is in line with the human capital theory, discussed in Chapter 2. In many countries the level of financial support available to students is dependent on income. This may either be parental income or personal income, although this varies between countries and according to age. Family income and job security may, therefore, influence a person's decision regarding post-compulsory education.

In the UK the maximum student loan for students living away from home, outside of London, for 1999–2000, was £3635 (for 1999–2000), which is well below the state welfare benefit level. For younger students, the likelihood of parents being able to top up their income may be a significant factor, in which case parental income and job security may influence their decisions. For independent students, financial support from a partner, or access to benefits, may be determining factors; so, once again, the labour market is important.

The young and mature students involved in the research in South Yorkshire, (Thomas, E., 1996), discussed above, all commented on the financial barriers to participation. This is significant given the high levels of unemployment in the area where the research was conducted. The area, called the Dearne Valley, was a traditional coal-mining area for over 100 years. There were twelve collieries, employing over 100,000 people directly, while thousands more were employed in related and dependent industries. Following the closure of the mines, a report on the area noted that in it, unemployment was consistently twice the national average, self-employment half the national average, the skill-base was traditional, there were very low staying-on rates at schools, and higher education attainment rates were among the lowest in the country (Dearne Valley Partnership, 1995). Students from this economic climate were acutely aware of the costs of participating in education.

Another relevant labour market issue is the availability of part-time work to help finance studying. If students are readily able to secure part-time work during term-time, and casual work during vacations, they are far more likely to be able to finance studying, than if such employment opportunities are in short supply. It was noted in the previous chapter that in the UK there has been a dramatic increase in part-time employment by higher education students. For this reason, at least in the UK, some colleges, universities and student unions are assisting students to find part-time and holiday employment. In the past, such practices, particularly working part-time while studying full-time, would have been discouraged. Staffordshire University is working in partnership with a private sector recruitment company to help find employment for students *during* their course of study, in an initiative called the 'WorkBank'. 'The WorkBank will draw on its extensive recruitment expertise to match skilled students with local companies seeking part-time or temporary staff' (Regional Office Staffordshire University, 2000).

The University Careers Service, the Students' Union and the National Union of Students, as well as the University itself, support this initiative.

If part-time work is not facilitated by educational institutions, this may penalize students from poorer backgrounds if they rely on part-time employment to contribute to the direct or indirect costs of participating in post-compulsory learning. Institutions can facilitate employment by being flexible with regard to the time and location of teaching, and primary resources that students need to access (e.g. library and computer lab opening times), and through more proactive initiatives such as Staffordshire University's WorkBank partnership.

It was noted above that lack of opportunities in the graduate labour market encourages students to participate in postgraduate education and training. This trend may, however, be stifled to some extent, especially among students from lower socio-economic classes and among mature students with fewer familial resources or other sources of financial support. Lack of access to an income (generated from the labour market) tends to discourage people from investing in postgraduate learning. Furthermore, if debts have already been incurred, by 'investing' in undergraduate education, the incentive for further investment seems to decline. Purcell and Pitcher reported, in 1996, that graduates were postponing further education and training on graduation due to the debt they incurred as under-graduates. Similarly, Dugdale (1997) notes that student debt is likely to be a contributory factor to the 'dramatic fall' in the number of applications for legal training: 'Graduates already in debt are reluctant to incur a further £10,000 debt to train for a career in law at a time when the market is clearly over-subscribed and an immediate return on their investment cannot be guaranteed' (*ibid.*, 1997, p. 161).

Thus, the evidence seems to suggest that the income available to invest in learning opportunities influences the extent to which people participate in education and training at all levels. It must be assumed that the primary source of income, from which a 'surplus' may be available to invest in learning, will, for the majority of students, be the labour market, either directly, through students' own participation or eligibility for benefits, or indirectly via parents or partners. Students from lower socio-economic backgrounds are less likely to have access to a sufficient 'surplus' to feel confident about investing in education or training, and therefore may be discouraged from participating in post-compulsory learning, especially in full-time study and for prolonged periods.

Returns on investments in education and training

In addition to the opportunity and actual costs of education and training, there is a further link between the labour market and participation. The willingness of potential students to accrue debt for the sake of education is related to their perceptions about the likely returns on their investment. Many people 'invest' in education with a view to receiving enhanced salaries from the labour market, and this effectively provides an economic 'return' on their investment. The anticipated size of the investment return helps people to calculate whether the opportunity cost (e.g. income forgone) and the actual cost (e.g. tuition fees, living costs etc.) are worth incurring.

A lack of graduate labour market opportunities, and insecurity about employment prospects, may make people more reluctant to take out loans to subsidize or fund education, as they may worry that the returns on their investment will not be sufficient to meet these costs. This analysis is based on the human capital approach to labour, education and training, and takes no account of the non-economic returns that individuals gain from learning (see Chapters 2 and 3 respectively).

People's perceptions of the economic returns to education and training are, at least partially, influenced by the graduate and 'post-compulsory certificated' labour market; in other words, people's potential employment prospects once they have participated in learning and obtained qualifications. Unemployment and under-employment (i.e. employment in a job that does not require the level of qualifications held by the employee) of qualified labour may discourage people from entering or continuing in post-compulsory education.

Discriminations in the labour market – which are discussed in Chapter 2 in relation to class, gender, ethnicity and age – may also act as barriers to some groups in society more than others. In Germany for example, many first-generation higher education students choose to be teachers because they are familiar with what teachers do, even though this is outside of their own family experience. Subsequently, a contraction in the demand for teachers deters these young people from entering higher education.

The link between age and the labour market may be an important factor influencing decisions about embarking on further study for mature students. Many older people, from the age of 50 onwards (or earlier), are excluded from the labour market (DfEE, 1998b). Hence, they are less likely to be able to recoup their investment in education from returns in the labour market. Similarly, as Adnett and Coates (1999) discuss, the economic returns to mature women via the labour market are lower than to men and younger women, and so higher education may not be a sound economic investment. Consequently, mature women tend to cite the private and social returns on higher education, rather than the economic benefits. In general, mature students are less likely to be able to earn sufficient income to compensate for lost earnings and to repay student loans and other debts incurred while studying, and this is particularly the case for women.

Many potential students, therefore, have to weigh up whether or not they think investing in education will reap sufficient returns via the labour market. This judgement may be influenced by the current operation of the labour market, but as 'perfect' information is never available, this decision will also be based on previous personal and family experience. These latter issues are examined in the next chapter. It should also be borne in mind that many returns to education are personal and social, rather than economic.

Conclusions about the labour market and participation in education and training

The labour market can be seen to influence the decisions people make about employment, education and training in a number of ways. First, the opportunity cost of education and training compared to employment. Unemployment seems to encourage people of all ages to pursue education and training, as there is a lack of employment alternatives. Conversely, a buoyant labour market may discourage participation.

Second, the affordability of education will be determined, to some extent, by access to surplus income to invest in education (assuming that the direct and indirect costs of education are borne, at least in part, by the individual, rather than the state or another body). In the main, income is derived from the labour market, and so students from lower socio-economic groups have less access to financial support from their families, which may act as a barrier to participation. Students may engage in the labour market conjointly with education to assuage the negative impact of this barrier, but this is dependent on the availability of suitable employment options in the local economy. It is therefore imperative that institutions do not make combining studying with full- or part-time employment difficult or impossible.

Finally, potential students may also take into consideration the economic returns they are likely to gain by participating in further education and training. A weak labour market for qualified staff and, more pertinently, labour market discrimination, may present barriers to participation in post-compulsory learning, especially for students from lower-income groups for whom the investment is more significant. Likewise, discrimination is more prevalent for certain social groups, such as older people, students from lower socio-economic classes and ethnic-minority groups.

The impact of the labour market for qualified staff is likely to be greater when education is not free of charge, and there is limited financial support for students. In this situation students not only incur the opportunity costs of forfeiting employment, but they must also pay for their education and their living costs. This in turn leads potential students and their families to 'calculate' the cost of learning, and the likely returns on their 'investment'. Discrimination against certain groups may help to explain persistent under-representation of certain socio-cultural groups. This issue is further explored in the next chapter with respect to the value of education to different groups, based on Bourdieu's analysis of the education system.

It can be concluded that economic and labour market factors are highly likely to affect participation in post-compulsory education, either directly, by shaping the decisions that potential students make, or indirectly, via government policy. If institutions are to continue to expand and widen access the impact of the labour market must be taken into account. It may be unrealistic to expect students, especially those who have little or no experience of post-compulsory education, to forfeit or reduce their earning capacity now, for potential, but uncertain, gains in the future. Other factors, such as few opportunities for part-time work, may also discourage or prevent students from participating in education and training beyond the age of 16. This chapter, however, has largely ignored the non-economic returns from education that are discussed in Chapter 3.

Key questions in relation to overcoming barriers created by the labour market:

- Are the expected economic and non-economic returns realistic and explicit?
- In what ways does your work help to reduce the cost of education to individuals?
- Is the initiative sufficiently flexible to enable (full- or part-time)

participation in the labour market? Is this facilitated or discouraged?

- Do the courses available provide labour market opportunities to those who want them (e.g. what are the requirements of the local economy)?
- In what ways is labour market discrimination tackled?

CHAPTER 9

The Influence of Social and Cultural Factors on Participation in Post-compulsory Education

Introduction

This chapter considers some of the influences of social and cultural factors on participation in post-compulsory education, using Bourdieu's analysis, and with particular reference to class. As was noted in Chapter 5, recruiting students from lower social classes is an enduring failing of post-compulsory education. It can be argued that in addition to the barriers emanating from the education system and the labour market there are other social and cultural barriers that impinge on non-traditional students, including those from low-income groups.

In democratic countries some people assert that the education system does not create barriers to post-compulsory education because everyone has access to compulsory education provided by and regulated by the state, and tertiary education institutions are open to all, irrespective of class, gender, ethnicity, (dis)ability, faith, sexuality etc. Furthermore, everyone is able to compete 'fairly' in the labour market; this is premised on the notion of equality of opportunity and a human capital approach, and it ignores discrimination in the labour market (see Chapter 2).

Thus, rather than there being faults with the education system and imperfections in the labour market, it may be claimed that different social and cultural groups have norms or characteristics that constrain participation in post-compulsory education. For example, people from lower socio-economic classes may be perceived not to value education as highly as other groups, and so be less willing to forfeit other activities (including employment) in preference to education or to borrow money to pay for education; or they may simply have no experience of it. Similarly, women may be traditionally disinclined to participate in science and engineering, having been socialized into notions of femininity and perceived lack of ability in these subjects.

This chapter examines Bourdieu's concepts of 'habitus' and 'cultural capital', which are used to demonstrate that education is biased in favour of dominant groups in society, at the expense of others. This disparity is reproduced in the labour market through discriminatory practices, which value certain attributes (called cultural capital) more than qualifications or other proxies of ability/suitability for the job. Consequently, some sectors of society effectively collude in their own exclusion from post-compulsory education (especially higher education), partly because it is outside of their experience (habitus) and second because it is of little value to them. Using this framework, the chapter proceeds to consider the impact of pre-entry contact and experience of post-compulsory education, and the related issues of foregoing employment in favour of studying, and/or borrowing money to fund educational participation. Finally, the chapter considers the importance of developing further and higher education that is of value to the intended beneficiaries, and discusses examples that build on familiarity and develop appropriate curricula.

'Habitus' and 'cultural capital'

Social and cultural barriers emphasize the importance of the social construction of reality, especially by distinct groups, who reinforce and perpetuate these norms. Pierre Bourdieu, the influential French sociologist, has described this as the 'habitus' of a class or group (see Bourdieu and Passeron, 1977). The habitus means 'the disposition to act which individuals acquire in the earliest stages of socialisation and which they consolidate by their subsequent choices in life' (Robbins, 1993, p. 159). These are ultimate values that inform classes or social groups, which are historically and socially constructed, and although change is possible, it is a slow process.

Central to Bourdieu's notion of habitus are two ideas. First, is the need of classes and groups to reproduce themselves. Second, in society, certain classes and groups are dominant and so control access to educational and career opportunities. Bourdieu attributes this to the dominance of 'cultural capital' which legitimizes the maintenance of the status and power of the controlling classes. The dominant classes have symbols such as language, culture and artefacts that enable them to subjugate other social classes.

Bourdieu argues that the education system is the primary institution through which class order is maintained. He analysed students in French higher education institutions, and concluded that working class students were less successful not because they were of inferior intelligence or not gifted, but because the curriculum was 'biased in favour of those things with which middle-class students were already ex-curricularly familiar' (Robbins, 1993, p. 153). In other words, educational institutions favour knowledge and experiences of dominant social groups (e.g. white, middle-class men) to the detriment of other groups. Hence, the education system is socially and culturally biased.

This is possible as educational institutions are able to determine what values, language and knowledge are regarded as legitimate, and therefore ascribe success and award certificates on this basis. Consequently, pedagogy is not an instrument of teaching, so much as of socialization and reinforcing status. This process ensures that the values of the dominant class are perpetuated and individuals who are inculcated in the dominant culture are the most likely to succeed, while other students are penalized. This is summarized by Derek Robbins:

> Bourdieu's conclusion seemed to suggest that the working-class students were at an unfair disadvantage and that there was a conspiratorial collusion between middle-class staff and middle-class students which meant that these students received a structurally preferential treatment which was a kind of cheating. (Robbins, 1993, p. 153)

Cultural capital, that only members of the dominant class possess, brings advantages in learning to these people, and, furthermore, it also helps to undervalue formal qualifications in the labour market. Bourdieu demonstrated that education institutions 'do not manu-facture students as products who possess universally valid – and validly graded – qualifications which offer correspondingly appro-priate opportunities for employment in the job market' (Robbins, 1993, pp. 155–6). Instead (some) employers prefer more loosely defined 'social characteristics', and so will discriminate against certain social groups, recruiting middle-class graduates from elite institutions rather than 'other' graduates with higher credentials, but less 'cultural capital'. Consequently: 'educational qualifications do not have an absolute value within the employment market but only have the value which the market assigns to them at any time' (*ibid.*, p. 156).

This, Bourdieu argues, is the mechanism that employers use to differentiate and reproduce themselves as a social group, and to retain their power and dominance.

Bourdieu also asserts that the education system alone does not perpetuate the status quo, but, for example, both religious teaching and technical training help to reinforce the world views held by the dominant group. Furthermore, 'cultural status and economic power are the joint keystones of class domination but they can only function jointly if they collude in concealing that they are mutually dependent' (*ibid.*, p. 156).

A simple, central conclusion that can be drawn from Bourdieu's work is that education is not neutral, but is value-laden. This has ramifications for people who are not members of the dominant class in terms of their success in education, and, subsequently, in the labour market, which is reinforced by collusion among employers and discrimination against members of other socio-cultural groups. Consequently, the working-classes (and other non-dominant groups) largely exclude themselves from post-compulsory education, especially higher education. This can be explained in two ways: first, education is outside of their habitus or experience, particularly some forms of learning, such as higher education; and second, education is of less value to them, as it serves the needs of the dominant sector of society, and this is reinforced by collusion in the labour market. These two reasons are mutually reinforcing, and are discussed below.

The 'habitus' of non-traditional students

This section of the chapter contends that the fact that many aspects of participation in post-compulsory education are outside of the experience or habitus of social and cultural groups that are under-represented in education is the *cause* of low rates of participation.

Pre-entry contact and experience of post-compulsory education

Using Bourdieu's analyses of the function and practice of the education system, post-compulsory education in general, and higher education in particular, can be said to be outside of non-traditional students' habitus. In other words, it is not within their cultural experience. For example, Sowinska (1993) comments: 'much of what students from middle – or upper – class backgrounds take for granted or expect to be part of college life is quite outside the experience of those of us who were first in our families to attend college' (p. 155). This lack of exposure to post-compulsory education is cited as a barrier to participation, and in order to overcome this disadvantage increased contact with and experience of post-compulsory education is said to be essential.

To reinforce and illustrate this point it is useful to return to John Knowles' (2000) study of Year 12 pupils, that was discussed in Chapter

7. As the year progressed, and more knowledge of higher education was gained, some pupils were less likely to apply for higher education than at the beginning of the academic year. The extent to which this was true was not only affected by 'disadvantage' (most prevalent among the 'college' students), but also prior contact with higher education. Knowles's results are shown in Table 9.1.

Table 9.1: Effect of prior contact with HE on the likelihood of students applying

	Independent	State	College
% of those with parental HE contact less likely to apply now	12%	16%	44%
% of those with other HE contact less likely to apply now	11%	25%	42%
% of those with no HE contact less likely to apply now	17%	38%	100%

Source: Knowles, 2000, p. 21, Table 9

From Table 9.1 it can be seen that having a graduate parent and other contact with higher education both appear to be important factors in influencing pupils' decisions about whether or not to pursue an application to higher education. Although 'disadvantage' substantially increases the likelihood of students deciding not to pursue an application to higher education, this is reduced by over 50 per cent when students have had prior contact with higher education. This helps to emphasize the importance of parental experience of education on the decisions young people make about further learning.

A range of other research, including substantial research carried out by the Institute for Access Studies in Stoke-on-Trent and North Staffordshire demonstrates the influence of parents on pupils' decision-making (Thomas and Slack, 1999a and 2000b). In research with over 300 Year 9 pupils (aged 13–14) in two consecutive years (1998–9 and 1999–2000), over half of the pupils surveyed felt that the main influence on their decision-making with regard to education, training and employment was their parents. Almost all pupils conceded that their parents had some influence on this decision-making process. This view was confirmed during the group discussions. For example, one pupil said, 'my dad would rather me go into FE than just get a job'. Some pupils reported that their parents encouraged them towards education, citing themselves as negative role models: 'They say, don't do that, 'cos I did that, and look where I've become.' Pupils also learnt from the negative experiences of family members, such as those in 'dead-end' jobs: 'I've got an older brother and sister ... my brother didn't do too well in school, messed about and I suppose that swayed me and I don't want to be like that.' Often, however, the support of parents tended to be less directive; parents were quoted as saying 'Do what you want to do', or do 'whatever you're happy at'. 'Your parents just tell you to wait and see what happens. They say "Just do what you want", but I don't know what I want to do.' Parents were perceived by the young people to be supportive. But the majority of parents were either in jobs that could be classified as low-status (Classes V–VII, after Goldthorpe and Llewellyn 1980), or were unemployed, and so did not have experience of post-compulsory education, and were not actively encouraging pupils to participate in further learning or training.

This and other research (cf. Hodkinson and Sparkes, 1997), suggests that decision-making by young people is context-related: it cannot be separated from the culture, life history and family background of the individual. Decisions relate to the life history of the person making them, their interaction with significant others, such as their parents and siblings, and the culture in which they have lived and are living. It can be concluded that parents and culture may act as a barrier to some people accessing post-compulsory education. This is certainly the assumption underpinning some programmes intended to promote participation among non-traditional student groups.

Access summer schools are at least partially premised on the notion that if the target group is exposed to the 'unfamiliar', then some disinclinations will be overcome. This is assumed with respect to 'disadvantaged' pupils (Blicharski, 1998) and women (Kosuch, 2000), who are exposed to university life in the former case, and non-traditional subjects for women to study in the latter; and, indeed, both schemes have demonstrated success in this respect. Other initiatives also seek to expose non-traditional potential students to post-compulsory education to overcome their lack of experience or contact with this type of institution and learning. For example, the University of Glamorgan organizes a range of activities that are available to pupils from under-achieving schools in south-east Wales; one of the functions of these activities is to introduce the university to these pupils. Two examples are provided in Box 9.1.

Lack of experience of debt (with regard to education)

In addition to lack of exposure to post-compulsory education in general, some commentators make a further case that the financial

Box 9.1 Examples from the University of Glamorgan of activities designed to familiarize 'non-traditional' students with higher education

---

Aiming for a College Education (ACE) Days

'The ACE days bring pupils from Year 9 and Year 10 on visits to the University where they meet staff and students, as part of longer term developmental work to introduce them to the notion of higher education. Participants are provided with written information about university life ... Thus, progression routes after A-levels are normalised through a process of informal awareness'. (Woodrow, 1998, p. 38)

'Master Classes'

'These are specific lectures given at the University at the request of schools in subject areas which would enhance the school's curriculum. They give the compact pupils an opportunity to visit the campus and to experience a formal lecture at a higher education level. Such curriculum developments not only begin the process of familiarisation with an HE institution, but also introduce students to the style of delivery in HE and to some of the demands that will be made upon them as undergraduates'. (*ibid.*, p. 39).

---

implications of entering education, as opposed to participating in the labour market, are outside the habitus of non-traditional student groups. Education usually involves forgoing or reducing current earnings (the opportunity cost of education). Furthermore, it often involves investment and debt, especially for students who do not have access to other 'funds', to cover the costs of education. (The links between the opportunity cost of education and the need to invest in education and the labour market are discussed in the previous chapter.) It can be claimed that debt, especially for education, is not the norm for some social and cultural groups. A report on access in Spain notes that 'families there with higher educational levels are more likely to invest in higher education, reflecting their understanding of the advantages and returns' (cited in Skilbeck and Connell, 2000, p. 31). This again suggests that family experience of post-compulsory education contributes to willingness to invest in education, and even to accrue debt. Similarly, commenting on the situation that confronts potential entrants from lower socio-economic groups with regard to finance, Knowles notes: 'Both the size of the debt and its long-term nature are outside the cultural experience of most of this target group, whose only experience of credit may be just a few pounds a week into a shopping catalogue' (Knowles, 2000, p. 15).

This situation is contrasted with the position of middle-class students:

> Better off students, with family experience of mortgages and investment, will have less resistance to taking out these loans, and many of them will have less need to do so, having families that can afford to support them. (*ibid.*)

The idea that borrowing money to fund participation in post-compulsory education is outside the habitus of some students is summed up in John Knowles's research. He cites the case of 'the father of a bright 15 year old in an inner city comprehensive who was being encouraged to consider aiming for university entry: "No daughter of mine is getting into debt just for education!" ' (Knowles, 2000, p. 23).

Similar sentiments are reported by Maggie Woodrow (1999b) to the Scottish Parliament's Independent Committee of Inquiry into Student Finance:

> If your sole experience of credit is 35p a week into Woolworth's catalogue, then the notion of taking on that level of debt before you've even got a job, is just horrific. It's totally outside your cultural experience. (Access Project Leader)

> But no-one in our family has ever been in debt. You can't start work and set up a home owing all that. (mother of a Compact pupil)

> In working-class communities, and particularly in Muslim working-class communities, there's an aversion to debt, a very strong aversion to debt. (Vice-chancellor)

Thus, student loans and debt may be particularly unacceptable to many non-traditional student groups as they are outside of their habitus. More generally, using Bourdieu's notion of 'habitus' and research evidence, it can be suggested that post-compulsory education, particularly higher education, is outside of some potential students' life experience, and this exerts a strong disincentive to participate.

Culturally relevant post-compulsory education
The second strand of the argument relating to social and cultural barriers and Bourdieu's analysis of the problem concerns the *value* of

post-compulsory education to different social groups. Bourdieu argues that traditional, middle-class students possess cultural capital that gives them an unfair advantage in comparison to other groups in the school sector, in post-compulsory education and in the labour market. Consequently, education is of less value to some social groups than others. If post-compulsory education is of less value to some groups than others, and of little value to particular groups, this provides a further disincentive to postpone entering the labour market and earning a wage, and simultaneously accruing debt.

From an instrumental perspective, it could be argued that the international expansion of the post-compulsory sector, including the promotion and importance of lifelong learning and the massification of higher education mean that, increasingly, 'everybody' needs qualifications at a higher level. More and higher qualifications are required for employment that previously did not require such a level of certification. This change can either be seen as a consequence of the growth of the 'knowledge economy' or simply the result of credentialism (see Chapter 2). Furthermore, the non-economic benefits of education relating to personal development and societal gains could all be viewed as reasons why post-compulsory education is of value to all students, including those from non-traditional groups.

But if Bourdieu is correct, in that education serves to reinforce the status and position of the dominant social group, and that this is coupled with discrimination in the labour market, education may indeed be of little value to many socio-cultural groups. Post-compulsory education will remain of little value, and thus be irrelevant, and this will continue to be a barrier to participation by some groups, unless institutions change to providing socially and culturally relevant curricula. These issues have been discussed in Chapter 7, but the need for an appropriate curriculum will be illustrated here by an example based on the work of Trish Spedding and Maggie Gregson (2000) in the north-east of England.

Spedding and Gregson (2000) argue that educational institutions are more aware of the need for structural change than they were in the past, and are '"reaching out" to educationally under represented groups' (p. 4), but they are 'still unable to maintain their engagement in learning' (*ibid.*). Although Spedding and Gregson accept the importance of structural barriers to participation, they reject the notion 'that structural deterrents are the only factors in play' (*ibid.*, p. 5). Instead, they argue that there is a 'missing curriculum' (p. 3) that 'recognises and values the everyday life experiences, needs and interests of local people' (p. 4). This assertion echoes the work of

Bourdieu, which recognizes the cultural bias inherent in the education system, prioritizing and validating the knowledge and skills of the dominant class, at the expense of other knowledges and experiences.

Spedding and Gregson (2000, p. 13) advocate 'starting with people's "stories" and their immediate needs and interests'. They consider using the approach suggested by Lipman (1995) and Sharp (1993): 'talking about their life experiences and sharing their understandings of these together' (Spedding and Gregson, 2000, p. 13), and this encourages both them and others to learn. Through their experiences, Spedding and Gregson found that the 'social relations of learning were perhaps the most crucial factor in decisions to come to, stay [in], or leave widening participation programmes of learning' (*ibid.*, p. 14). By this they suggest that learning environments and student–tutor relations need to 'look, sound, feel and smell close to home' (*ibid.*). The importance of students feeling 'comfortable' in their learning environment is reflected in this comment from a mature student on a maths summer school:

> I thought it would just be like going back to school, however it was totally different. I didn't feel pressured, it was a comfortable way of doing maths, the tutors were very helpful and made you feel good about yourself and also it was good because everybody was in the same boat as you. (Thomas and Slack, 2000c, p. 7)

Spedding and Gregson argue that learning needs to be in local venues; learning needs to involve friends and allies and learning needs to be relevant (which may be to help children or grandchildren or to improve employment prospects and so forth). Furthermore, learning is often triggered by changing life circumstances and so needs to be available at the right time in people's lives. They conclude:

> Educationally under-represented people need increased opportunities and social space to shape their social relations of learning alongside people who look and sound like them and who may have shared similar life experiences or 'organising circumstances' and not to find their learning and themselves jeopardised or colonised by the social power and dominant discourses of others. (Spedding and Gregson, 2000, p. 18)

A further example helps to demonstrate the value of developing curricula that are of relevance to particular target communities, rather than reinforcing traditional and elite forms of knowledge and patterns of learning. In South Wales, the Penderry Project (Trotman and Pudner, 2000) has sought to work with socially excluded communities who have little confidence that education is of value to them. Members of these communities have been reached through the provision of learning that is relevant to them – learning that will assist their children. Trotman and Pudner write:

> Even when groups of adults have all the appearance of being totally disaffected and alienated from education in all its guises, it is still possible to invigorate them educationally. What matters to them, is the education of their children. We can reach them as adult students through their concerns for their children, through the abilities, skills, and resources that they apply on a daily basis, to counter social and economic deprivation. (Trotman and Pudner, 2000, p. 169; cf. Trotman and Pudner, 1998)

Spedding and Gregson conclude that in the field of widening participation more work is 'urgently needed' to develop and, crucially, apply appropriate pedagogies and curricula to engage non-traditional student groups. They comment on the poor practices they witnessed in the communities in which they were working:

> We also found examples of FE colleges trying to maximise funding, by simply offering existing courses in community settings with apparently little recognition of the pedagogical issues in terms of the interests, needs and demands of working with educationally under represented groups. (Spedding and Gregson, 2000, p. 16)

The lack of appropriate curricula is reinforced by the low status that is often accorded to widening participation work. Consequently, less-experienced staff are utilized (on low rates of pay), and the level of training and staff development that is offered is minimal or non-existent. (The need for staff development and institutional learning is considered in Chapter 11.) It is therefore not surprising that there is often a mismatch between the courses that are delivered and the requirements of the learners (or potential learners). Chapter 14, however, is based on a case study in which community groups are actively involved in determining both the contents and structure of a programme of courses.

Conclusions about the social and cultural barriers to participating in formal learning

Two key points can be concluded from Bourdieu's writing, and demonstrated by the experiences and applied research of practitioners. First, many of the learning opportunities that are available to people from 'different' socio-cultural groups (i.e. not the dominant group, and, therefore, non-traditional students) are outside of their experiences, or habitus. And second, this learning is of little or no value to them, as they do not possess the relevant cultural capital. These points are summarized by David Davies: 'to many people, the lifelong learning prospectus makes little economic or financial sense and the 'rules of the game', that is the meanings of what is on offer are not clear' (2000, p. 42). Solutions involve bringing education to these groups (as discussed in Chapter 7), enabling similar learners to study together and to gain support, familiarizing people with learning and the associated institutions and practices, and, perhaps most importantly, changing the curricula to develop learning that is of value to non-traditional groups of students.

Key questions to overcome social and cultural barriers to participation:

- To what extent does learning familiarize people with the 'world' of post-compulsory education (e.g. to facilitate progression)?
- Does the initiative involve 'others' who influence the decision-making of potential learners?
- Are the expected economic and non-economic returns realistic and explicit?
- Is the curriculum socially and culturally relevant (is it free from cultural bias)? Is it of 'value' to the learners?
- Does the initiative allow similar groups to work together to gain confidence?

CHAPTER 10

Individualizing the Problem, or Problematizing the Individual?

Introduction

The fourth category of barriers to participation in post-compulsory education, discussed in this chapter, is those that can be said to exist at the level of the individual. Rather than attributing barriers to participation to the education system, the labour market, or social and cultural issues, this stance places responsibility onto individual students who choose whether or not to participate. This position may emanate from the fact that there are examples of individuals from all walks of life that have overcome disadvantages and have successfully accessed education to the highest level. This, however, ignores the very significant impact of the other issues that impinge on and limit the opportunities available and the types of decisions that people are able to take.

Proponents of this view seem to assume that individuals are to blame for not participating in post-compulsory education, which implies that non-participation should be attributed to personal inadequacy, and responsibility for overcoming this is placed with the individual. In other words, this approach reduces the issue of non-participation to the level of the individual, and tends to *problematize* the individual, for example, by blaming individuals for having low aspirations, or for simply being ignorant about the opportunities that exist. Malcolm Tight (1998) describes this process as 'victim blaming', and comments that: 'stigmatizing non-participants from the start hardly seems the most sensible approach' (quoted in Parry and Fry, 1999, p. 109). Two issues – low aspirations and motivation, and lack of information – are now discussed.

Low aspirations and motivation

The intention of programmes that address aspirations and motivation is to *change* attitudes and cultures (towards learning), rather than to acknowledge difference. This, for example, is demonstrated by the comment below, which suggests that increased motivation is all that people require in order to enable participation in post-compulsory education, irrespective of their different life experiences and social and cultural positions:

> we need to create incentives and to ensure that they are effective in motivating everybody in society to go into learning, irrespective of where they live, how old they are, what their ethnic background, gender or economic and personal circumstances are, or their existing level of achievement. (Paul Hamlyn Foundation, 1993, p. 247)

This statement ignores the barriers created by the education system, the restrictions imposed on people by the labour market and the differences between social groups, which means, for some people, post-compulsory education is outside of their experience and of little value. Assumptions of this sort – that people need to change – underlie a wide range of policy and practice initiatives. But, as this book has aimed to demonstrate, people are constrained by a range of factors, and these impinge on the opportunities available to them and the subsequent decisions they make. The importance and implications of this observation is illustrated by using an example from my own research, which demonstrates that formal equality or equality of opportunity is insufficient to ensure equality of results.

The initiative in question operates with Year 9 school pupils, aged 13 and 14 years, and offers a programme of activities that are intended to raise aspirations. The primary aim of the project is 'raising the aspirations and ambition of young people in the area to encourage them to achieve their full potential regardless of ability' (Thomas and Slack, 1999a, p. 16). The scheme works with the whole Year 9 cohort, incorporating both private and state schools, across a reasonably large geographical area including urban and rural settings. The activities include inspirational speakers and arts activities, such as music, singing, dance and set-building, and culminate in a public concert performed by pupils in partnership with arts professionals in an impressive city-centre venue.

Although this scheme has strengths, one of the difficulties encountered is the assumption that all pupils will benefit equally from the initiative; or, indeed, that those children with low aspirations will benefit in particular. Two related factors contribute to this assumption not being realized; moreover, those pupils who are already performing well at school benefit the most. First, pupils either volunteer to take part in some activities, or they are selected by school staff, and this helps to determine who benefits from the scheme. Second, with respect to activities in which all pupils participate, there appear to be differential benefits that pupils gain from the same activities. These two issues are discussed briefly below. The relevance of Bourdieu's notion of cultural capital – the built-in advantage that middle-class children have in education, and, conversely, the disadvantage that working-class children face (discussed in Chapter 9) – is reiterated.

The research involved conducting surveys with pupils, both before and after the programme of activities took place, and focus groups with young people, some of whom had only attended the inspirational speaker sessions, and others of whom had participated more fully, including performing in the final concert. (The former are referred to as 'non-performers', and the latter as 'performers' from here on.) Many pupils – both performers and non-performers – felt that the project only appealed to those interested in music. These children were described as more 'academic' than their peers, and were observed to be more interested in, and motivated by, their schoolwork. In the group discussions, some non-performers labelled these pupils as 'keenos' and 'swots'. In fact, in one school, pupils felt that the scheme was only intended for high-achievers, and, consequently, those who did not participate in the final performance felt that they lacked the ability and skill, and that this labelled them 'non-achievers'. Irrespective of whether pupils volunteered to take part, or whether they were selected by the teaching staff, performers were identified by their peers as those who achieved the highest grades in their schoolwork.

In some schools, pupils were selected by teaching staff, who devised their own methods and criteria (Thomas and Slack, 2000b). Although some staff expressed regret, most schools chose pupils who could be relied upon to behave well in public, and who had some musical ability. In other schools, pupils were able to volunteer to participate. The research suggested that those pupils who were already successful were the ones who tended to put themselves forward, thus enabling them to further improve their 'advantage'. It appears that some pupils possessed the relevant 'cultural capital' (see Chapter 9) to take advantage of the opportunities provided by the scheme, while others did not. Both pupils and teachers said that they did not believe academically successful pupils should be the focus of the project because they were already motivated and were likely to stay on at school – they were already 'dead good'. But this is what happened in the majority of schools, and can be illustrated by a more specific example from the initiative.

A central element of the programme was a concert that involved the BBC Philharmonic Orchestra and school pupils performing together in public. Unfortunately, in many schools both teachers and pupils felt that a certain level of musical literacy (gained from formal learning) was a prerequisite to participate. Indeed, some non-performers said they would have liked to have volunteered, but that they could not because they did not play an instrument. Most of the pupils who participated were chosen for their musical ability and the majority had attended music lessons for a number of years.

This scheme offers formal equality (see Chapter 3), in that everyone is offered the same chance to participate, but, it does not achieve equality of results. This is because of pre-existing inequality and disadvantage, and so some pupils are better able to take advantage of the opportunities offered than others. Learning to play a musical instrument, and practising regularly, demonstrates a relatively high level of commitment and motivation in the pupils themselves, and is likely to indicate good levels of parental support and encouragement. It is also expensive to buy or rent the instrument and pay for the music lessons. During focus-group discussions pupils confirmed that encouragement and financial support for music lessons came from parents.

Often teachers corroborated that many of the musicians taking part represented the top end of the ability range within the Year 9 cohort. For example, in one school the majority of the musicians were in the 'A' band. The perception that pupils who play instruments were already high achievers was further demonstrated in focus group discussions about future plans. Pupils were asked what they wanted to do after their final year in school. Many of the pupils involved as musicians were already considering going on to university and considered this the next step in their education. For example, in one focus group only one girl had had any experience of music, having taken lessons for a number of years; she was also the only one in the group who said she was going to go on to university.

Although schools do not have to put forward their most able pupils, in a competitive environment, one can argue that some schools felt they were left with little choice. The public concert offered a 'showcase' for local schools and, therefore, they needed to select pupils to participate on the basis of ability to promote a positive image of the school.

This discussion demonstrates that there are educational factors, financial (labour market) issues and social and cultural advantages that contribute to middle-class pupils being far more likely to play a musical instrument than their working-class peers. This enables the former to benefit from this scheme more than pupils from other backgrounds. As a result of their possessing cultural capital, pupils from the dominant social group are also more able to succeed at school. The combination of economic and cultural capital, coupled with educational achievement, facilitates the participation of these pupils in the project.

Further evidence of the operation of cultural capital, and the ability of some pupils to benefit more from the scheme than others, is provided by the examination of an activity in which all pupils participated. The majority of Year 9 pupils attend two inspirational speaker sessions. However, the benefits gained by pupils varied. One teacher commented that pupils who 'don't want to know' do not 'suddenly become "wanting to know"' following the sessions. Similarly, pupils said that the sessions 'appeal to those who want to listen and not to those who don't', and 'it is for everyone, but those who don't want to listen ... it doesn't reach them'. However, these pupils felt that they had benefited from the talks because they had gone and sat and listened, but, they said, 'you have to be ready to do this'.

Some pupils were able to listen to the inspirational speakers and synthesize the ideas from the talks and apply them to their own lives, while other pupils were unable to do this, and could only link the concept of working hard to achieve their aspirations to the activities being discussed. These pupils only understood a speech from an Olympic swimmer as relating to the objective of being a successful swimmer. Another pupil commented that most pupils would not face a situation similar to that faced by Simon Weston (a soldier who was badly burned and had struggled to rebuild his life), so his story and its associated message did not really apply to them. Pupils who were able to extrapolate the concepts from the presentations said that listening to the inspirational speakers had made them 'feel like going out and getting a future', and they 'made you want to go back to school and learn a lot so you can get a good job'.

The way pupils responded to the inspirational speakers appeared to be influenced by their own level of academic maturity and their school culture. Some schools prepared pupils for the talks beforehand, and, consequently, they gained more from the speakers. This can be contrasted with schools that gave pupils no information about the speaker sessions, and where the pupils had negative responses to the sessions. Again, there appear to be both social and cultural factors, and features of the education system that affect the ability of pupils to benefit from the inspirational speakers.

Although raising aspirations may appear to be a solution to low participation in post-compulsory education, the example above illustrates that 'low aspirations' are not the cause of this predicament. Instead, the education system, the labour market and social and cultural factors all shape the ability of people to benefit from opportunities available. Hence, formal equality is insufficient, and actually enables the advantaged and dominant social groups to consolidate their position. It is therefore essential that the scheme is carefully and effectively targeted to avoid consolidating the position of the dominant classes, and that sufficient account is taken of the other types of barriers that people face, particularly the need for structural change. It is instructive to consider the issues raised in Chapter 5 regarding the assumptions that underpin attempts to widen participation. The need for awareness of the range of constraints that operate to inhibit participation is returned to in Chapter 11.

Information, guidance and awareness

A further explanation for the low take-up of opportunities, including post-compulsory education and training, is that certain groups in society lack information about the opportunities that are available, and so the provision of information, guidance and awareness-raising are central to widening participation in learning. For example, it may not be known that you do not necessarily require the standard entry qualifications to embark on a university or college course. Or that, in the UK, if your parental income is below £17,370, you do not have to pay fees for university tuition and you are entitled to a full student loan, which is only repayable when you are earning £10,000 or more. Certainly, the school pupils involved in the aspiration raising initiative, discussed above, felt that they had insufficient information to make decisions about their futures, as this extract from the report illustrates:

> During group discussions many pupils felt that they had a relatively low level of information and knowledge relating to employment opportunities and pathways. Pupils frequently said they did not know what they ought to do to get the job they would like. Similarly, they did not know what they 'needed' in terms of qualifications, or which subjects they should be opting

to study at GCSE level. Although pupils were aware that they would receive more careers information as they progressed through school, many felt that it would be beneficial to have more information earlier. This is illustrated by this comment made by a Year 9 pupil: 'The project shows what other people have done but it doesn't show us how to do it ... the speakers are saying when you get to here, try really hard, but I want to know how to get to "here".' Indeed, 76.5 per cent of Year 9 pupils said that they would like to speak to a careers teacher or advisor to receive information about both post-16 education and careers. (Adapted from Thomas and Slack, 2000b, p. 11)

More specifically, small-scale research carried out by the Institute for Access Studies (Thomas and Slack, 1999b) with 17- and 18-year-olds preparing for higher education in the UK suggested that there are serious gaps in many young people's knowledge of university that relate directly to financial issues. Furthermore, earlier research by Keen and Higgins (1990, 1992) found that both young people and adults have very inadequate knowledge of higher education, and the same can be assumed to be true of other forms of post-compulsory education.

As participation in further and higher education expands, and the notion of a 'job for life' gives way to the need for lifelong learning and career change, the role of improved information and guidance expands. These changes are features of a more individualized society, which expects individuals to take responsibility for and manage their work, learning and finances (discussed in Chapter 2). Tony Watts and Brian Stevens (1999) elucidate that not only is there a growing need for educational and careers guidance, but also for financial guidance, with regard to both direct and indirect costs of learning, and the lack of financial security associated with the decline of continuous and sustained employment. Information and guidance facilitates potential students to make choices and participate more fully in post-compulsory educational opportunities, but some people may be able to make better use of the information than others, unless such support is carefully targeted.

Harte and Jordan (1999) reiterate these arguments in relation to a guidance service that targets adults at risk from social exclusion:

Cutting edge technology, industrial re-organisation and changing patterns in family and community life bring many changes and transitions, and create a continuous need to learn, to re-train, to adapt, in order to cope with the demands of everyday living. Support and guidance during each transition helps in the making of informed decisions, in creating the confidence and self-belief to explore new options and to commit to them ... People who have missed out on education the first time around need to acquire both information and skills, the actual currency that allows them to negotiate and ultimately participate fully in education. Guidance is a way of bridging the gap. (p. 43)

The initiative they discuss prioritizes working with individuals, but these are carefully targeted, and it can be seen from the above quote that Harte and Jordan view information and guidance as a 'bridge' that enables people to move from where they are now to other opportunities (cf. Johnston and Croft, 1998). When information and guidance is conceptualized and delivered in this way it can be viewed as a link between people's habitus and the world of education, and, concomitantly, it provides them with skills to 'negotiate', which may be part of the cultural capital that certain socio-cultural groups lack. Thus, the boundaries between individual and socio-cultural barriers become blurred. It is, however, necessary to ensure that providing information and guidance does not allow dominant groups to improve their advantage. By recognizing the other types of barriers present, and targeting recipients carefully, an individually directed initiative can have positive benefits.

Many prospective students do not go to the most appropriate sources for information and guidance (Percy et al., 1982; Woodley et al., 1987; Tuckett and Sargant, 1996). Instead, people prefer to go for help to organizations and individuals that they are familiar with. Consequently, certain socio-cultural groups are likely to be further disadvantaged as the people they know and are familiar with may have little or no experience or knowledge of post-compulsory education. Sarah Williams comments that 'with the myriad of changes [within the higher education sector] the information that enquirers receive from these sources is likely to be at best patchy, and in some cases unhelpful, out-of-date or mis-leading' (Williams, 1999, p. 21).

Conclusions
The danger with individualizing the problem, and thus problematizing the individual, is that it allows traditional, elitist and exclusionary practices to continue within the education system and the labour market. This approach does not acknowledge that it is these very practices, rather than the individuals themselves, which are to blame for the under-representation of certain social and cultural groups in

post-compulsory education. There is a danger that solutions premised on assumptions that individualize the problem exacerbate the situation, as some people (particularly those who possess greater cultural capital) are able to make better use of opportunities that are available.

There are indeed arguments for both seeking to raise aspirations and motivation, and for providing better information about educational opportunities, careers and related financial issues, and targeting these services on non-traditional student groups in particular to help them adapt to fit in with the 'rules' of the current education system. The solutions, however, are not simply about ensuring that individuals are better motivated and better informed. As the previous chapters have demonstrated, changes in structures and institutional cultures are also required. For this reason, attempts to facilitate access to, and improve the delivery of, information and guidance must not be 'stand alone projects' but part of a comprehensive strategy. This theme is returned to in the next chapter.

Key questions relating to individuals:

- How does the initiative target the intended beneficiaries, and is it effective? Who benefits most from the programme?
- Does the scheme avoid blaming individuals, and seeking to change them without changing the institution?
- Is information about programmes and learning opportunities available to non-traditional learners?
- Is sufficient account taken of the other types of barriers limiting the participation of non-traditional students?

CHAPTER 11

A Strategic Approach – But Whose Strategy?

Introduction

The last five chapters reviewed barriers to participation in post-compulsory education as they arise in the contexts of the education system, the labour market, social and cultural norms and at the level of the individual. This chapter considers the importance of developing a strategic approach to widening participation. 'Strategic' is defined here to imply an awareness of the inter-relationship between different barriers to participation, a need for coherence between different policies and projects and longer-term sustainability. This chapter argues that a strategic approach can be developed first at the level of the project, and second, on a broader scale, such as the institutional, regional or national level. Of paramount importance in the creation of a strategic approach is to consider *who* is involved in the planning and implementation of policies and practices directed towards widening participation. This issue relates to the discussion in Chapter 5 regarding the assumptions underpinning policies and practice, and suggests that assumptions made, for example, by a provider may not coincide with those of the intended beneficiary group. Thus, a policy or initiative founded on assumptions, rather than consultation, research and user participation may be, at best, less effective and possibly damaging.

First, this chapter considers the inter-relationship of the different types of barriers, and, in particular, the need to develop a coherent project. This is illustrated by reference to an example of a project that is trying to recognize and take into account the range of issues confronting young people who come from families and schools without a tradition of participation in third-level education. Second, the chapter turns to the need for coherence and complementarity *between* projects and policies. It is particularly important that *institutional* policies and practices are consistent and mutually reinforcing, and that widening participation activities are not marginalized or reserved for disciplines that are struggling to recruit a sufficient number of traditional students. An example is therefore used of an Australian university, which offers both further and higher education courses, that has attempted to develop a strategic approach to widening participation. Then the issue of sustainability is discussed. Sustainability is not easily defined, but this chapter considers a number of components: financial autonomy, ownership by stakeholders (particularly those who traditionally lack authority), the extent to which the capacity of a stakeholder is developed and evidence of institutional learning and change (see Thomas and Slack, forthcoming). Finally, attention is turned towards 'who' is involved in developing a strategy.

The inter-relationship between different types of barriers: developing a coherent project

The distinctions between the different categories of barriers (within the education system, the labour market, social and cultural factors, and the individual) are somewhat artificial, as was acknowledged in Chapter 5. There are certainly areas of overlap, which have been noted in the previous five chapters, and this is illustrated in the previous chapter in particular. The process of differentiating types of barriers raises awareness of the range of issues that confront learners and provides a mechanism to think about and unpack the assumptions that are made, and to critically challenge solutions, with the aim of improving the benefits to potential new learners. Simply changing the institutional structure will not ensure a diversity of students – it is a necessary condition, but it is not sufficient. Similarly, providing more information about educational opportunities will not, on its own, stimulate an increase in participation by non-traditional student groups unless there are structural changes to cope with the needs of non-traditional students. There is thus an inter-relationship between institutional, labour market, social and cultural and individual issues that can either inhibit or facilitate participation. Figure 11.1, reproduced from Chapter 5, represents this inter-relationship. A central question for practitioners and policy-makers to bear in mind is whether due accord has been given to the different types of barriers that potential learners face.

A single project can develop a strategic approach to widening participation by helping to overcome a range of barriers facing

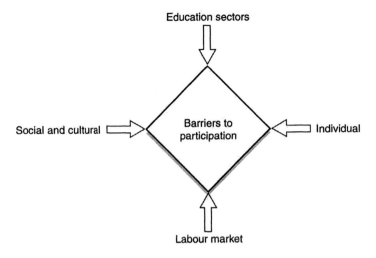

Figure 11.1   *Categories of barriers to participation*

potential entrants, rather than simply addressing one particular issue. The extent to which the impact of the range of barriers to participation is embraced is reviewed as part of the analysis of the case studies in Chapters 12, 13 and 14. But an example of a project that is trying to recognize and take into account the complexity of issues confronting young people who come from families and schools without a tradition of participation in third-level education is presented here to clarify the discussion.

The Schools Partnership Programme (SPP): an example of a project trying to embrace a range of factors impeding participation

The Schools Partnership Programme (SPP), initiated in 1998, is a partnership between a modern university in the UK and a number of schools in the area. The overall aim is to work together to raise the awareness of pupils and parents, to encourage them to plan for their post-compulsory education and to ensure that all those with the ability are given the knowledge, confidence and opportunity to progress into further and higher education. The scheme works with a cohort of pupils selected from the partner schools each year who, traditionally, would not have aspired to post-16 education, and supports and tracks their progress from Year 10 (age 14/15) onwards.

The initiative provides a *programme* of activities (and indeed integrates and builds on a number of existing projects), rather than simply addressing one barrier (such as the school-based scheme relating to low aspirations that is discussed in the previous chapter). In the first year of operation activities included: campus visits, including university-based social events; media projects; engineering workshops and group work; and mentoring with pupils by university students. This is supplemented by university compact agreements (see Chapter 7), that guarantee pupils a reduced-points entry offer, taking account of other qualities demonstrated by pupils through participation in extra-curricular activities such as the Schools Partnership Programme. The programme organizers are expanding the range of activities offered, and, in the future, parental involvement is to be explored. There are other initiatives already in existence in the area that have complementary aims, while the project aims to work in close association with the schools and other partners to try to avoid duplication of activities.

Although this project is still largely focusing on the individual, by raising awareness, developing skills and providing information, it demonstrates awareness of the need for a strategic or coherent project that addresses more than one type of barrier. It seeks to work with pupils in the school system, and the compact arrangement acknowledges that previous educational performance is not necessarily a good indicator of potential. The compact arrangement also provides a progression ladder that removes some of the uncertainty and barriers associated with accessing higher education.

The project provides support to similar groups of pupils in school and, subsequently, in further education, to assist them to secure and take up a higher education place. This is facilitated by student-mentors, who are often students who have come from similar backgrounds (such as the same school or a family with no previous experience of higher education). Visits to the university and subject workshops (usually requested by the schools) help to familiarize pupils with the university culture. Besides, if the scheme achieves its goal of involving parents this will further help to overcome some social and cultural barriers, as parents are very influential on the decisions young people make about future education and careers (Thomas and Slack, 1999a). The project selects the young people carefully, and tries to raise pupils' confidence, without blaming them for not necessarily contemplating further and higher education. It can, therefore, be seen that this scheme seeks to address a range of barriers that impede these young people from progressing from school into further and higher education (although there are issues that are not contemplated).

Coherence and complementarity *between* projects and policies

This section contends that not only should individual projects seek to take account of the different types of barriers that exist, but there should also be coherence and complementarity between different projects and policies. This book focuses largely on *projects* that aim to widen participation. One reason for this is the huge expansion in the number of projects that are intended to expand access to further and higher education and promote lifelong learning. Christine Davies, of the National Task Group for Widening Participation, commented that there have never been so many projects (Davies, C., 2000). In 2000–1 there were 77 special-initiative projects funded by HEFCE in England, and there are numerous others.

Much of the work concerned with widening participation and promoting lifelong learning concentrates on projects and special initiatives. Widening participation *projects*, however, often focus on overcoming one or two particular barriers, and there is a tendency to overstate the importance of one type of barrier and to minimize or ignore the significance of other barriers. Although it may be comforting for all concerned to blame someone or something else for the still comparatively narrow patterns of participation in post-compulsory education, this is not an effective strategy for those genuinely concerned to achieve greater social equality. Targeted widening participation *projects* are important, but they have to be part of a coherent *strategy*, seeking to address different aspects of this complex issue. There is a tendency for practitioners to become absorbed in the day-to-day tasks, and for policy-makers to consider the success of individual initiatives at the expense of more strategic thinking. Many small-scale projects are successful in meeting their aims and objectives, but these do not challenge the structures and the distribution of power that allows elitism to prevail for the majority. It is not always possible for one project to address all barriers relating to low participation, but projects and policies may complement each other, and, similarly, avoid duplication of comparable services. Strategic thinking helps to locate a project within a wider context, and helps to achieve greater impact.

In the UK, the White Paper, *Learning to Succeed: A New Framework for Post-16 Learning* (DfEE, 1999), proposes that all pupils, rather than the minority, should be encouraged to participate in post-16 education. It goes on to recommend that initiatives should 'cut out fragmentation, bureaucracy and duplication' to 'deliver improvements that benefit the learner' (*ibid.*, section 2.12).

The HEFCE acknowledges the value of individual projects, but also the need for a more strategic approach to widening participation: 'while individual projects can do excellent work, there are additional benefits if the work is co-ordinated and good practice is shared' (HEFCE, preface in Harrison *et al.*, 2000, p. 8).

This recognition led to the HEFCE taking steps to encourage 'institutions to adopt a more strategic approach to widening participation' (*ibid.*, p. 9). This included providing mainstream funding incentives, requesting institutions to prepare an 'Initial Statement' on widening participation (HEFCE 99/33) and seeking synergy between institutional policies:

> We are keen to see the question of widening participation being addressed at the highest level, and for each institution to develop an approach that is in accordance with its mission, corporate plan and more general strategic development. (HEFCE, preface in Harrison *et al.*, 2000, p. 10)

The move towards a more strategic approach to widening participation was stimulated and informed by the policy climate of the time (Storan, 2000). The Kennedy Report noted the lack of a strategic approach to widening participation, for example the report said: 'The absence of a strategic dimension at local level, in our view, is a major weakness in the system which significantly reduces the potential for widening participation' (Kennedy, 1997, p. 39).

More specifically, the Dearing Report (NCIHE, 1997) recommended that greater financial support should be accorded to institutions that have a coherent strategy towards widening participation:

> We recommend to the Government and the Funding Bodies that, when allocating funds for the expansion of higher education, they give priority to those institutions which can demonstrate a commitment to widening participation, and have in place a participation strategy, a mechanism for monitoring progress, and a provision for review by the governing body of achievement. (*ibid.*, 1997, p. 14)

Ward and Steele (1999) have noted that the further and higher education funding councils in the UK have promoted wider participation, but they question the extent to which senior staff in institutions support and embrace this mission:

> WP [widening participation] policies and strategies have clearly moved from marginalisation to expansion, at least as far as the Government and Funding Council in England are concerned. What will need to be monitored closely in the near future, however, is the extent to which this key 'policy objective' (of WP) has been approved of, and embraced by senior management and academics in universities [and colleges]. (p. 197)

It is only if widening participation policies and practices within institutions are centralized and fully embraced that widespread change will take place. The HEFCE recommends synergy between institutional policies, such as recruitment, teaching and learning and financial plans. The example of an Australian institution that has attempted to create a 'culturally inclusive university' is now discussed to exemplify the points made above.

Creating a culturally diverse and inclusive HEI

Victoria University is located in the western region of Melbourne, Australia, which is an area that has a higher than average proportion of its population from immigrant non-English-speaking backgrounds. The area also has lower income levels and lower rates of participation in post-compulsory education than the rest of the state of Victoria. Victoria University is a dual sector institution, which means it provides higher education, and vocational education and training, known as Technical and Further Education (TAFE). The institution has attempted to create a 'culturally inclusive university' (Ronayne, 2000, p. 143) by 'developing multi-faceted policy approaches which meet the needs of its diverse student population' (p. 146).

Over approximately the last twenty years the University has sought to develop relationships with different communities in its locale, 'based on partnership and mutual support' (*ibid.*, p. 148). This, in turn, has led to the development of the Personalised Access and Study (PAS) policy:

> PAS comprises a complex set of processes focused around the inter-related issues of access (creating alternative mechanisms for students to enter the institution) and study (assisting them to stay in the institution once they arrive). (p. 149)

Access initiatives include developing alternative entry arrangements, interviewing students to assess their point-of-entry learning needs and developing a 'personal student compact' that details how the institution will attempt to address these requirements.

The 'study' elements of the policy have been addressed through a reworking and enhancement of institutional policies relating to the design and delivery of the curriculum: student progress procedures, study pathways between the TAFE and HE components, and student learning support at course and subject levels. (p. 149)

Jarlath Ronayne describes a number of examples of how this set of institutional policies has been used to effectively engage groups of students from different social and cultural backgrounds, such as recently arrived communities from the Horn of Africa and Kosovar refugees who sought a 'safe haven' in Australia (see Box 11.1).

The projects and policies developed by Victoria University help to demonstrate a coherent approach to widening participation, and complementarity between projects and policies. For example, the University has developed alternative entry and Recognition of Prior Learning policies that can they be combined and utilized in a range of specific situations, and the University has a policy oriented towards developing culturally sensitive curricula that can accommodate the needs of different learner groups. The University has also developed links with other bodies, such as employers, to provide learners with employment opportunities and so enhance the value of learning to them. Hence, the University can be described as having a strategic approach to widening participation, which is endorsed by the senior management and supported by policy and practices throughout the institution.

Complementarity between projects and policies is not only beneficial at the level of the institution, but in broader contexts too. For example, Jan Smith has undertaken research in one region in the UK intended to 'identify and evaluate the impact of widening participation strategies in the sub-region and to inform the development of a regional strategy' (Smith, 2000, p. 23). Similar approaches could be employed at the national level. The PERACH scheme in Israel attempts to link together two issues relating to widening participation (Carmeli, 2000a). This is a national tutoring and mentoring scheme, which employs less-well-off university students (thus helping them to meet the costs of higher education) to tutor and mentor school pupils from disadvantaged backgrounds to aspire to post-compulsory education.

Longer-term sustainability

There is a danger that projects that aim to widen participation and promote lifelong learning are short term, and that the benefits do not

Box 11.1: Using a strategic approach to promote learning: examples from Victoria University, Australia

Horn of Africa Communities

Extensive consultation with the region's recently arrived communities from the Horn of Africa resulted in the design and delivery of culturally-sensitive curricula in a range of TAFE and HE courses provided specifically for these communities. Negotiations, largely conducted by a cultural support worker whose role is to liaise between the communities and the teaching staff, resulted in some course components being taught in one of the mother tongues (Amharic). English-language support was integrated at all levels, and content areas were recontextualized to take account of African cultural mores, beliefs and practices. Components of the course were also taught, where possible, by community leaders.

The partnership between the Horn of Africa communities and the University resulted in a range of outcomes, including the establishment of a University-African Community Advisory Committee, a forum that discusses and negotiates the education, training and employment needs of the African communities. A subsequent partnership between the African communities, the University, the Electrical Trade Union and a Group Training Company resulted in the development of a pre-apprenticeship programme for African young people, who were guaranteed apprenticeships on successful completion of the programme. Within the HE division of the University, refugees have taken advantage of the Recognition of Prior Learning (RPL) scheme, and targeted bridging programmes to access courses such as the Community Development degree, which enables students to use their experience of working in refugee camps.

Kosovar Refugees

Kosovar refugees arrived in Victoria in 1999. A meeting was held between senior university staff and a delegation of fifteen Kosovar academics from one of the refugee communities to devise a strategic plan for those Kosovars whose education and training has been disrupted by the war. At the local level, these initiatives were supported by the local Albanian community, and at the international level links were made with the University of Tirana and the Polytechnic University of Tirana. Credit transfer arrangements were developed so that Kosovar refugees could be linked with academic study on their return to the Balkans.

Source: Adapted from Ronayne, 2000, pp. 149–51

last beyond the life of the project and so genuine change is not achieved. Kennedy notes the prevalence of short-termism: 'the FE landscape is littered with examples of short term initiatives which show little evidence of coherence ... and often stop abruptly once the funds expire' (1997, p. 37).

Sustainability is not easily defined, and is context related. In the case of widening participation, I think it is composed of a number of elements. These include financial autonomy, promoting ownership amongst the stakeholders, developing the capacity of the stakeholders and ensuring that institutional learning takes place.

Many contemporary widening participation initiatives are dependent on external funding to meet their running costs, and their continued existence. These projects are therefore not financially autonomous, or sustainable. A financially sustainable initiative may use start-up or 'pump-priming' finance to set up an income-generating initiative, which would then be capable of covering its ongoing running costs. In the field of widening participation, however, it is unlikely that projects could generate sufficient income, and it is questionable whether this should be their aim. This presents two ways in which an initiative can be judged to be financially sustainable. In the first instance a project might be seen to be sustainable if it is supported not by short-term project funding, but if there is a commitment from an institution's core budget. Such a funding arrangement would help to change the status of the scheme away from being a short-lived, marginal project that is only undertaken if project funding is provided, to part of an institution's 'core business'. A second criteria that could be applied to projects that are not financially sustainable in the strictest sense of the term would be to examine what will remain after the initial funding period. Some projects can have a finite life, but contribute to overcoming barriers to participation. This could, for example, include developing an information pack that will still be available to potential learners, providing training for institution staff (e.g. about alternative entry mechanisms or pedagogical requirements of a non-traditional learner group) or developing, piloting and evaluating good practice.

A second aspect of sustainability is 'ownership' or 'governance'; in other words, to what extent do the people affected by the scheme feel that they own it, or have a stake in it? The people affected by a scheme include intended beneficiaries, practitioners, institution staff and others whose support is often paramount to ensuring that an initiative is successful. Ownership tends to promote commitment, and people work harder to ensure that an initiative succeeds. A sense of ownership can stem from consultation and involvement in decision-making as equals. For example, if staff in institutions do not feel that they have a stake in widening-participation initiatives they are less likely to co-operate. Appropriate recruitment, teaching and learning and support strategies should be developed in consultation with staff and potential students, rather than imposed by managers (cf. Cotterill and Waterhouse, 1998). Similar responses can be identified in relation to learners. In research about work-based learning for support staff in schools (Thomas and Slack, 1999c), it was apparent that staff who had chosen to participate in the scheme, either to improve their skills or to develop their self-confidence, were complimentary about the learning experience and often planned to undertake further learning. But those learners who had been required to participate in the programme were critical and were far less likely to engage in further learning of any sort. Guba and Lincoln (1989) state that involving people as equals is likely to 'unleash energy, stimulate creativity, instil pride, build commit-ment, prompt the taking of responsibility, and evoke a sense of investment and ownership' (p. 227).

Participation and ownership can be enhanced by the development of the capacity of the different stakeholders. 'Capacity' refers to the ability of participants to carry on with positive elements of the scheme, even when the project organizers or initiators are no longer involved. A key way in which participants are able to continue and develop a project, and promote changes is if part of the initial programme includes training to enhance the relevant skills of group members. Training and development for staff, community leaders and learners could all be an integral part of a widening-participation scheme. For example, in a pilot project a university was working with a Muslim community, attempting to promote higher education by delivering selected courses with modified curricula in community locations. One way of developing the capacity of the community leaders was to educate them about higher education in general, the opportunities provided by this institution in particular, and to familiarize them with the campus. The community leaders felt this would enable them to talk authoritatively to other community members, and this would encourage some local learners to access HE, irrespective of the provision of community-based courses.

Not only do individuals need to learn for an initiative to be sustainable, but so, too, do organizations. Organizational learning refers to the way and extent to which the institutions involved 'learn the lessons' that occur during the project. The reality of a project differs from the theory, as implementation is unlikely to be exactly as planned. Outcomes in reality will not match planned outcomes and problems will be encountered. Korten (1984) defines three types of organizations indicated by their response to problems or 'error'. The first is the *self-deceiving organization*, which hides error, or blames another party. 'Those in authority, thus removed from operating reality, are reassured that as a result of their "brilliant" leadership everything is going just as intended' (p. 185). The *defeated organization* sees error as beyond their control, and 'thus while adverse factors may be discussed in rich detail, no action is taken' (*ibid.*). 'In the *learning organization* error is treated as an essential source of information. Since some margin of error is treated as inevitable, particularly in the early stages of the learning process, it is viewed neither as a sign of failure, nor of environmental perversity. Error is discussed candidly in such organizations, but in the context of lessons learned and corrective actions being attempted' (*ibid.*). Institutions that encourage organizational learning with respect to projects, initiatives and policies are responsive to the needs of learners, the concerns of staff and other stakeholders. Hence they help to develop better policies and practices, which are ultimately more sustainable (see Thomas, 2000).

Who is involved in developing a strategy?

There is a danger inherent in proposing a strategic approach to widening participation. That is, that it is 'disempowering' to the intended beneficiaries. A strategy suggests that a prescriptive 'blue-print' is devised and implemented, rather than allowing organic and pragmatic actions to develop and be refined in response to the diverse and changing needs of non-traditional learning communities. For this reason, it is essential to ask the question, '*Who* is involved in developing the strategy?'

Although institutional change is far easier when it is supported by the senior management team, this must be balanced by genuine participation by all stakeholders. Stakeholders are *all* the groups of people who are likely to be affected by or involved in a project or policy. The intended beneficiaries are the 'primary stakeholders' and, therefore, priority should be given to them. Stringer (1996, p. 25) notes that many people react negatively to authoritarian processes. This helps to explain why widening participation initiatives that are imposed from 'above' (with the best of intentions), rather than developed from a grass-roots approach, fail. There is a danger that decision-making processes are dominated by managerial and profes-sional classes, to the detriment of people from lower socio-economic groups or cultural minorities. Opening up the process allows the formation of services that are socially and culturally appropriate for diverse client groups and promotes sustainability.

A participatory approach reduces the reliance on traditional or 'expert' knowledge, which is often the knowledge of the elite, and legitimizes the experiences and knowledge of other stakeholders, such as community members and practitioners working in the field (De Koning and Martin, 1996). Participation can be at a range of stages, including identification of the barriers, the development and implementation of new practices, the collection of feedback, and the development of revised action. A continuum of participation can be conceptualized ranging from information sharing, to consultation to collaboration to empowerment. Knowledge gained from a diversity of sources helps to improve a policy or initiative and make it more effective in overcoming the barriers to participation in the particular community concerned.

Community involvement in, and ownership of, initiatives is clearly advantageous if participation in education is going to continue and expand beyond the life of a single project. Long-term participation in educational opportunities is only going to occur if there is a cultural shift in favour of education and learning in the communities concerned. A participatory approach offers a means to not only develop more effective strategies to promote wider participation in education in the short term, but reinforces the value of learning as part of the whole process, and is more likely to result in sustainable changes in attitudes in the communities involved. (These ideas are discussed more fully in Thomas, 2000.)

Conclusions

This chapter has argued for the development of strategic projects and policies that are integrated with other initiatives, and that complement each other but avoid duplication. It has also considered the importance of developing sustainable initiatives, and particularly the importance of involving a range of stakeholders in the planning, implementation, assessment and revision of policies and practices that aim to widen participation.

Three case studies are now examined in relation to the different types of barriers to participation that have been identified in the preceding chapters. These initiatives are all very different, and have not been selected as 'models of good practice'. Instead, they are used to examine the extent to which projects address the range of barriers facing potential learners, to demonstrate the need for initiators to be aware of the wider context in which they are operating and to consider issues of sustainability.

Key questions about strategy:

- Has due accord been given to the different types of barriers that potential learners face?
- What levels of synergy are there between different projects and policies at the institutional level and in the region?
- Sustainability: What will remain after the funding period? Is ownership promoted? Is the capacity of stakeholders developed? And are the institutions involved 'learning organisations'?
- Are the intended beneficiaries involved in the planning and implementation of widening-participation strategies?

CHAPTER 12

Case Study 1: Regional Distance Learning Scheme

Introduction

This chapter is the first of three case studies from Sweden, the UK and Ireland. Each initiative aims to extend participation in tertiary education to groups of learners that are under-represented, and living in communities that are isolated geographically and socially from post-compulsory education institutions and practices. Each case study provides a description of the initiative, using the following headings:

- Project organizers and other partners;
- What does it do?
- Who does it target?
- Why was it initiated?
- Success of the programme.

The descriptive data have been gained from a range of sources, including interviews, evaluation reports and other documentary evidence, but obviously these are not definitive accounts. Nor are these chapters presented as 'best practice'. Instead, the intention is to use the framework of analysis that has been advocated and developed in the preceding chapters to think about genuine initiatives that are being, or have been, implemented. Each case study is, therefore, considered in relation to the assumptions that underpin it. Each is then analysed in relation to its attempt to overcome the four categories of barriers: those created by the education system, the labour market, social and cultural norms, and by individuals. Finally, the extent to which a widening-participation strategy, rather than a short-term and marginal project, has been implemented is reviewed.

As was noted in Chapter 5, each case study concludes with a table and a 'score' of how well I think the scheme rates in relation to the key questions posed (see Appendix 1). This is NOT an objective score, and as such is of no value. Instead, the *process* of answering the key questions and completing the grid is of value – particularly if it is undertaken as a group activity and used to stimulate reflection and debate between stakeholders. The scores indicated in the grids relate to my perceptions and are based on my limited and necessarily biased information about the projects.

The first case study is a distance-learning programme using information computer technology (ICT) and video-conferencing to deliver higher education modules in one province in Sweden. This programme has accommodated the needs of part-time learners in the region who are unable to travel to the university. There is a range of higher education courses on offer, but they particularly qualify graduates for employment in the public sector. This project is primarily a response to demographic change and labour market shortages. It focuses on structural change (i.e. in the mode of delivery) at the institutional level.

Details of the scheme

Project organizers and other partners
The regional distance learning scheme is essentially an initiative developed by a Swedish university. The university is a state-controlled (rather than a private) institution, although it has a large degree of autonomy; its status was recently changed from that of university-college to a university. The university works in partnership with the municipalities in the province in which it is located. The University provides the distance learning teaching, while the municipalities have set up the learning centres, where the students meet together and access their learning. The learning centres are well-established in providing basic-level adult education, but currently only a minority are developing as university-centres, so they are keen to work in partnership with the university to offer courses at this level.

What does it do?
The scheme delivers distance-learning higher education courses via ICT to students who are unable to travel to the university. The students learn in regional learning centres outside the immediate university district. 'The use of information technology in distance education has made it possible to bring higher education to every part of the region' (university document). The closest study centre is about 60 km from the University, and the furthest is 150 km away.

The teaching and learning includes computer conferencing, using FirstClass software, e-mail contact with tutors, and lectures and seminars through video-conference links. In addition, the university library distributes requested books and literature to students via the learning centres. The majority of courses delivered are one-semester (20 weeks) first- or basic-level (known as the 'A level' in the Swedish system) courses in a range of subjects, which are requested by the learning centres in the municipalities.

For example, a fully accredited teacher-training programme is due to be delivered shortly. Usually this course would take a full-time student three-and-a-half years to complete, but the whole course will be delivered via ICT distance learning, enabling students to learn according to their own time-scale. The students will be based in seven learning centres in the municipalities, and there will be at least five students in each group. Thus a minimum of 35 students will be enrolled on the course. Teaching and learning will be composed of video-conference lectures, school teaching practice, group studying and computer conferencing. The teacher-training course is of particular significance, as there is a shortage of trained teachers in Sweden, especially in the less urbanized areas such as the municipalities, where the course is being delivered.

The university is not actively involved in the promotion of the distance learning programmes, as this is the responsibility of the municipal learning centres. The courses are advertised in the local newspapers, information is sent via video-conferencing to the learning centres, and university staff visit the centres to meet with prospective students.

It is anticipated that students who study by distance learning at the outreach centres will achieve a degree qualification equivalent to their peers who study at the main university site. There is no expectation that these students will achieve a lower qualification (such as a diploma rather than a degree, which is sometimes the case) or that the qualification will have less kudos, as it is a university award. The university provides support services at the main site, but it does not provide special support services for students studying at the distance-learning centres. The local-learning centres organize learning-support courses to assist people returning to education and undertaking higher education for the first time, and to help them gain the entry qualifications required for HE courses.

Who does it target?

The distance-learning scheme targets students who cannot leave their geographical area and travel to the university for a range of reasons, such as employment commitments, unemployment and other economic restrictions, cultural reasons (e.g. 'they are not prepared to go to university') and domestic responsibilities. Currently, students participating in courses include a significant number of mature people (aged 25–40), and more women than men.

The courses are open to anyone who lives in the areas where the learning centres are located, but in order to participate in the distance-learning programme students must have successfully completed their upper-secondary school education in an appropriate combination of subjects. Alternatively, they need to have attended one of the recognized courses (offered in the last three years at the learning centres) for people who do not have the upper-secondary school certificate to prepare them to the requisite entrance level for higher education.

Why was it initiated?
Three inter-related reasons can be identified for the establishment of this initiative. First, a national decline in the number of young people entering higher education, and, second, labour market shortages, particularly in the public sector. Both of these factors are attributable to demographic changes resulting in an ageing population. Thirdly, these issues prompted the government, and consequently institutions, to look at ways of widening participation in post-compulsory education.

Across Sweden there was decline in the number of applicants for higher education in 2000–1. This was primarily due to the fall in the number of young people as a result of the declining birth rate, and this was accompanied by a strong economy with low unemployment rates that further reduced the number of young applicants. This was reflected in the university by a decline in student recruitment of approximately 30 per cent. Hence, the university became increasingly aware that it needed to change in order to provide more attractive learning opportunities to a wider range of potential students.

As a result of demographic issues there will be a significant demand in the labour market for public sector staff – teachers, doctors, nurses, municipality employees, engineers in the coming 5–10 years, when the large group of people born in the 1940s reaches retirement age. Simultaneously, there has been a decline in the birth rate, so there are fewer young people to meet the demands of society and to fill these public sector jobs. Remote areas, such as the province in which the university is located, lack teachers and nurses more than the urban areas, as qualified professionals tend not to want to live in these regions.

This approach to widening participation was chosen primarily in response to a government directive that places responsibility on universities to become more *regional*. Swedish universities traditionally have had to undertake two core functions: teaching and research. A third task has been added to these obligations, which is 'networking with the region'. It is for this reason that the university decided to prioritize the development of distance-learning programmes, in partnership with learning centres in the province. Thus, when the university was reorganized recently, its core activities were divided into five boards, and to facilitate the development of distance learning a board was created with responsibility for developing and delivering these types of courses.

Success of the programme
The scheme has not been rigorously evaluated, but it is deemed to be successful in terms of the number of students enrolling on the courses offered: 1500 students enrolled in less than six months.

Examining the assumptions
This scheme assumes that there are potential students in the province to participate in higher education courses. In particular, it assumes the following:

- The primary barrier to participation is the *distance* people live from the university;
- The secondary barrier identified is *attitudes* towards higher education (i.e. not prioritizing it over employment or family commitments and being prepared to study full-time, which would involve moving away or commuting and taking a student loan);
- People have the necessary entry qualifications for HE;
- People will not be put off by technology and distance learning;
- Students want and are able to study part-time;
- Students want or need higher education qualifications;
- The university can deliver distance learning programmes using ICT and video-conferencing;
- The municipal learning centres will work in partnership with the university and promote the courses.

These assumptions have been made primarily by the university, in response to the decline in student applications and the government edict to take on a regional focus. Potential learners and their families have not been consulted about any of these presumptions. Although there is evidence to suggest that some conjectures will hold true, this is not so for all the assumptions. For example, the scheme assumes that people will have the necessary entry qualifications. This is supported to some extent by the fact that people in the province have participated in courses leading to higher education entry qualifications, and so want to continue their studies.

But the university also assumed that students want higher education qualifications. The evidence so far suggests that although people are participating in the HE courses, they are less concerned about accreditation. A significant number of students study the course, but opt not to be assessed. The reasons for non-participation in the assessment seem to relate to the academic confidence of the students and/or their instrumental requirements. Non-traditional students are unused to academic assessment, and often lack confidence in their own ability to perform well, and so study for interest and other reasons, rather than certification. As a corollary, or in addition, some students do not need to participate in the course assessment; for example, students in some employment situations do not require certification, but the course does provide them with knowledge and skills to assist them in their work.

Non-participation in the assessment has negative financial implications for the university. Fifty per cent of funding per student is paid for delivering the course, and the second payment is made if the student successfully undertakes the assessment. This, therefore, is calling into question the financial viability of the scheme, and could be seen as a 'killer assumption'. The senior administrator said:

> I think we are doing a good job in developing distance courses, but the more students the worse business for us! So that's why the board of the university has decided that we will stop at 400 full-time students per year for the moment, and we need to develop the assessment of the students and we need to develop the most popular courses.

Overcoming barriers created by the education system

This scheme makes significant changes to the way higher education courses are traditionally delivered in Sweden in general, and in this university in particular. It does not, however, directly address previous educational disadvantage; for example, adults who left school without their upper-secondary school certificate. This will affect students who left school at 16 (currently about 10 per cent of the year group) and those people who failed to attain the certificate. Potential mature students require the upper-secondary school certificate or an equivalent qualification, as this is the only entry route into higher education in Sweden. Thus, educational achievements are taken as an indicator of potential in further learning. However, once students have entered the higher education system they are not differentiated from contemporaries who are learning through alternative delivery modes (i.e. traditional HE at the main university site).

The main strength of this programme is that it departs from the traditional structure of higher education in terms of delivery patterns and pedagogy (although not in terms of admission procedure or course contents), and so goes some way to meeting the needs of non-traditional students. The courses are delivered away from the university, in learning centres that are close to where students live. Students are able to study part-time, many are studying only 0.25 of a full-time course; this is comparatively unusual in Sweden, where 90 per cent of students study full-time. This allows students flexibility for employment and family commitments, and allows them to study at their own pace. The courses also utilize open learning, enabling students to study mostly at times convenient to them, rather than those determined by teaching staff or the university organization. This has involved the development and utilization of new pedagogical approaches, which are discussed below.

There are only limited support services available for students on the distance-learning programme, and, in particular, fewer services are provided for these students, compared with 'traditional' students studying at the university's main site. The local learning centres do offer learning-support courses to assist people returning to education and undertaking higher education for the first time, and to help them gain the entry qualifications required for HE courses.

This scheme helps to reduce the indirect costs of higher education to students. It has reduced the opportunity cost of higher education as students are able to continuing working while they are studying. In addition, some of the indirect costs, such as travel and childcare, are reduced. Students do not have to travel long distances to access university courses, and for some students this may mean that they do not need to move away from their home to the provincial capital (or another university town) and incur higher living costs. Reduced travel time and flexible learning patterns lessen the need for childcare, and thus, for some students at least, lowers the cost. There are difficulties for students studying scientific subjects, where there is an expectation that students will travel to the university to access specialist equipment and no practical or financial assistance is provided.

The need for organizational learning and change is paramount in this case study, as it is reliant on institutional change. The university has re-structured to include a 'distance learning board' that is responsible for the provision of distance and open learning. But a number of internal difficulties have been encountered, which the university is seeking to overcome, and so it can be seen to be learning from its experiences and seeking change.

One difficulty of the programme is the timescale. Courses are currently being planned over one year in advance of when the courses will be offered. The planning finishes in December for courses to commence the following September. It is therefore difficult to respond flexibly to the requirements of students with regard to course type; for example, level and, particularly, subject. The distance- and open-learning board feels that they need the ability to make decisions in a shorter time-frame, to 'change directions, open up and be more flexible' in response to students' needs. This, however, is not currently possible within the university's organizational structure.

Distance learning involves change on the part of teaching staff. For example, lecturers must be prepared to deliver lectures by video link and reply to e-mails on a daily basis, as the computer is the primary method of teaching. The senior administrator commented: 'Some university staff think of this as a new and very interesting form of teaching, and some don't ... We don't want them.' The distance-learning board, however, is not able to select the teaching staff allocated to the distance-learning programmes. Staff need particular skills, such as teaching via a video link and the ability to facilitate computer conferencing, and they need positive attitudes to these changes and towards non-traditional students. Lectures delivered by video-conference need to be planned thoroughly and well structured, and are less open to distraction.

The distance-learning board has developed pedagogic courses for lecturers involved in distance learning and training to develop their technical knowledge. Although not all courses involve video-conferencing, training staff to be effective video-conferencing lecturers is crucial. The current training is described as 'sufficient', but the programme organizers believe that ideally more staff development is required. The need for new teaching methods is paramount in scientific subjects to overcome the limitation of not having access to laboratories and other technical resources. Hence the university must invest in developing appropriate forms of pedagogy and related staff training.

The university has responded to the shortage of students and the associated need to broaden participation to new groups of potential learners by making radical changes to its mode of delivery. This has required significant change throughout the institution, including restructuring and staff development training. The university, however, does not seek to compensate for previous educational disadvantage, and it provides less support to students on the distance-learning programme than is available to students based at the main campus.

Labour market issues

As this programme has been developed at least partially in response to labour market requirements, the economic returns to education may be realistic, although further investigation into discrimination in the labour market would be required before this can be verified. Although the programme organizers admit there are issues regarding their ability to respond to students' demands regarding course type, there is evidence to suggest that the opportunities provided enable people to study to enhance their current employment and to access new employment, especially in the public sector. This is eased by the fact that unemployment is low in Sweden.

This scheme facilitates the continuation of labour market participation by students while they are studying as all the courses are part-time, and much of the learning (except lectures delivered by video-conference) can be structured flexibly to meet different work patterns. This is particularly important if participation in higher education is to be increased (and, potentially, widened). Participation in higher education in Sweden is amongst the lowest in Europe, at about 25 per cent, as the majority of the population enters employment at the age of 19, and most employers require upper-secondary qualifications, as opposed to a higher-level course. This provides young people with economic independence, which cannot be equalled by a combination of student grants and loans and the prospect of improved employment prospects in the future.

Overcoming social and cultural barriers to participation

The programme organizers say that many of the people living in the more rural areas of the province lack the tradition of entering higher education, and often believe that higher education is too difficult for them. In addition, borrowing money is, culturally, alien to them. The senior programme administrator commented:

The problem is their attitudes, their culture. In a working-class family, for example, there are very strong hesitations about taking loans, and also in the old farming society – 'You should not borrow money, it's dangerous.' You still hear this argument – 'I don't want to borrow money.'

Although there appear to be social and cultural barriers to participation, overcoming these is not the focus of the distance-learning programme. The university does not undertake any outreach work, or other attempts to familiarize people with higher education. The aim of the distance-learning programme is not to familiarize people with education to facilitate progression, but rather to offer them HE courses. The course curricula are not revised to be socially or culturally relevant to the new constituencies of learners, although programme choices are influenced by what students want to learn, and perceived labour market needs. These decisions are reached in consultation with the local learning centres, rather than with potential students or employers directly. One, perhaps unintended, consequence of this model of learning is that similar groups of students are able to work together and gain confidence.

Individualizing the problem

The distance-learning programme does not have a clearly defined and targeted priority group, beyond people who live in the province where it is located. It is assumed that it will be attractive to people who are unable to travel or relocate to the main university site. Research and targeting could potentially enable the scheme to include more students from under-represented groups than it currently does. It is acknowledged by the university that, with sufficient funds, more could be done to reach non-traditional student groups.

The distance-learning programme does not directly try to change attitudes towards learning in general and higher education in particular. However, efforts are made in the municipalities to affect people's aspirations and perceptions; research in Sweden is showing that men are more entrenched in traditional attitudes, while women are more flexible (hence the high proportion of women compared to men participating in the distance-learning programme).

The university's distance-learning programme does not have the money to target specific groups and provide them with information about distance-learning higher-education courses, but it is hoped that the learning centres do reach these people. For example, the learning centres liaise with the employment service, which provides information to unemployed people and unemployment benefits can be converted to a grant for studying. The unemployment service, however, will not compel people to participate in education and training. Information about the services available is limited, and, in general, people will need to be looking for information if they are to find it.

From project to strategy

The distance-learning programme overcomes the barrier of geographical distance from the university. To some extent it alleviates the labour market and associated financial barriers: students are able to continue working full- or part-time, young people do not have to relocate to the university town (and incur additional costs), and travel and other indirect costs are removed or substantially reduced. It provides a second opportunity for students to participate in higher education, but this is not facilitated through alternative entry routes. Thus, past educational performance is still used as an indicator of potential for future learning. Although some university staff recognize the social and cultural barriers to participation that exist, the programme does not seek to overcome or compensate for these types of barriers. Nor does it seek to overcome barriers at the individual level; in particular, relatively little information is provided about the higher-education courses on offer, as dissemination is left to the municipal learning centres, and there is no targeting of particular under-represented groups. This initiative tackles a range of issues, and can be seen to be moderately comprehensive at the level of the project.

It can be surmised that there is synergy between policies at both the institutional and regional level. The distance-learning programme was developed in response to the requirement made by the Ministry of Education that universities should expand HE provision in their regions. The university works in partnership with the learning centres in the municipalities in the province. When the university was reorganized, a distance-learning board was created with responsibility for this type of provision. There is, however, little evidence of links with other widening-participation initiatives, which would help to create a more coherent package for learners. There is clearly scope for a more strategic approach both within the institution, and in partnership with other agencies in the region.

The financial sustainability of the programme is questionable. The university funds the distance-learning scheme, and funding for students is drawn down from the national funding body. But more funding is required to develop and promote this programme.

Furthermore, there is currently a difficulty regarding the receipt of payment from the funding council. Fifty per cent of funding per student is paid for delivering the course, and the second payment is made if the student successfully undertakes the assessment. As a significant number of students opt not to be assessed, the university forfeits 50 per cent of fees from the funding council. This creates negative financial implications for the university, which call into question the viability of the scheme. The university distance-learning board has subsequently decided not to recruit more than 400 full-time-equivalent students per year.

The distance-learning programmes are co-owned by the university and the municipal learning centres, but there is no role for the learners in the governance of the scheme. Potential students or their representatives are not involved in the planning or the implementation of the programme, and are not consulted about course choices. Within the university, training helps to ensure that staff capacity to deliver distance-learning courses is developed and maintained, and the university is having to tailor its staff-development programme in response to the difficulties that have been identified so far. Thus, in many senses, the university can be described as a learning organization. The extent to which these changes have been accepted within the university is, however, questionable.

To summarize, although the institution and its staff are learning from the experiences of implementing distance-learning programmes, this project has poor financial sustainability and no input from the intended beneficiaries. Its prognosis for longer-term sustainability, therefore, is not very favourable, which could be to the detriment to members of the communities currently benefiting from the scheme.

Conclusions

The scheme focuses on new modes of delivery, and to this end is supported within the university through the development of a distance-learning board and staff-development training. This approach overcomes the barrier of distance of learners from the university, and labour market barriers, as people can study part-time and flexibly, and the courses on offer enable people to secure public sector employment. There is, however, little curricula change to accommodate diversity, there is little targeting of specific social and cultural groups or individuals, and only limited information is available. Although the scheme has policy links at the regional and institutional level, there is little evidence of integrated practices. There is a danger that in the long term the scheme will not be sustainable due to the financial problems that are being experienced. A summary of my assessment of the strengths and weakness of the distance-learning programme are presented in the table below. It must be remembered that the grid below is not an objective assessment of the case study, but should be used as an aid to thinking.

A summary of the strengths and weaknesses of the Regional Distance Learning Scheme

Issue	Rating	Comments
EDUCATION SYSTEM		FOCUSES ON CHANGING MODE OF DELIVERY
How are stereotypes about 'good learners' and 'bad learners' challenged at the institutional and individual level?	☑☑☑	Students are not singled out as 'different . No positive action taken to boost self-image etc.
In what ways does your work help to reduce the cost of education to individuals?	☑☑☑	Reduces indirect and opportunity costs of education.
Have you developed a range of entry routes that meet the needs of all the potential students you are targeting?	☑	No flexibility with regard to entry qualifications. Pre-entry qualification course available at the same learning site.
Is learning appropriate and flexible with regard to the curriculum?	☑☑	The curriculum has not been altered to meet the needs of the students, but different teaching methods are used to accommodate the mode of delivery.
Is learning appropriate and flexible with regard to the location?	☑☑☑☑	Teaching is delivered in learning centres close to where people live.
Is learning appropriate and flexible with regard to the timing?	☑☑☑☑	Timing is flexible, but there are some restrictions, such as when lectures are delivered by video-conferencing.

Issue	Rating	Comments
Is learning appropriate and flexible with regard to the pace?	☑☑☑	Pace is flexible in that students can choose how many modules they undertake at the same time.
Are personal and academic support services provided at all sites to meet the needs of your students?	☑	No support is provided by the university. Academic support only provided by the learning centres.
How is organizational learning and change with respect to diversity encouraged?	☑☑☑☑	Scheme requires organizational change and learning. University has restructured to create a distance-learning board. Staff development is provided, although could be expanded.
LABOUR MARKET		RESPONDED TO LABOUR MARKET NEEDS AND ENABLES STUDENTS TO CONTINUE IN EMPLOYMENT
Are the expected economic and non-economic returns realistic and explicit?	☑☑☑	Returns appear realistic. Low unemployment rates.
Is the initiative sufficiently flexible to enable (full- or part-time) participation in the labour market? Is this facilitated or discouraged?	☑☑☑☑	Students are able to continue participating in full- or part-time employment.
Do the courses available provide labour market opportunities to those who want them (e.g. what are the requirements of the local economy)?	☑☑☑☑	Good employment opportunities on completion.
In what ways is labour market discrimination tackled?	☒	No evidence of efforts made to tackle discrimination.

Issue	Rating	Comments
SOCIAL AND CULTURAL		THE SCHEME IS NOT TRYING TO ADDRESS ISSUES AT THIS LEVEL
To what extent does learning familiarize people with the 'world' of post-compulsory education (e.g. to facilitate progression)?	☑☑☑	Students study at HE level, but no attempts to familiarize them with main institution site.
Does the initiative involve 'others' who influence the decision-making of potential learners?	☒	No.
Is the curriculum socially and culturally relevant (is it free from cultural bias)? Is it of 'value' to the learners?	☑☑	Local learning centres are consulted about preferences that students have expressed. No evidence of how these are identified.
Does the initiative allow similar groups to work together to gain confidence?	☑☑☑	Groups of students do work together in the learning centres.
INDIVIDUAL		THE SCHEME DOES NOT OPERATE AT THE LEVEL OF THE INDIVIDUAL
How does the initiative target the intended beneficiaries, and is it effective? Who benefits most from the programme?	☑	The scheme does not target groups beyond those who live in the areas of the learning centres.
Does the scheme avoid blaming individuals, and seeking to change them without changing the institution?	☒	The scheme does not seek to change views – or blame people.
Is information about programme and learning opportunities available to non-traditional learners?	☑	Very little information about the scheme is provided.

Issue	Rating	Comments
STRATEGY		QUITE STRATEGIC AT THE LEVEL OF INSTITUTION, BUT LACK OF BENEFICIARY INVOLVEMENT.
Has due accord been given to the different types of barriers that potential learners face?	☑☑	Takes account of some structural and labour market barriers, but does not address other barriers.
What levels of synergy are there between different projects and policies at the institutional level and in the region?	☑☑☑	Institutional and regional policy synergy; limited evidence of links with other projects.
Sustainability: What will remain after the funding period? Is ownership promoted? Is the capacity of stakeholders developed? And are the institutions involved 'learning organizations'?	☑☑☑	Scheme is funded by the university, but poor financial sustainability due to limitations of funding arrangements, related to student assessment. Very limited stakeholder ownership. Learning centres are consulted about course choices, but does this represent learners' views? Some staff do not want to participate. Capacity of staff is developed through training. Organizational learning is taking place, e.g. recognition of the need for staff training, assessment approach and pedagogical methods for scientific subjects.
Are the intended beneficiaries involved in the planning and implementation of widening participation strategies?	☒	Beneficiaries are not involved in planning and implementation.

Guide to the ratings

☑☑☑☑	–	excellent	☑☑	–	weak
☑☑☑☑	–	good	☑	–	very poor
☑☑☑	–	average	☒	–	not addressed

CHAPTER 13

Case Study 2: Community Outreach Partnership

Introduction

This case study focuses on an initiative providing outreach education in selected geographical communities in one county of the UK. The scheme recruited education community link-workers, based in targeted communities, in order to raise awareness of educational opportunities, assess needs and to make arrangements for community-based course provision. The programme sought to organize, primarily, short, and invariably leisure-orientated, courses for small groups of adults. The aim was to introduce, maintain and develop courses at community locations away from the main campus, thus surmounting certain social and cultural barriers.

Details of the scheme

Project organizers and other partners

The scheme was organized by a concordat of local partners, including eight further education colleges, two local education authorities, two universities, the Careers Service, the Training and Enterprise Council, the Employment Service and the Open College Network. Representatives of these organizations formed a steering group, who contributed to the co-ordination of the programme. Networks were created with other partners, such as voluntary groups and public sector service providers, during the life of the scheme. Funding was provided by the Further Education Funding Council (FEFC), in response to the Kennedy Report (1997) and the idea of 'strategic partnerships' advanced therein.

What does it do?

Each of the eight further education colleges received funding to employ a part-time education community link-worker. Link-workers 'personalized' the potentially faceless bureaucratic side of college recruitment, and helped to overcome the recalcitrance of the target communities towards formal learning. One link-worker commented that

> The community thinks that the college is ... not someone they can talk to on an equal level ... [And it is seen as] too high and mighty ... A lot of people [in the community] think of college as the same as school and many ... have bad memories of school.

Each link-worker was based in a geographical community, identified by post-code analysis (see Tonks, 1999 and Batey *et al.*, 1998) as having low rates of participation in further education. Through contacts with individuals and groups in these areas the link-workers' task was to gain information of educational requirements and relay this to the college, thus helping prospective students to overcome cultural and structural barriers. In practice, link-workers undertook a wide range of tasks, including establishing and developing links in the community, assessing learners' needs, and course provision. Perhaps their most central task was to establish contacts with the community, which was achieved through networking with other agencies and by one-to-one contact with potential learners. In fact, as the project progressed, workers tended to favour one of these two approaches.

Networking generally involved making links with other agencies and organizations operating in the area, either to gain access to groups of potential students directly, or, less directly, to secure referrals. Link-workers liaised with a range of bodies, including voluntary organizations (such as ethnic minority associations, educational organizations and playgroups); religious groups; public sector agencies (schools, health, social services and employment offices), and development and regeneration initiatives. Some link-workers obtained a base in the targeted locale that was shared with colleagues from other agencies, allowing members of the community to contact them (rather than workers having to make speculative, ad hoc, visits to schools, community groups and other meeting places).

Other link-workers, however, preferred to establish one-to-one contact with potential entrants. This, perhaps, was the original intention of the partnership, given that the initial funding bid proposed to employ link-workers *from* the target communities. In fact, only a quarter (i.e. two) of the link-workers were drawn from the designated areas (for whatever reasons). In both cases, these link-workers prioritized face-to-face contact, and seemed to have less difficulty breaking down some of the barriers that other link-workers experienced. For example, one link-worker commented how she had to be prepared to deal with inquiries at all times, and remarked: 'people are stopping me in the streets to ask about the courses. I carry information about with me everywhere, even collecting my children or going to the shops'.

With regard to assessing learners' needs, some link-workers made use of questionnaires, either with members of the community or employers, but rates of return were generally low. Consequently, there was a tendency to rely on more informal methods, such as meetings with individuals and agency referrals. Also, link-workers were often involved in operational matters relating to course provision; for example, identifying suitable locations, enrolling students, collecting course fees and overcoming organizational difficulties.

A further feature of the project was an Open College Network (OCN) Level 2 qualification undertaken by each link-worker while in post. This was designed to provide training to assist with their work. The course was assessed via a portfolio handbook of their work relating to community development and learning in the post-compulsory sector, to demonstrate predetermined competencies.

Who does it target?

The scheme targeted eight discrete geographical communities, with clear boundaries, but without designating particular socio-cultural groups within these locations. In the early stages of the scheme, link-workers named the following as possible target groups: lone parents, unemployed people, people on low incomes, working-class people, people without qualifications, people who lack basic skills, people who lack motivation, ethnic and religious groups, people aged 18–25 years and middle-class women. This, it must be said, is a somewhat disparate list of potential entrants, which is not based on any formal research or analysis by the partnered institutions. It is possible that this lack of clarity regarding targeting focus compromised the effectiveness of the initiative, as is discussed below.

Why was it initiated?

This project was one of 26 second-wave Widening Participation Strategic Partnerships emanating from the Kennedy Committee's report into widening participation in further education, *Learning Works* (Kennedy, 1997), and was funded by the FEFC (see Chapter 7 of this book). Kennedy *et al.* advocated partnerships, partly because a collaborative approach was considered to be more productive in realizing the objective of widening participation in further education than a disparate and unco-ordinated range of initiatives or projects. It avoids duplication, and targets activities more carefully. Furthermore, partnerships were seen as an antidote to the increase in competition in the further education sector that had arisen in the 1980s (see Ainley, 1999).

Success of the programme

There was debate within the partnership regarding how success should be assessed. The partnership included a universities-based research team, and utilized a process model of evaluation (see Thomas, 2000). Using this approach, data were collected throughout the first year of the scheme, and ideas and good practice were shared with partnership members. In addition, the college's MIS (management information systems) collected statistical data relating to course enrolments, and some link-workers recorded how many individuals and agencies they had contact with. The success of the programme is therefore assessed using a number of criteria that arose from the research process.

Perhaps the most obvious criteria for success was to measure the number of course enrolments from the targeted communities during the lifetime of the project, and to compare these with previous figures. Indeed, link-workers reported considerable success with regard to setting up new community-based courses and enrolling students in the first nine months, and this was supported by analysis of the statistical data collected by MIS. Increases ranged from a gain of ten students in one ward to 109 students in another; and percentage increases ranged from 2% to 28% (these figures are obviously partly determined by the baseline participation levels). It is, however, impossible to reach useful conclusions from these data, as the size of each area, the number of other initiatives in each area, the initial participation levels and other factors all varied between the targeted communities.

Link-workers and their line managers also believed that it was important to look at 'less immediately tangible' results, including the extent to which 'the culture of the community changes towards education'. One link-worker commented that a positive reception in community groups might indicate changing attitudes towards education and/or the college:

> I think sometimes you're surprised how you are welcomed in a group or something. You might think, 'oh, I'm not going to get spoken to', you think, 'this is going to be a grind, I'm going to

represent authority', and the rest of it, but actually people are, 'oh, right, you're from college', college in the community sort of thing, the penny's sort of dropping, people are beginning to realise that education is for them, and it's not elitist and it's not inaccessible. I think it is, certainly, within the area I'm working in, it's happening slowly, but I think a project like this has to be delivered ... each institution should be committed to offering.

The initiative did not, however, assess the extent to which attitudes had been changed. This process was hampered by a lack of appropriate baseline data existing prior to the project commencing.

In addition to increasing enrolments and engendering positive attitudes to learning, some outcomes were 'unexpected'. An interesting example of 'success' was recounted by one link-worker: 'A success to me is when one of the courses, they're going into a small business, but that's taking them away from the college. It's built their confidence up, it really has, they've found something they're good at'. This particular group of students attended a leisure course – Painting on Glass – and, subsequently, started up a small business.

Some senior college managers felt that the true value, and thus success, of the scheme was not the number of students recruited – primarily because this type of work was already taking place – and the sum of money involved was so small. Instead, increased co-operation between colleges was valued, both at the management level and at that of practitioners. One principal commented:

It brings back an element of cohesion into post-16 education – a lot of cohesion was wrecked 6 or 7 years ago when we went through the process of incorporation ... prior to that we all had this common link whereby we all had the same employer ... This partnership is a small building block moving us back the other way ... it's been good in that sense.

Another principal felt that the benefits of a strategic partnership had been experienced primarily at lower levels:

I think it's created a good network for people at an operational level ... People are doing similar things in colleges and I think that has been very valuable ... I think the real benefit has been for people who are networking and working with actual communities ... and that, after all, is where a lot of the work is done. It's that area where I'd see a lot of benefit. But that's for them to judge, rather than me surmise.

Overall, link-workers, line managers and principals believed that the project was successful in terms of widening participation in learning, but that the time-scale was too short, as it takes time to change attitudes. This is borne out by the statistical and qualitative evidence generated by the scheme.

Examining assumptions

In Chapter 5 the discussion turned to raising awareness of the assumptions underpinning projects and policies aiming to widen participation. Having described the key features of the Community Outreach Partnership, this section examines the assumptions that underpinned the scheme, and, in particular, notes those that did not hold true.

In general, this scheme assumes that there are potential learners in the targeted communities who were willing to participate in further education. More specifically, assumptions made included:

- People do not participate in education as colleges are located away from the communities, and formal learning is therefore unfamiliar to them;
- Link-workers could and would be recruited from the community;
- Communities are more or less homogeneous;
- One link-worker would be able to communicate with assess a targeted locale's 'needs';
- Link-workers would enable potential students to overcome barriers related to the unfamiliarity of formal education;
- People will participate in courses if they are based in their communities;
- The college can run courses based in the community;
- Competition was not entrenched in the system, so colleges and other agencies would co-operate together.

Most of these assumptions may have arisen from past institutional experience, but not pre-project research. Partly as a consequence of this, the veracity of some assumptions was tested as the project progressed.

The Partnership's intention was to recruit link-workers from each of the target communities, but despite the fact that shared criteria were drawn up to assist the selection process, they were not adhered to closely by colleges. The funding received was small, and so was either combined with other income to create a more substantial, full-time post, or was used to supplement or sustain existing posts. When interviewed, only two line managers spoke of the need to attract and recruit candidates from the target community, and only two of the eight link-workers were from the target communities.

It was implicitly assumed that the geographical communities were homogeneous, and, consequently, particular social or cultural groups were not identified within the locales. It also presumed that community members would agree about the types of courses that they wanted, including curricular content, level, accreditation, venue etc. In the event, consensus was seldom evident, and difficulties were faced in terms of forming financially viable cohorts of students for each course (as colleges had minimum group sizes). Some link-workers resorted to negotiation, amalgamating students with different requirements to create a sufficiently large cohort, and then offering a 'package of courses'. Leney et al. (1998) have noted these practices within FE provision.

In some colleges problems were encountered when delivering courses in the community, as this required suitable venues and staff to work flexible hours (who could also travel from the main campus). Furthermore, colleges needed to respond flexibly and quickly to the needs of these students. In some colleges, staff attitudes and bureaucratic frameworks seemed to militate against a fast, appropriate (and inventive) response. For example, students wanted courses to start at times suitable to them, rather than to coincide with college terms, for a duration that matched their other commitments (e.g. school holidays) and to be delivered in locations selected by the participants (sometimes they even sought to specify the tutor). Some colleges were able to react positively, while others found it more challenging to accommodate some of the more unorthodox requirements (e.g. to override the traditional validation timescale for new courses or to find suitable tutors to teach 'unsociable' hours in a community location).

A further misplaced assumption was that significantly higher levels of co-operation between providers and other agencies would emerge. Or, more accurately, those degrees of competition and suspicion were not as heavily entrenched. Hence, a primary rationale underlying the notion of strategic partnerships, as conceived by Kennedy et al. was to overcome the 'excesses of competition' (Kennedy, 1997). Link-workers displayed awareness of the potential benefits of 'networking' with agencies, thus contributing to a 'holistic partnership approach'. This was in keeping with the over-arching objective of the project and strategic partnerships in general. Nevertheless, evidence of competition between agencies can be found in the context of this partnership, which, ultimately, limited the efficacy of the Partnership.

In most of the targeted locations there were other initiatives already in operation. One line-manager therefore advised the link-worker to 'proceed with caution', in order to avoid 'stepping on toes or even confrontation'. Another line manager told her link-worker to learn to 'weave your way around', whilst a further line manager reported that other agencies could be quite 'territorial and protective'. She remarked that 'the first barrier that she has had to face, and shouldn't have, is another organization'.

Competition was also apparent in the low number of referrals arising from other agencies. On this issue, one link-worker commented: 'It's not a question of people being not helpful, it's just that they've got their own agenda, they've got their own job to do'.

There was also some evidence of competition, or at least a dearth of co-operation, between colleges. So, for example, the link-workers did not regard themselves as members of an inter-college initiative. Sometimes this became quite explicit, as in the following: 'I think I'm a bit wary of getting together (e.g. with other link-workers) 'cos those two training days I felt like it was a competition to see who could do best.' Another link-worker professed to feel closer to local agencies, than to colleagues in partner colleges.

There is a danger that institutions join together to bid for funding on the basis of a notional partnership only, and, subsequently, co-operative alliances do not develop. In this initiative it is apparent that partnerships and alliances could operate at a number of levels within the college sector, and with partners outside of this category, but that competition was prevalent.

This case study illustrates a number of assumptions that underpinned the Community Outreach Partnership. These were not investigated from the perspectives of different stakeholders, particularly the targeted communities and other agencies, and this confounded the success of the scheme.

Overcoming barriers created by the education system

Chapters 6 and 7 discussed the barriers and opportunities created by the compulsory and post-compulsory education systems respectively. In summary, compulsory education has the potential to provide learners both with qualifications (that act as a 'passport' to post-compulsory education) and with positive or negative images of individuals as learners that influence people's perceptions about future formal learning. Post-compulsory education institutions can develop policies that facilitate or hinder participation by non-traditional student groups. Barriers can also be erected in relation to the cost of education and there are constraints associated with entry qualification requirements. Particularly appropriate to this case study is the need for appropriate and flexible learning opportunities and the provision of support services. The extent to which institutions engage with and accommodate diversity reflects the institutional culture, and can be anywhere on a continuum from highly inclusive to elitist. This section now examines the extent to which the Community Outreach Partnership succeeded in overcoming these types of barriers.

This scheme makes no requirements regarding previous educational attainment, but this is primarily because courses are not accredited, or are only offered at a low level so that no previous educational experience/achievement is required. As was noted above though, this does assume that the targeted communities are rather homogenous, and may perpetuate stereotypes about 'good' and 'bad' learners, whereby non-traditional students are associated with the latter.

The courses provided are flexible with regard to location, although there were some tensions – for example, not all students in one community wanted to learn at the same venue. Most colleges have also sought to tailor the timing and pace of courses, but, as was discussed above, some colleges struggled to accommodate these needs, as structures were too rigid. Most colleges were poor at providing personal and academic support services to meet the needs of community-based students. Link-workers, however, have found themselves fulfilling the role of advice and guidance counsellors with regard to educational and career choices. There appears to have been relatively little organizational learning and change, although this varied significantly between institutions. The action research evaluation model (Thomas, 2000), feeding findings back to partnership members, facilitated learning, but some colleges did not want to learn.

Labour market issues

The second category of barrier considered in this book is that which is created by the labour market. This project, however, was largely divorced from labour market issues; some link-workers made contact with local employers, but courses were not set-up in response to their demands and there were no attempts to address labour market discrimination. Some courses, however, did fulfil the instrumental needs of students. For example, IT courses were popular as students perceived them to have value with regard to employment opportunities, and, more specifically, food hygiene courses provided a qualification for working in the food and catering industries, but the majority of courses were not vocational. The flexibility with regard to the timing and location of the courses will have enabled some students to continue working while attending a course.

In summary, although the scheme did not address labour market issues, these are less likely to be barriers to participation. Some vocational courses were set up in response to student demand, the indirect costs of participation were reduced (the majority of students did not pay direct costs as they were in receipt of benefit); and courses were timetabled flexibly.

Overcoming social and cultural barriers to participation

The third category of barrier that is examined is 'social and cultural' issues. In Chapter 9 these are discussed in relation to the work of Pierre Bourdieu. First, further and higher education may be unfamiliar to students, and second, formal learning of this nature may be of little value to non-traditional student groups, unless there is a relevant curriculum.

In many ways, this scheme focused on overcoming the social and cultural barriers to participation. This is illustrated by the intention to recruit link-workers from the targeted communities, because: 'people drawn from the community are most successful in working with that community and find successful solutions in increasing participation' (proposal for funding, 1998). Thus, the scheme attempted to involve a range of people from the community who might help to influence the decisions that people make. Indeed, where link-workers were drawn from the communities in which they were working, communication and cultural barriers were reduced. They did not have to spend time familiarizing themselves with relevant people and places. One remarked: 'I don't need to get over that barrier.' By contrast, a link-worker who lived some distance from the community did not feel 'any affiliation with these groups'. After six or seven months, two link-workers who did not live in the target community commented:

> It's only really in the last, sort of, month-and-a-half, two months, that I know what I should be doing ... The initial sort of four months was just setting up your contacts, just getting on the ground and getting noticed by whatever organizations and individuals you're trying to contact ... It's been a lot of trust building, and that takes time; you can't just do it overnight. And I think that may be partly because I don't live in a [targeted geographical community]. It takes time to actually get to know your community, to actually get to know where the groups meet .[interrupted], to know what its needs are, to be able to really get

to grips with the sort of value systems, I know that sounds academic, but the culture within your area – what people believe in.

A link-worker from the community felt that s/he had an advantage, as s/he knew most people in the community:

> They knew me as 'me' in the community, they didn't know my job. It's a pretty small community, and even if I didn't know them by name, I knew them by sight.
>
> That made it easier actually, being known. I used to just go to mother and toddlers. After a couple of hours, mention what I'm about and everything. Let them get to know me first. Because people round here are a bit anti-college, they see them all as stuck up.

The project did not familiarize students with educational opportunities outside of their community – it did not, for example, involve students visiting the main college sites. But working in groups in the community did seem to build their confidence and allow them to progress within the community. One link-worker explained that, initially, people had lacked the confidence to enrol on an accredited course, but the experience of attending a course had emboldened them to consider progressing to another level:

> We found a lot of people didn't have the confidence to actually go straight into an accredited course. But the courses have all finished now, and they've all showed an interest in going on to the next stage. They've had a taste of it now, they know pretty much what it involves, they know it's not going to be that difficult really.

There is a danger that progression will become increasingly difficult as the funding stops and community-based courses are not available.

The Kennedy Report (1997) and the Further Education Funding Council (FEFC, 1997b, 1997c) both talk of necessity to 'identify the learning needs of these groups' (FEFC, 1997b, p. 13). This raises difficulties, such as how needs are identified, and by whom. Link-workers relied on individuals and referral agencies to identify and express needs. Thus it can be argued that in many ways the courses provided were not socially and culturally relevant. The only curriculum alteration that tended to occur was the provision of short 'taster' courses, modelled on the longer courses delivered at the main college sites. Some colleges did try to select tutors who they felt would be more supportive of the needs of students learning in the community, but other colleges were unable or unwilling to make such arrangements.

If a broader definition of 'participation' – including visiting a drop-in session or requesting information, in addition to more traditional course enrolment – is adopted, it can be seen that there has been greater accommodation of the needs of the local communities. Most link-workers developed a version of these services to meet the needs of their communities.

Individualizing the problem

The final category of barrier is those levied at individuals. Chapter 10 discusses barriers created by low aspirations and motivation, and a lack of information, guidance and awareness relating to educational opportunities.

As noted above, the community outreach scheme had identifiable geographical communities, but within these there was no discrimination. This suggests that the project may not have benefited the more marginalized or reticent adults in these communities. Link-workers adopted a pragmatic approach, often working with established groups, and whichever ones would co-operate with them. One link-worker rationalized:

> I found, because of lack of time, that I have gone to already established groups. I've actually been to young mums and I've been to older people – like luncheon clubs. But I also made sure I included unemployed men by going to the Job Centre.

In some instances link-workers did try to target certain socio-cultural groups that they perceived to be under-represented in further education, but in the particular instance described below this was difficult to achieve. The link-worker explained:

> I've tried to target this group, but I haven't been able to, I encountered a barrier. And that is ethnic minorities, whether it's Bangladeshi or Pakistanis or whatever, I've found a bit of a stumbling block trying to access ethnic minorities on these cases. Because, you know, your first port of call is to go down to the mosque or whatever, but being white – it's difficult, you know ... I haven't had any success ... which is a shame. But there's only so far, you know, if you can't get access into that group because of the cultural barriers, then you can't widen participation with that group either.

The lack of targeting may also impinge on the information that individuals received, as the main source of information was link-workers.

Although the scheme attempts to bring educational opportunities to communities, this does involve individuals 'taking a risk' and participating, perhaps for the first time. There is, therefore, some obligation on individuals to change, but this is not matched by changes within college; overall, they were reluctant to alter.

From project to strategy

Chapter 11 stressed the importance of developing a strategic approach to widening participation. In particular, this embraces the notion of developing, first, a coherent project; second, ensuring complementarity *between* projects; and, third, moving towards longer-term sustainability. Sustainability includes financial sustainability, ownership among stakeholders, developing the capacity of the stakeholders and ensuring that institutional learning takes place.

The extent to which this partnership could be viewed as a strategy varied between colleges. Overall, there was a series of eight widening-participation projects, with limited liaison between them and within colleges. The appointment of a project manager part way through the initiative helped to unite link-workers, as did the joint training sessions and research seminars, although there was still competition between colleges. Within institutions the attitudes and support of senior management was a key factor – for example whether or not they would change structures to facilitate inclusion of these learners. Although strategic partnerships were intended to overcome competition, within the community there was competition between agencies. There have been exceptions, but, overall, there was little or no synergy between policies and practices at either the institutional or regional level. Thus, insufficient attention was given to the range of barriers limiting participation.

With regards to sustainability, this initiative has significant strengths and weaknesses. The programme was only funded for one year, which promoted financial insecurity, and had negative consequences. For example, one college principal felt that short-term funding detracted from colleges' abilities to develop coherent and appropriate approaches to widening participation in the communities they serve:

> I'm not a great enthusiast, ... for several reasons really, often the initiatives are rushed in the first place, so they don't always get

thought through clearly enough. The national agenda and the regional agenda may not always coincide with the local agenda, so you try to bend ... to what's happening at a regional or national level ... there's always a feeling with an initiative that you set up a special team; you justify it, you cost it, you prove you've spent the money in the right way and at the end of it, if you're not very careful, the project doesn't live on because it hasn't been properly integrated, 'cos the whole approach to the project is to discourage integration and make it something that can be clearly evaluated and, in fact, that's something I don't think we want; we want a seamless provision where we're doing things in a coherent fashion over an extended period of time. Having said that, the way the world operates, if you don't participate you'll lose out on a lot of resources that can help you tackle things that we want.

Towards the very end of the funding period there was no certainty of further financial support for this particular initiative. Link-workers, in particular, were consequently left in a somewhat precarious position. It is, therefore, not surprising that some key staff (notably a link-worker and the project manager) secured alternative employment. Short-term funding does not promote sustainability, and funding insecurity leads to a loss of capacity.

On the other hand, the OCN course has helped to develop local capacity, and the compilation of a link-workers handbook will, subsequently assist people working in these communities. One link-worker said:

The actual section [of the training course] that is 'the role of the community link-worker', now that section, I think, is quite useful because of putting the handbook together, because if anyone follows on from you, you've got a map of all the provision, and all the providers, and also the other stuff will be going into the handbook. So that section, yes, I think it's very useful.

The value of the course to individual workers depended, in part, on their previous educational experience, as noted by this link-worker:

I think it all depends on what you've got and what you've done before. I mean, I've had a lot of experience in community development type work. I found it a bind, to do it – but it depends what you've done. I've got a degree in sociology, so when they're asking me about stereotyping and all of these sorts of things, it's at quite a basic level.

Additional training needs were, however, identified. For example, most link-workers organized sessions where local people could drop-in and ask for information and advice, but the training course did not provide training relating specifically to this:

> We've been expected to do drop-in sessions, where you give advice and guidance – well, that's one thing I haven't had training in, so that's definitely some thing that should be included in the course, advice and guidance training.
>
> In some cases, you are an educational careers adviser. Somebody asks you questions like 'What can I do with this course?' 'Where will it take me?' You need to be able to respond properly to people's questions ... You need to be able to guide somebody and empower somebody.

The training, therefore, helps to develop capacity and promote ownership (although both of these would be enhanced if the link-workers had all been recruited from the target communities). But care needs to be taken to ensure that the training matches needs. Furthermore, the majority of the learning was focused on the link-workers, not on others in the institutions, and so the extent to which they can be described as learning organizations is questionable. Some senior managers did not prioritize the initiative, and only attended the Steering Group meeting sporadically.

The intended beneficiaries were not directly involved in the planning and implementation of the initiative, but link-workers played a central role in the day-to-day operation of the scheme, and, particularly when they were recruited from the community, they were representing the voices of local people.

Conclusions

This scheme identified communities that were socially isolated from post-compulsory education, and to sought to discover their needs and deliver education via community outreach. This did involve some change on the part of institutions, but, on the whole, the emphasis was on overcoming social and cultural barriers by familarizing people with education through the services of a link-worker and community-based services (particularly informal drop-ins and short courses). The degree of change at the level of the institution varied, and was largely determined by the attitudes of senior management. But, for the most part, the partnership was peripheral to the work of the colleges for one reason or another. The scheme did not directly tackle labour market issues, but was significantly flexible to overcome these barriers. The scheme did not problematize the individual, but there was poor targeting within communities. Despite Kennedy's intentions, this scheme was not very strategic. My perceptions of the main strengths and weakness are summarized in the table below.

A summary of the strengths and weaknesses of the Community Outreach Partnership

Issue	Rating	Comments
EDUCATION SYSTEM		MAKES SOME CHANGES TO THE WAY EDUCATION IS DELIVERED, BUT THESE ARE NOT FUNDAMENTAL TO THE ORGANIZATION OF INSTITUTIONS.
How are stereotypes about 'good learners' and 'bad learners' challenged at the institutional and individual level?	☑	Community-based students are seen as different.
In what ways does your work help to reduce the cost of education to individuals?	☑	Reduces indirect costs of (low-level) education.
Have you developed a range of entry routes that meet the needs of all the potential students you are targeting?	☑☑☑	There are no entry requirements for the courses, but only low-level courses offered.
Is learning appropriate and flexible with regard to the curriculum?	☑☑	Minimal curriculum changes – such as taster courses, but mostly traditional courses delivered in the community.
Is learning appropriate and flexible with regard to the location?	☑☑☑	Location of courses was fully flexible, and left to the discretion of the link workers and/or their managers. Variable learner input.

Issue	Rating	Comments
Is learning appropriate and flexible with regard to the timing?	☑☑☑	The timing of courses was established in the community locations, usually in consultation with participants.
Is learning appropriate and flexible with regard to the pace?	☑☑	There was some variation in pace – for example short courses.
Are personal and academic support services provided at all sites to meet the needs of your students?	☑☑	Link-workers were able to provide support, but support services (e.g. available at college sites) were not provided in the community.
How is organizational learning and change with respect to diversity encouraged?	☑☑	Limited organizational learning and change – but this varied significantly between institutions.
LABOUR MARKET		DID NOT DEAL DIRECTLY WITH LABOUR MARKET ISSUES.
Are the expected economic and non-economic returns realistic and explicit?	☑☑☑	Courses provided in response to students' wants, but not tailor-made, so may meet students' expectations.
Is the initiative sufficiently flexible to enable (full- or part-time) participation in the labour market? Is this facilitated or discouraged?	☑☑	The courses were not specifically designed to facilitate participation.
Do the courses available provide labour market opportunities to those who want them (e.g. what are the requirements of the local economy)?	☑☑	Some courses provide labour market opportunities, but this is not the focus of the scheme.
In what ways is labour market discrimination tackled?	☒	No evidence of efforts made to tackle discrimination.

Issue	Rating	Comments
SOCIAL AND CULTURAL		THIS SCHEME FOCUSES ON OVERCOMING SOCIAL AND CULTURAL BARRIERS.
To what extent does learning familiarize people with the 'world' of post-compulsory education (e.g. to facilitate progression)?	☑☑	Familiarization with low-level, community-based learning only.
Does the initiative involve 'others' who influence the decision-making of potential learners?	☑☑☑	Scheme attempted to engage community, using community link-worker. This was only partially successful.
Is the curriculum socially and culturally relevant (is it free from cultural bias)? Is it of 'value' to the learners?	☑☑☑	Courses tended not to be created specifically, but other services were developed to meet community needs.
Does the initiative allow similar groups to work together to gain confidence?	☑☑☑☑	The project was excellent with regard to enabling similar learners to work together and gain confidence.
INDIVIDUAL		THE SCHEME IS NOT PARTICULARLY INDIVIDUALISTIC.
How does the initiative target the intended beneficiaries, and is it effective? Who benefits most from the programme?	☑☑	Geographical communities with low participation were clearly defined, but not specific social or cultural groups within them.
Does the scheme avoid blaming individuals, and seeking to change them without changing the institution?	☑☑☑	Students were not blamed, although they were often perceived to be different, and they were expected to change more than colleges themselves were prepared to do so.

Issue	Rating	Comments
Is information about programme and learning opportunities available to non-traditional learners?	☑☑☑	Link-workers were the primary source, so varied between sites. Targeting impacted on availability of information to relevant groups.
STRATEGY		DESPITE INTENTIONS, THIS SCHEME WAS NOT VERY STRATEGIC.
Has due accord been given to the different types of barriers that potential learners face?	☑☑	Limited account of the range of barriers facing potential students.
What levels of synergy are there between different projects and policies at the institutional level and in the region?	☑☑	Despite intentions, only limited synergy – evidence of competition within the partnership, and with other agencies.
Sustainability: What will remain after the funding period? Is ownership promoted? Is the capacity of stakeholders developed? And are the institutions involved 'learning organizations'?	☑☑	Poor financial sustainability. Ownership by community and college not promoted. Good attempt at capacity building of link-workers, but not staff. Most institutions did not change, although a few did.
Are the intended beneficiaries involved in the planning and implementation of widening participation strategies?	☑☑☑	Beneficiaries not included, but link-workers from community were intended to implement project, and consult with potential learners.

Guide to the ratings

☑☑☑☑	–	excellent
☑☑☑	–	good
☑☑☑	–	average
☑☑	–	weak
☑	–	very poor
☒	–	not addressed

CHAPTER 14

Case Study 3: A Tailor-made Programme of Courses

Introduction

This case study focuses on a programme of higher education courses in Community Education and Development that is delivered in outreach locations in the south-east of Ireland by an Institute of Technology and community group partners. The form and the contents of the courses are strongly influenced by the participants. The first programme was designed for and with women working as volunteers in the community through a partnership with ACCESS 2000 (a network of women's groups). The women were all socially and/or financially disadvantaged (Murphy, 2000), and lacked confidence and experience of formal education. The course has now been extended to other community groups, and so includes men as well as women. This scheme is based on pre-project research, and provides an example of an initiative that is seeking to overcome different types of barriers confronting potential participants.

Details of the scheme
Project organizers and other partners

The programme is a partnership between an Institute of Technology and voluntary agencies. The courses commenced in 1996, when the college was approached by ACCESS 2000, a community partnership of women's groups (see Blackmore and Heynen, 1998) that wanted a higher-education programme to qualify people as community educationalists and development workers. The original programme was, therefore, designed collaboratively by the HEI and a particular community group, and now involves other groups.

What does it do?
In partnership with community and voluntary groups the HEI has developed, and delivers, a programme in Community Education and Development, leading to, first, a National Certificate and then a National Diploma, and, finally, a degree (which is under development). The initial aim of the programme of courses was to engage women who had a wealth of practical experience as community activist volunteers, but who were excluded from the labour market because they lacked formal qualifications. The course, therefore, targeted part-time adult learners who were often working (but not necessarily in community-related employment) and who had domestic and family commitments. The intention was to build on their practical community action experience, often undertaken on a voluntary basis, and to integrate academic learning with these community activities. Former students explain: 'Assignment topics were negotiated between tutors and participants to provide the opportunity to relate theory to practice, to reflect on practice and, in turn, to generate new theory' (Blehein and O'Grady, 2000, p. iii).

The course is delivered in locations selected by the community groups who pay for their workers or volunteers to attend, and, usually, there are about fifteen students per group. The participants study for a National Certificate, which is a two-year higher-education qualification, which can be extended for a further year to attain a Diploma. It is anticipated that the course will be developed to enable students to gain a degree; this part of the programme is currently being designed by the HEI in partnership with the original community group, ACCESS 2000. Thus, progression is possible from the National Certificate to the National Diploma, and, in time, to a degree in Community Education and Development.

A key part of the programme is the recognition by the accrediting body that learning takes place *outside* of the classroom, in the community. This enables part-time students to complete each level of qualification in the same time-frame as a full-time student who is not undertaking relevant community work. For example, for a module taught only in the classroom, 200 teaching hours would be required, but for this course just 30 hours are classroom-based. The remaining 170 hours are notional hours of learning that occur outside of the classroom, in community groups, through community work and in people's own study time.

Many of the lecturers for the course are also community practitioners who are recruited especially for this course, as opposed to being mainstream lecturers based at the college's main sites. This policy ensures that the lecturers have relevant applied expertise – which is what the learners require. The co-ordinator emphasized this point:

> they need to be able to frame their own practice within the theoretical and academic framework ... They need to be able to reflect on their own learning to date, and then bring that new academic framework to bear on their work when they go back to the community.

Who does it target?

Much of the Irish government's efforts at widening participation (which has influenced institutional responses) has focused on young people, rather than mature students (e.g. Department of Education, 1995). But, this project was developed in response to an approach by ACCESS 2000, which has the explicit intention of providing training for disadvantaged women. The group targets lone parents, travellers, women without formal qualifications, women with literacy problems, women experiencing poverty and unemployed women (Murphy, 2000, p. 1). The women who participated in the first courses were all involved in community work, but largely in an unpaid capacity. 'It was identified that the work which the women had done on a voluntary basis was now being paid for. However, people with qualifications were getting the work, not the women volunteers' (*ibid.*). The scheme, therefore, targets people who are working in the community, in either a voluntary or a paid capacity, and who would not otherwise be able to access a higher-education course – either for practical reasons or due to a lack of confidence. In the first instance, ACCESS 2000 identified women who were ready to participate in the programme, and this model was adopted in relation to other community groups. Thus, voluntary organizations themselves play a leading role in the recruitment and selection of course participants.

Why was it initiated?

ACCESS 2000 undertook research into the needs of the women's groups, and the barriers that prevented their members from accessing traditional higher-education. This identified confidence, time and distance from higher education provision as key barriers to participation by these women. Cost was assumed to be a barrier, given the socio-economic background of the women concerned. This scheme seeks to overcome all of these barriers. With regard to confidence, course participants confirmed that previous educational experiences acted as disincentives to participation. Many course participants have work and family commitments, and so they would not be able to undertake a full-time course. Furthermore, some of the groups studying for the course are based more than three hours' travel away from the main university site, and this qualification is not available in a college closer to where they live. Thus, distance from an HEI can be cited as a barrier related to the limitations of time and other commitments that are typical of the students targeted.

Success of the programme

The programme itself has not been formally evaluated, but the course can be judged to be successful using a number of criteria, which are discussed below.

The most obvious criteria is demand for the course by community groups, which is limited by the availability of external funding. Since the programme was developed in 1996 the certificate and diploma programmes have been requested by a wide range of groups, and have been delivered in diverse locations. The sustained level of interest by community groups, support from external funding bodies and subsequent enrolments by individuals endorse the success of the course in meeting genuine and valuable needs by three stakeholder groups. If funding was not an issue, the demand would be even greater.

Completions are another quantitative method of assessing the scheme. Although there is some concern regarding the students who do not complete the course, retention is high. Given the complicated and sometimes difficult circumstances faced by these mature students, this can be regarded as an indicator of success.

A further measure of success is the extent to which participants have progressed, both to other courses, and to employment. The initial group of students comprised nineteen women, and all of them completed the programme (although they had full support mechanisms in place). In 1999, sixteen of the nineteen students were employed in 'community or related areas', in either a full-time or a part-time capacity, whereas before they undertook the course, most were only engaged in the community as volunteers.

Anecdotal evidence reports that employers are 'really happy' with the work of graduates from the programme, and that they are 'very familiar with the field' and 'they know their stuff'. Participants who complete the course also say how much it has meant to them, and that it has changed their way of thinking, and this has given them confidence to go for jobs that they would not have previously considered.

The benefits for participants can be seen to be operating at different levels. First, the self-confidence of course participants increases; secondly, they learn new skills that directly assist with their community work; and, thirdly, they can place their own practice within a theoretical framework. In addition, students have the opportunity to obtain a qualification in community education and development, and to progress into further study and into enhanced employment.

The course helps to build up the confidence of the participants in their own skills and abilities, both in relation to community work and academic studying. The programme co-ordinator commented:

> As an individual their confidence goes up hugely, particularly in what they already know. One of the very early pieces of work we ask them to do is to compile a personal portfolio where they detail their life history, the skills that they have developed over the years, and there's quite a bit of work on understanding. They name skills that they use everyday in their family work, for example.

Through the course, participants develop 'core skills' – group work, facilitation, communication skills, interviewing skills, dealing with people on a one-to-one basis, curriculum design, and so on. These help them in their community education and development work.

The conceptual elements of the course enable course participants to understand and place their own practice within a broader theoretical framework. People who have participated in the course say that they 'now know what they know'. This is undoubtedly linked to the point that studying the course improves confidence in academic and vocational terms. The co-ordinator said:

> They now know that what they have done, maybe as a matter of form, or because they've always done it that way, or because they believe that's the way it should be done, is based very solidly on a particular theory, or on a particular line of thinking. So that they are now able to place their own practice within that context, and that's valuable.

Although the course is 'process-focused', successful completion also results in certification. The programme is modular, and each module is certificated, allowing students to achieve and progress to a range of qualifications. Working towards (and attaining) a qualification is an important aspect of the original conceptualization of the course by

ACCESS 2000, who noticed that people with qualifications, rather than people with voluntary experience, were securing jobs in community education and development. Indeed, students and graduates of the programme have been more able to secure employment related to this field of work.

Examining the assumptions
This scheme has fewer assumptions than the other case studies as it was initially based on a direct approach from a community organization, and continues in response to demand from voluntary groups. Furthermore, ACCESS 2000 undertook research into the barriers facing their members. The assumptions underpinning the scheme include:

- The target group is willing and able to study in higher education – if the courses are tailored to meet their needs;
- Community groups are able to identify suitable participants;
- Suitable venues and tutors can be found;
- Sufficient funding is available to support the course;
- The HEI will continue to support the course.

These assumptions have all held true. The most problematic issue has been funding. In Ireland there has been extensive European funding since 1990 for community-based partnerships, and this is a primary source of support for this course, but there are implications for its viability in the longer term. College support is limited, but does not prevent the course from taking place and being effective. These two issues are discussed below in relation to developing a strategic approach.

Overcoming barriers created by the education system
This scheme actively challenges the barriers created by compulsory education, and those subsequently posed by the post-compulsory sector. Past educational achievements are not taken as an indicator of potential in further learning. The course does not require any formal entry qualifications, and approximately half of the students in each learner group left school without any formal qualifications. There is less need for people to overcome their own self-images as poor learners, as they are approached by the community organizations they are involved with, rather than having to put themselves forward, and this reduces the limitations created by low self-esteem and lack of confidence.

Once students have been recommended, they must comply with

quite a detailed application procedure, which includes submitting a written passage regarding the motivations for undertaking community work in general and, more specifically, their reasons for wanting to participate in the course. This gives an indication of students' ability to express their thoughts in writing, and, more importantly, highlights literacy difficulties, as the course is unsuitable for such students. Following the submission of an application, a representative of the community group and the programme co-ordinator conduct a face-to-face interview. This interview provides an opportunity for candidates who are not ready for higher education study to be guided towards other courses before attempting the National Certificate programme.

The majority of applicants are accepted, primarily because the community groups identify them as potentially suitable candidates at the first informal stage of the procedure; literacy is the single most important reason why people do not participate. The programme co-ordinator said:

> It's our responsibility to advise somebody in relation to the course, whether the course is suitable or not. Once we have accepted them on to the course it is our responsibility to make sure that we do everything possible so that they can succeed in their studies, but if the course is really going to be a bad experience ... [we wouldn't encourage them to do it].

In addition, to help overcome perceived and actual limitations of previous educational experiences, on-course support is provided. For the first cohort of students, one-to-one mentoring was available. Unfortunately, the funding is no longer available for this activity, so the HEI sets up study groups of three or four students who live in a close geographical area, and the course co-ordinator meets each group once or twice per month. In addition, informal evaluation sessions are held twice per term. The evaluation sessions last for between one and two hours, and enable students to raise issues that have arisen during the course, and to make comments about the contents, organizational issues and their own experience of the programme. The course co-ordinator is in phone contact with students, and they can ring him. But he feels the mentoring scheme is preferable.

The demand for the course is sufficiently high, however, to ensure that the withdrawal of the support services has not reduced the number of people participating. But, from both informal evidence and a common-sense perspective, it must be surmised that there are people who would have enrolled, or who have been forced to drop out, who would have benefited from extra support. Consequently, the most disadvantaged may have been excluded from the programme.

The curriculum has been designed specifically for voluntary groups, and to be delivered on a part-time basis in community locations. In terms of location, timing and pace, the course is highly flexible.

When each new study group is formed, the tutors negotiate with the course members regarding the best time for the formal teaching to take place and the most appropriate pace (i.e. the overall duration of the course). Some groups complete the certificate programme in two academic years, while other groups take longer: one group has successfully completed the National Certificate in less than two years. The programme co-ordinator said, 'We try to work around people's lives.' This means that the timetable can be complicated. After consultation, one group decided to have lectures on Wednesday night, one week, and Tuesday night the following week. This compromise allowed course members with a regular community commitment on one of these nights to attend this from time to time to retain their involvement. School holidays and family commitments can also be worked around to enable as many people as possible to attend the course.

In addition to time and pace, place is also important. The college tries to find venues with which each student group is comfortable, and which has appropriate facilities. There are no outreach campuses, but pre-existing venues are utilized, such as community training facilities. The co-ordinator comments:

> I think there's a reluctance among the more traditional educators to support those type of outreach programmes, and yet the facilities in those centres are at times way better than are available in the classroom here. There are tea-making facilities on site, they have video and TV in the room, overhead projector, the whole lot. Very comfortable seating, flexible seating, you can move the chairs around so that you can do group work, and yet if you had to run it in some of the lecture halls here you couldn't do that.

No matter how flexible the programme is, the time commitment does remain too great for some students, and ultimately prevents or curtails their participation.

A fee is not levied on students directly, as this would prevent members of the target group from participating. Initially, a training allowance and support with the costs of childcare, travel and books were provided, which reduced the indirect and opportunity costs of learning too. It is not known what impact the withdrawal of these financial benefits has had on participants. The programme co-ordinator commented that often 'people cope, they make arrangements, and you don't know how much they're sacrificing on the side. And I don't know how many people would be on the course if there was childcare.'

The aim is for the programme to be self-financing, and so the sponsoring community groups do pay for the courses in which their members participate, and must secure funding from external sources for payment to the college. (The HEI is not able to claim state funding as adult education courses are not currently centrally financed in the Republic of Ireland.) This means that some people may be excluded, because the community group with which they are involved is unable to raise the necessary finance.

A weakness of the programme is its inefficacy to promote institutional learning and change, and to develop a culture that supports and values diversity. The programme is peripheral within the HEI. One member of staff commented: 'Within the institution this work is seen as marginal and these courses are seen as marginal.' There is a perception that staff not involved in community outreach work, and some members of senior management do not value the contribution of the Community Education and Development programme. Although some staff are supportive, many are indifferent and some are opposed to this type of learning: 'Just in conversations you get the impression that they are actively against these types of initiatives because of the question of standards dropping.'

Similarly, part-time community education tutors feel that they are

> kind of excluded from the mainstream life of the college, that they are really on the margins and that there isn't a place for them. There is no meeting room, for example ... And those small factors make a big difference. The fact that they are spread all around the country too makes it very difficult to bring them all together at any one time, apart from course board meetings ... There are opportunities that are being lost.

The co-ordinator attributes this lack of support to the radical nature of the programme, which challenges the orthodoxy of traditional higher education provision. The scheme gave control to a community organization (because they had the money):

> if you gave the funding to the college I don't think that the course the college would put in place would be anything like ...

It changes an awful lot of things about the way the other courses are run, and I think it's in those changes that a lot of the suspicion and lack of understanding lies. (programme co-ordinator)

Labour market issues

As has been noted above, all the students who participate in the course gain both economic and non-economic returns. The programme was developed as there was an increase of employment opportunities in the field of community education and development, but preference was given to applicants with qualifications, which many volunteers working in the community lacked.

The programme has helped to overcome this labour market discrimination, and graduates have secured employment, that matches their requirements, in the field of community education and development. The experience of programme participants demonstrates that success in the labour market is not solely dependent on the possession of relevant qualifications, but the course develops self-confidence, so that candidates are self-assured and cope better with interview situations. It is, therefore, the personal development elements of the programme that are assisting participants as much, if not more, than job-related skills and certification. The co-ordinator explained:

Often people will get work, get jobs *during* the programme, even though they don't have the qualification, but when they're going into the interviews, they tell me that they just know their stuff and they're confident about what they know. And the way they present themselves at interview then means that they have been able to access employment, even though they don't have the qualification at that stage ... One of the good things, I suppose is that they have been able to access employment that suits them: part-time, job-share, etc. It's not all full-time, and change everything to do with their family involvement and their community involvement.

Overcoming social and cultural barriers to participation

For many students participation in this programme is their first experience of post-compulsory education, and many students want to progress. Initially they enrol on the certificate, and then they can undertake the diploma; a degree programme is currently being developed (collaboratively with ACCESS 2000). There have, however, been difficulties establishing direct lines of progression to courses at other universities. Other institutions have 'demanded' students 'go back to day one as if they had done no other course'.

The programme has familiarized students with post-compulsory education, but progression is hampered by barriers in the education system, and insufficient funding. For example, there are currently two cohorts of students who have completed the National Certificate and would like to progress to the diploma course, but there is no funding available.

This scheme involves others from the local community. In the original programme, course participants selected mentors from the community. This system had advantages; in particular that the students felt confident to work with their mentor, and the mentors had first-hand experience relevant to each student. But it is acknowledged that, had the one-to-one mentoring system continued, steps would need to have been taken to integrate the mentors into the course more fully. It is hoped that in the near future it may be possible to introduce a revised mentor system with funding from an alternative source. Furthermore, all the tutors are recruited from the local community. The scheme, however, does not involve 'others' such as family members.

As discussed above, the curriculum was specifically developed to meet the needs of community group volunteers, and so is socially and culturally relevant. The HEI was effectively 'forced' to work with community groups, which significantly influenced many features of the course. The co-ordinator commented: 'It's been fundamental, a radical way of developing things. You give the money to the community group, who then demand exactly what they are looking for.'

The course is of value, allowing personal development and enhancing employment possibilities. A former course participant sums up how the course was right for her:

> I always knew I wasn't 'brainy' not like the others who could say things properly and sound really intelligent. I wanted to be like that. I wanted to use those big words and understand them. I wanted to come across as intelligent, and stand up for what I believed in. My schooling only lasted until I reached the first month of Intercert class when I was offered a job. Knowing that I wouldn't do well in my exams I was encouraged to take the job. I was over the moon, I had never liked school and school never liked me and my ambition was never to return.

However, 'never say never': Community Education was there for me when I needed something more in my life. It brought me along step by step from where I was at, up to the completion of this Diploma Course. I now know that I am intelligent, because I have a stack of assignments full of work that I did and that I know about. I may have complained (a little) about doing the assignments, but the satisfaction of knowing that these assignments are written proof of what I know and are now a resource for me to work with – was worth it. (Nuncie Murphy, in Blenhein and O'Grady, 2000, pp. i–ii)

A further strength of the scheme is the fact that it allows similar groups of learners to work together and gain confidence, with the support of local tutors.

Individualizing the problem

The scheme targets individuals very carefully, and overall this is effective. Voluntary groups identify people that they feel would benefit from participating on the course, and would be able to cope with it. All the community partners in this programme work with disadvantaged and marginalized individuals and communities, which is where the students, who are mostly volunteers, are drawn from. Very few applicants are not accepted, and most students achieve at least the National Certificate, while many progress further.

There is a danger that the scheme does not reach potential beneficiaries if the organizations or groups of which they are members do not have sufficient funds to enable them to participate. Larger and better-organized community groups are more likely to be able to obtain external funding (in general) and to support the development of staff and volunteers, as they have sufficient time and skills (Thomas, forthcoming). To some extent at least, smaller community groups are highly likely to be missing out on funding opportunities, and so their volunteers will not be participating in the Community Education and Development courses.

The scheme does not blame individuals at all, but provides opportunities for change, as a direct consequence of substantial change on the part of the institution.

The HEI does not provide extensive information about the programme of courses, but voluntary groups approach them. There may, therefore, be a lack of information and guidance for potential students – for example, is this the best option for them? The admissions procedure is intended to identify these issues, and the HEI does have outreach information and guidance centres that some potential students may have access to (cf. Harte and Jordan, 1999).

From project to strategy

Research in Ireland by Lynch and O'Riordan (1998) showed that economic barriers were the most significant obstacles to participation in post-compulsory education by students from lower socio-economic groups, and other class-related barriers reinforce these financial problems. The findings of their research are summarized by O'Brien and O'Byrne (2000):

> These economic barriers are compounded by a series of inter-related obstacles which are social, cultural and educational. Community activists believed that working-class culture is not valued in schools or elsewhere in society, while teachers believed that there is a 'cultural deficit' among students due to the fact that many parents had a negative experience of the education system. A lack of information about how the education system works and about life at third-level in general was identified as another barrier leading to a fear of isolation among second-level students and a sense of alienation from third-level institutions. The middle-class culture of the school, teacher expectation and the quality of schooling in terms of curriculum and subject choice were identified as some of the educational constraints. At post-entry level, working-class students identified the role of lecturers and support in college as very important as they came from families with little previous experience of third level. (p. 80)

This scheme can be seen to be addressing the different types of barriers faced by the target groups.

One weakness in this programme is its lack of linkages, particularly at the institutional level. As is noted above, community outreach work does not appear to be central to the work of the institution. This isolation means that the programme of Community Education and Development courses is not integrated into an institutional strategy. And although the programme has good links with the regions, there is no evidence of synergy with other adult education initiatives at this level either.

A further problem of this scheme is its potential lack of sustainability. As was noted above, community groups must secure external funding for their members to attend the course, and European funding is a primary source of support. This dependence on one, finite funding source means that the programme is financially unsustainable. The programme co-ordinator is aware of this short-coming and comments:

> Those types of barriers [i.e. course funding] have been by-passed by European funding, which may not be there long-term, and I'm not happy that the college hasn't bought into it ... the college isn't putting on these courses from its own resources.

Initially, the course was developed collaboratively with ACCESS 2000. But there is a feeling among some members of the group that 'the college has taken their course, and owns it now and is benefiting from it ... and there's a lot of truth in that' (programme co-ordinator). The original course model has been utilized by the HEI in partnership with other community groups. This, perhaps, is the consequence of 'success' – but these grievances should be addressed to help ensure effective working relationships in the future, and to promote sustainability.

The capacity of community tutors has not been developed – they feel isolated, and teaching contracts are precarious – they do not know from year to year whether particular courses will be delivered, and what their level of involvement will be. It is argued that part-time tutors are a strength, because, in addition to teaching, they all work in a relevant community capacity. Furthermore, the tutors have embraced the ethos of the programme, for example with regard to teaching style, timetabling flexibility and so forth. The programme co-ordinator commented that 'the tutors make it or break it'.

These tutors would like to participate in the development of the programme to meet the needs of the community in general and the course participants in particular, but the funding regime and the attitude of the HEI limit further remunerated involvement. In this way, the HEI cannot be described as a learning organization, although the voluntary and community groups can. A strength of the scheme, however, is the involvement of the community organizations in the development of this programme.

Conclusions

This programme has faced some difficulties, but it is an example of initiative that is based on pre-course research and involves students and community groups in the process of addressing a broad range of barriers that potential learners face within one project. There is, however, very little evidence of coherence and complementarity between projects and policies at the level of the institution, indeed the project is marginalized with the HEI, and this helps to contribute to its potential insustainability. This is an excellent project, but the institution has demonstrated a lack of commitment to the initiative which limits is effectiveness. My perceptions of the main strengths and weakness are shown in the table below.

A summary of the strengths and weaknesses of the Community Outreach Partnership

Issue	Rating	Comments
EDUCATION SYSTEM		RADICALLY ALTERS AND CHALLENGES FUNDAMENTAL ELEMENTS OF HE SECTOR PROVISION.
How are stereotypes about 'good learners' and 'bad learners' challenged at the institutional and individual level?	☑☑☑	Students do learn in community groups, but stereotypes are overcome by ignoring past academic performance.
In what ways does your work help to reduce the cost of education to individuals?	☑☑☑	Course fee is paid by community groups, rather than participants. Indirect costs reduced as course is based in community and timetabled very flexibly.
Have you developed a range of entry routes that meet the needs of all the potential students you are targeting?	☑☑☑☑	Past achievements are not taken as an indicator of potential (except in the case of literacy difficulties), and there are no entry requirements, beyond commitment to participation.
Is learning appropriate and flexible with regard to the curriculum?	☑☑☑	Curriculum was developed in response to, and in partnership with a community group. It is not altered for each cohort of students.
Is learning appropriate and flexible with regard to the location?	☑☑☑☑	Community location negotiated with each cohort.

Issue	Rating	Comments
Is learning appropriate and flexible with regard to the timing?	☑☑☑☑	Completely flexible timetable.
Is learning appropriate and flexible with regard to the pace?	☑☑☑	Learner group determines pace, therefore will suit majority of students.
Are personal and academic support services provided at all sites to meet the needs of your students?	☑☑☑	The first cohort of students received comprehensive academic and personal support, and childcare and travel costs etc. were paid. Reduced support is now available, due to lack of funding.
How is organizational learning and change with respect to diversity encouraged?	☑	Lack of organizational learning and change.
LABOUR MARKET		EFFECTIVELY OVERCOMES MOST OF THE LABOUR MARKET BARRIERS.
Are the expected economic and non-economic returns realistic and explicit?	☑☑☑	Developed in response to trends in the labour market, and to fulfil personal development needs.
Is the initiative sufficiently flexible to enable (full- or part-time) participation in the labour market? Is this facilitated or discouraged?	☑☑☑☑	Fully flexible delivery enables people to continue in full- or part-time employment
Do the courses available provide labour market opportunities to those who want them (e.g. what are the requirements of the local economy)?	☑☑☑☑	Graduates of the programme have secured work in community education and development, and it has matched their needs – e.g. part-time, in their communities etc.

Issue	Rating	Comments
In what ways is labour market discrimination tackled?	☑☑☑	Contributes to overcoming discrimination. Employers prefer those with formal qualifications, as opposed to practical experience.
SOCIAL AND CULTURAL		OVERCOMES MANY OF THE BARRIERS CREATED BY THE SOCIAL AND CULTURAL CONTEXT.
To what extent does learning familiarize people with the 'world' of post-compulsory education (e.g. to facilitate progression)?	☑☑☑	Builds confidence and encourages progression, but some difficulties have been faced developing degree programme. No contact with main institution site.
Does the initiative involve 'others' who influence the decision-making of potential learners?	☑☑☑	Utilizes community tutors. First scheme had community mentors. No involvement of 'others'.
Is the curriculum socially and culturally relevant (is it free from cultural bias)? Is it of 'value' to the learners?	☑☑☑☑	Socially and culturally relevant and meets genuine needs.
Does the initiative allow similar groups to work together to gain confidence?	☑☑☑☑☑	Similar groups work together in their communities, with local tutors.
INDIVIDUAL		LESS INDIVIDUALLY FOCUSED.
How does the initiative target the intended beneficiaries, and is it effective? Who benefits most from the programme?	☑☑☑☑	Effective targeting, but volunteers in smaller community groups may be missing out.
Does the scheme avoid blaming individuals, and seeking to change them without changing the institution?	☑☑☑☑☑	There is no evidence that students are blamed – the institution provides opportunities as it has radically restructured delivery.

Issue	Rating	Comments
Is information about programme and learning opportunities available to non-traditional learners?	☑☑	Community groups inform members. Lack of information about alternatives available.
STRATEGY		STRATEGICALLY WEAK, ESPECIALLY WITHIN THE INSTITUTION.
Has due accord been given to the different types of barriers that potential learners face?	☑☑☑	Comprehensive at the project level.
What levels of synergy are there between different projects and policies at the institutional level and in the region?	☑	Lack of synergy, especially at the institutional level.
Sustainability: What will remain after the funding period? Is ownership promoted? Is the capacity of stakeholders developed? Are the institutions involved learning organizations'?	☑	Poor financial sustainability, ownership tensions, lack of capacity development and little institutional learning by HEI.
Are the intended beneficiaries involved in the planning and implementation of widening participation strategies?	☑☑☑☑	High level of beneficiary involvement. Could contribute to contents on an ongoing basis.

Guide to the ratings

☑☑☑☑☑	–	excellent	☑☑	–	weak
☑☑☑☑	–	good	☑	–	very poor
☑☑☑	–	average	☒	–	not addressed

CHAPTER 15

This Approach to Widening Participation

Introduction

This final chapter draws together the ideas discussed in the preceding chapters and considers how this approach to widening participation can be used by practitioners, policy-makers and researchers. First, it offers some general conclusions about the three case studies examined in Chapters 12–14. It then returns to the limitations of developing a blueprint to widen participation and recommends a strategic, participatory process, as a superior alternative.

Learning from the case studies

The case studies presented were not intended as examples of best, or necessarily good, practice, but rather as examples to illustrate the approach to widening participation as discussed in this book. The three examples share some common features. In particular, each initiative aims to extend participation in tertiary education to student groups that are under-represented, and living in communities that are geographically and/or socially isolated from post-compulsory education institutions and practices. Despite this similarity, each scheme attempts to achieve this generic goal in distinct ways, and, in particular, greater attention is focused on different barriers in each project. For instance, the Regional Distance Learning Scheme has been developed, at least in part, to address constraints associated with the labour market, and so enables students to continue living and working in their domicile. This is primarily achieved by changing the mode of delivery, thus introducing greater flexibility with regard to the location, timing and pace of the delivery of the course. By contrast, the Community Outreach Partnership takes little account of the barriers created by the labour market, and instead emphasizes the importance of social and cultural barriers. This encourages similar groups of students to learn together in community settings. Indeed, working with peers in the locale is given greater priority than subject or level of study. Both initiatives can, in turn be seen to differ from the Tailor-made Programme of Courses, as this is more strategic at the project level, addressing, as it does most of the barriers facing potential learners.

However, although the Tailor-made Programme of Courses is comprehensive at the project level, it is not strategic at the level of the institution, as there is little coherence or complementarity between projects and policies within the college. The institution itself has undergone virtually no organizational learning or change (except in the project, which is marginalized). The initiative has not positively influenced access and participation for other groups of non-traditional students in the college, unless they participate in this particular programme of courses. For example, the admissions procedure for the project is progressive, but this is not reflected throughout the institution. Conversely, the Regional Distance Learning Scheme only addressed a limited number of barriers within the project, but this was accompanied by significant organizational change: the creation of the distance-learning board, the inclusion of lecturers from across the university and the development of staff-training programmes. Such an approach helps to promote change throughout the university, rather than in a single project only, thus improving its chance of long-term sustainability. Although the Community Outreach Partnership was intended to be a 'strategic partnership' (after Kennedy, 1997) it largely failed to be strategic at the levels of the project, the institution and the sub-region. First, it failed to take account of the range of barriers facing potential students; second, there is evidence of competition between the colleges and other agencies; and third, in most institutions the project work has been marginalized and it has not stimulated internal change.

These types of comparison help to highlight the limitations of initiatives and indicate ways in which there is scope for improvement in each scheme to meet the needs of beneficiaries more effectively. For example, if the Regional Distance Learning Scheme had undertaken pre-project research, and included intended beneficiaries in the planning and implementation of the scheme the disinclination of students to participate in the assessment, and the associated negative financial implications, could have been foreseen, and potentially avoided. Furthermore, community involvement may improve the selection of courses to maximize the uptake by students. Similarly, recommendations could be made for each case study. But the aim of this chapter is not to pass judgement on these examples, but to illustrate the utility of the approach.

Blueprint or process? The value of a participatory tool

In Chapter 1 it is noted that this book should not serve as a blueprint for widening participation. This is because a single detailed agenda for reform cannot hope to meet the diverse needs of a broader constituency of learners, and these groups must be involved in the processes of change. A blueprint is construed as a model, that once developed can be implemented again and again. Such an approach contends that if widening participation is only partially successful, it is just a question of redefining the model. This, however, assumes an unchanging environment, simplicity and homogeneous communities of 'non-learners'; whereas both society and the field of widening participation are dynamic, complex and diverse (see Ferrier and Heagney, 2000). For this reason the goal of widening participation must be conceived as a dynamic *process*, in which many people participate (in Chapter 5 the importance of involving stakeholders in the process of examining assumptions and planning projects was explored).

This book has argued throughout that overcoming the barriers to participation in post-compulsory education is complex. In particular, there is not a single barrier to be identified and rectified, but a whole range of issues that face different groups of potential students in various ways. These barriers were grouped into four broad and overlapping categories: the education system; the labour market; social and cultural issues; and the individual. A series of questions has been developed in relation to each of these, and the strategic approach. These questions have been used to examine the case studies, and can be used in the planning of other projects, programmes and policies. The list of questions has been reproduced in grid format in Appendix 1 to assist this process. Appendix 2 provides a list of examples that have been mentioned in this book and sources of further information. These initiatives could be analysed in relation to the above key questions.

Once again, it is important to stress that these key questions are not intended to serve as a checklist; but rather as an aid to thinking with a range of stakeholders. In the comparable field of development management, Alan Thomas has pointed to the importance of recognizing the variety of institutions and types of agencies involved in interventions (Thomas, A, 1996). It can be valuable to identify the individuals, groups and organizations that will either be affected by a widening participation initiative, or who can facilitate or hinder its implementation. The perceptions and objectives of these stakeholders, particularly those of beneficiaries, will not necessarily coincide, and may well conflict. Stakeholders include intended beneficiaries, the management group, staff, institutions, accreditation agencies, local authorities, other agencies, voluntary groups, and so forth. There are of course sub-groups within stakeholder categories. For this reason 'intended beneficiaries' is not of necessity a homogenous group. A useful starting point is, therefore, to list all the stakeholders, and make sure that representatives of these groups are involved in the planning and implementation of the initiative (cf. Montgomery, 1995). A participatory approach does not, naturally, guarantee consensus: conflicting interests may not be reconcilable, and hidden agendas may constrain progress. It is, therefore, important to decide the relative priority to be given to the needs and interests of different stakeholders in relation to the initiative. This should be done as a participatory activity, in which stakeholders discuss whose needs and interests are given priority, *before* the issues arise (a full discussion of conflicts and trade-offs is provided by Grimble, *et al.*, 1994, pp. 7–4).

Once stakeholders have been identified, it is easier to involve them in the planning and implementation process. The key questions can then be asked as part of this process to stimulate thinking about different ways in which the project, programme or policy could be designed. Before decisions are made, it is helpful to refer to the four questions about assumptions:

- What are the underlying assumptions?
- Who is making the assumptions?
- Have these assumptions been investigated?
- Are there likely to be any killer assumptions?

Conclusions

This book is written at a time when there is more interest in widening participation in post-compulsory learning than ever before, although it is not without its sceptics. The early chapters critiqued some of the reasons for this expansion, and, in particular, the distinctions between the agenda of the modernizers and that of the progressives. The former prioritize education and training for personal and national *economic* gain, but this may be compromised by a lack of suitable jobs and the existence of credentialism and inequalities in the labour market which act to maintain the status quo. The progressive, or liberal, agenda acknowledges a much broader range of benefits from learning, and thus asserts that education should be extended beyond traditional constituencies to non-traditional student groups. Such a division also challenges the subjects and types of learning that should be promoted: the former indicates that vocational education and training is paramount, whereas the latter promotes education that facilitates personal development and social cohesion. The dominance of economic motivations for expanding the post-compulsory education and training system have led to an increase in the number of students, but this has not ensured greater diversity and equality. The need for further efforts to widen, as opposed to simply increase, participation remains.

Attempts to redress the balance in participation in post-compulsory education often assume the causes and these dictate the solutions proffered. Assumptions, however, are determined by past experiences, role and position and vested interests. Awareness of assumptions and participation by stakeholders, especially intended beneficiaries, helps to improve the quality of decisions that are made. Furthermore, attempts to widen participation often focus on only one or a limited range of barriers to access and progression. This book has sought to demonstrate the broad number of issues that can inhibit participation, categorized as barriers created by the education system, the labour market, social and cultural norms, and individuals. Only acknowledging one category (especially just one particular barrier), is unlikely to be the most effective way of addressing the complex issues surrounding non-participation by some sectors of society. Only recognizing and remedying one of the barriers to access may be counter-productive, as non-traditional students may enter education but be unable to complete as other obstacles remain in place. An effective *strategy* to widen participation among under-represented groups of students must take account of the differing categories of barriers that exist, and seek to develop an approach that engages with as wide a range of factors as possible.

Widening participation is complex and dynamic. It is, therefore, essential that the views of as many different individuals and groups who are affected by widening participation initiatives be involved in the process of change. Institutions need to be flexible, accepting of diversity, and thus open to change, and not simply expecting 'others' to be normalized so that they can participate in an unreformed traditional education. It is hoped that the approach suggested and developed in this book will help this process of institutional change.

APPENDIX 1

Key Questions

In this book a number of 'key questions' have been asked to facilitate widening participation. These have been grouped together into a grid below (as in Chapters 12–14). This grid can be used to stimulate debate with stakeholders about an initiative, such as a project or a policy, with the aim of widening participation.

The first column of the grid lists the questions. The second column is used for a group-agreed score or 'rating'. The aim is not to identify an objective score, but to try to reach agreement about whether the initiative addresses this issue adequately to meet the needs of the target group of beneficiaries. The following ratings could be used:

☑☑☑☑	– excellent	☑☑	– weak
☑☑☑	– good	☑	– very poor
☑☑	– average	☒	– not addressed

This is NOT an objective score, and as such is of no value. Instead, the *process* of discussing and trying to agree a score is perceived to be of value.

The other questions to be borne in mind when addressing the questions in the grid are those relating to the assumptions that underpin the initiative. These are:

- What are the underlying assumptions?
- Who is making the assumptions?
- Have these assumptions been investigated?
- Are there likely to be any killer assumptions?

Key questions to assist with the identifying of strengths and weaknesses of widening participation initiatives

Issue	Rating	Comments
EDUCATION SYSTEM		
How are stereotypes about 'good learners' and 'bad learners' challenged at the institutional and individual level?		
In what ways does your work help to reduce the cost of education to individuals?		
Have you developed a range of entry routes that meet the needs of all the potential students you are targeting?		
Is learning appropriate and flexible with regard to the curriculum?		
Is learning appropriate and flexible with regard to the location?		
Is learning appropriate and flexible with regard to the timing?		
Is learning appropriate and flexible with regard to the pace?		
Are personal and academic support services provided at all sites to meet the needs of your students?		
How is organizational learning and change with respect to diversity encouraged?		
LABOUR MARKET		
Are the expected economic and non-economic returns realistic and explicit?		

Is the initiative sufficiently flexible to enable (full- or part-time) participation in the labour market? Is this facilitated or discouraged?		
Do the courses available provide labour market opportunities to those who want them (e.g. what are the requirements of the local economy)?		
In what ways is labour market discrimination tackled?		
SOCIAL AND CULTURAL		
To what extent does learning familiarize people with the 'world' of post-compulsory education (e.g. to facilitate progression)?		
Does the initiative involve 'others' who influence the decision-making of potential learners?		
Is the curriculum socially and culturally relevant (is it free from cultural bias)? Is it of 'value' to the learners?		
Does the initiative allow similar groups to work together to gain confidence?		
INDIVIDUAL		
How does the initiative target the intended beneficiaries, and is it effective? Who benefits most from the programme?		
Does the scheme avoid blaming individuals, and seeking to change them without changing the institution?		
Is information about programme and learning opportunities available to non-traditional learners?		

STRATEGY		
Has due accord been given to the different types of barriers that potential learners face?		
What levels of synergy are there between different projects and policies at the institutional level and in the region?		
Sustainability: What will remain after the funding period? Is ownership promoted? Is the capacity of stakeholders developed? And are the institutions involved 'learning organizations'?		
Are the intended beneficiaries involved in the planning and implementation of widening participation strategies?		

APPENDIX 2

Further Case Studies

This book has selected just three case studies to examine in depth; however, numerous other examples are referred to. Here is a list of other case studies – for which some published literature is available – that could be analysed using the framework developed in this book.

School-based programmes

The **Student Action Research for University Access** (SARUA) Project was established in 1992 at Queensland University of Technology, Australia. The aim is to engage students from under-represented groups in research on barriers to tertiary education in their own schools and communities, and in action to bridge the gap between their home and school cultures and that of the university. See Atweh and Bland (1999) for further details.

The **Aiming High** project was a five-year scheme based in Stoke-on-Trent and North Staffordshire (1995–2000). The intention was to raise the aspirations and ambitions of young people in the area by involving Year 9 pupils in a series of inspirational activities to encourage them to achieve their full potential, regardless of their ability. These activities varied from year to year, but included dance, theatre and music workshops; artwork; and inspirational speakers. Each year, some pupils were involved in a public concert in partnership with the BBC Philharmonic Orchestra and other professionals, such as the Birmingham Royal Ballet and the BBC Singers. See Thomas and Slack (1999a, 2000b).

PERACH is a national tutoring and mentoring scheme that has been developed in Israel, and is now used by other universities and countries. It recruits university students from poorer families, who do not have sufficient income to participate in higher education, and trains them as tutors and mentors to work with disadvantaged school pupils. The mentors work either individually or with small groups of pupils. The scheme can demonstrate high levels of success. See Carmeli (2000a, 2000b) for further details.

University-based schemes

The **Access Summer School** at the University of Dundee, Scotland, commenced in 1993 as a ten-week course for disadvantaged students aged between 17 and 24. It is designed for students who have had their educational development 'held back', and thus lack university entry qualifications. The course involves a wide range of subjects, the development of personal transferable skills, academic and personal support and guidance and guaranteed university places. See Blicharski (1998, 2000) and Woodrow (1998) for further details.

The **Tertiary Preparation Programme** (TPP) is a distance education Enabling Programme or Access course run since 1986 by the University of Southern Queensland, Australia. The programme is delivered externally, allowing students to study irrespective of location or social circumstances. It consists of a series of study packages, including study guides, books of readings, audio and video tapes and a supporting text book. Telephone tutorial support is offered, and optional on-campus seminars are available. There is also a freephone support service for students. The aim of the scheme is to prepare students to enter and succeed in undergraduate studies (see Bull, 2000).

In Germany, universities in Lower Saxony have worked together to create an **Access Summer School for Young Women in Science and Engineering**. Although the numbers of women participating in post-compulsory education is continuing to rise in Germany, female students continue to be under-represented in science, engineering and other 'technology-related' subjects. Week-long summer schools for female secondary-school pupils seek to redress the balance by introducing them to subjects in which women are traditionally under-represented. Since 1995, between 30 and 100 female pupils have participated in the summer school each year. The summer school has been evaluated, and shows not only that it is popular, but also enrolment in science and engineering subjects by women have increased (see Kosuch, 2000).

Maths summer schools. South Bank University, London and Staffordshire University, both in the UK, have developed maths summer schools for students who do not possess a GCSE or equivalent qualification in mathematics. Not only is a maths qualification a prerequisite for entry into a range of post-compulsory courses, but overcoming concerns about maths can contribute to developing self-confidence by individuals as learners. These are intensive courses that take place at university sites during the summer months. (See Paczuska (1999) and Thomas and Slack (2000) for further details of these schemes.)

Victoria University has tried to create a 'culturally diverse and inclusive higher education' by developing a range of **policies** that enable the institution to respond flexibly to the needs of individuals and groups who have not traditionally participated in higher education in Australia. (See Ronayne, 2000, for further details.)

Community-based programmes
The **Penderry Project** works in partnership with communities in the poorest areas of South Wales, with the aim of combating the effects of social exclusion on participation in education. Many of these people are not interested in learning, but 'we can reach them as adult students through their concerns for their children, through the abilities, skills, and resources that they apply on a daily basis, to counter social and economic deprivation'. (See Trotman and Pudner, 1998 and 2000.)

The **Cork Northside Education Initiative**, in Ireland promotes equality of access to third-level education for people who are marginalized from mainstream learning opportunities. It has adopted a dual policy of consultation with the community, and educational action based on action research and community development. It is, therefore, an initiative that is comprehensive and complementary. (See Powell 1999, and Forde, 1996.)

Information and guidance
The **Regional Educational Guidance Service for Adults** (REGSA) was set up in 1998 by Waterford Institute for Technology, Ireland, to provide a comprehensive and accessible adult guidance service in the south-east of Ireland. It is targeted proactively on adults at risk of social exclusion, who may be reluctant to access information and guidance. The service is free of charge, and is located in one central and three outreach locations, and there is close networking with other organizations to facilitate inter-agency co-operation. (See Harte and Jordan, 1999; Jordan, 1997; and Waterford Institute of Technology, 1999 for further details.)

Coventry University, UK, has developed two **IT-based guidance packages** to assist potential learners to access post-compulsory education. The first attempts to demystify the process of applying to, and accessing, a university. The second package examines the possibility of making a claim for the Accreditation of Prior Learning (APL). 'Both packages are designed to short-cut the first section of guidance interviews, which is often about ascertaining people's past achievements and aspirations for the future, thus allowing the guidance worker to spend time on action planning' (see Williams, 1999).

Work based learning

Middlesex University, UK, has introduced *work-based learning* as a new field of study in higher education, through Work Based Learning Studies. In order to create further inclusion the concept of 'work' is defined in a broad way: 'all purposeful activity', and includes work in the home and other unpaid activities. 'An inclusive definition of work is therefore important so higher education is not just acknowledging the work of the privileged or the work of the wage earners.' Students register as individuals, community groups or work teams at any level from pre-entry to postgraduate. The core modules are: recognition and accreditation of learning (RAL); programme planning, including a learning agreement; and research methods and work-based projects. (See Costley, 2000 and Doncaster, 2000, for further details.)

Further sources of information

There are many other case studies and examples. The following publications provide further examples:

Preece, J. with Weatherald, C. and Woodrow, M. (eds) (1998) *Beyond the Boundaries: Exploring the Potential of Widening Participation Provision in Higher Education.* Leicester: NIACE.

Thomas, E. and Cooper, M. (eds) (2000) *Changing the Culture of the Campus: Towards an Inclusive Higher Education.* Stoke-on-Trent: Staffordshire University Press.

Thomas, E., Cooper, M. and Quinn, J. (2001) *Access to Higher Education.* Stoke-on-Trent: The Institute for Access Studies and The European Access Network.

Widening Participation and Lifelong Learning: The Journal of The Institute for Access Studies and The European Access Network. Stoke-on-Trent: Staffordshire University Press HYPERLINK http://www.staffs.ac.uk/journal

Woodrow, M. (1998) *From Elitism to Inclusion: Good Practice in Widening Access to Higher Education.* London: CVCP.

Woodrow, M. (forthcoming) *Poverty and Participation: From Elitism to Inclusion II: Widening Access to Higher Education.* London: Universities UK.

Bibliography

Adnett, N. and Coates, G. (1999) 'Mature female entrants to higher education: matching theory, empirical analysis and policy'. Paper presented at the conference *Access: the Changing Face of Further and Higher Education & Lifelong Learning*, Staffordshire University, Stoke-on-Trent, April.

Adnett, N. and Coates, G. (2000) 'Mature female entrants to higher education: closing the gender gap in the UK labour market', *Higher Education Quarterly* 54.2 pp. 187–201.

Ainley, P. (1992) 'On the trail of that illusive first job', *Guardian*, 12 January 1992.

Ainley, P. (1998) 'Higher education in a right state: Professionalising the proletariat or proletarianising the professions' in Jary and Parker (op cit.).

Ainley, P. (1999) *Learning Policy: Towards the Certified Society*. Basingstoke: Macmillan.

Akinbolu, J. (1999) 'HEFCE performance indicators', presentation at SRHE Access Network Seminar, London, 23 June 1999.

Allman, P. (1987) 'Paulo Freire's education approach: a struggle for meaning', in G. Allen (ed.) *Community Education*. Milton Keynes: Open University Press.

Amano, M. (1997) 'Women in higher education' *Higher Education*, September, pp. 215–235.

Anderson, D. (1990) 'Access to university education in Australia 1852–1990: Changes in the undergraduate mix'. *Australian Universities Review*, 1 & 2, 37–50.

Angus, L. (1993) 'The sociology of school effectiveness' in *British Journal of Sociology of Education*, 14 (3), pp. 333–45.

Arulampalam, W. and Booth, A. (1998) 'Labour market flexibility and skills acquisition: Is there a trade-off?', in A. B. Atkinson and J. Hills (eds) *Exclusion, Employment and Opportunity*. CASE paper 4. London: Centre for Analysis of Social Exclusion, London School of Economics.

Ashton, D. and Maguire, M. (1983) *The Vanishing Youth Labour Market*. London: Youthaid Occasional Paper no. 3.

Association of Graduate Recruiters (AGR) (1996) *Graduate Salaries and Vacancies*, summer update. Cambridge: AGR.

Athey, C. (1990) *Extending Thought in Young Children*. London: Paul Chapman Publishing.

Atkinson, A. B. (1998) 'Social exclusion, poverty and unemployment', in Atkinson, A. B. and Hills, J. (eds) *Exclusion, Employment and Opportunity*. CASE paper 4. London: Centre for Analysis of Social Exclusion, London School of Economics.

Atweh, B. and Bland, D. (1999) 'Beyond access and participation towards social justice: the SARUA Project'. *Widening Participation and Lifelong Learning*, 1(1), 27–33.

Atweh, B., Kemmis, S. and Weeks, P. (eds) (1998) *Action Research in Practice: Partnerships for Social Justice in Education*. London and New York: Routledge.

Ball, C. (1995) 'Developing the learning society'. Presidential address. North of England Conference, University of York, 4 January.

Ball, S. J. (1990) *Politics and Policy-Making in Education: Explorations in Policy Sociology*. London and New York: Routledge.

Ball, S. J. (1993) 'Education, majorism and "the Curriculum of the Dead"', *Curriculum Studies*, 1(2), 195–214.

Ball, S. J. (1993) cited in Coffield and Williamson, 1997b.

Banks, M., Bates, I., Breakwell, G., Bynner, J., Emler, N., Jamieson, L., and Roberts, K. (1992) *Careers and Identities*. Milton Keynes and Philadelphia: Open University Press.

Batey, P., Brown, P. and Corver, M. (1998) 'Participation in higher education: a geodemographic perspective on the potential for further expansion in student numbers'. Paper presented at 38th Congress of the European Regional Science Association, 28 August–1 September, Vienna.

Beck, U. (1992) *The Risk Society: Towards a New Modernity*. London: Sage.

Bekhradnia, B. (2000a) 'A national model for monitoring institutional progress'. Key note speech at the ninth EAN Conference *Access to Higher Education: The Unfinished Business: An Evaluation for the Millennium*. University of Santiago de Compostela, Spain, 3–6 September.

Bekhradnia, B. (2000b) 'HEFCEs widening participation strategy'. Key note speech at the conference *Action on Access: From Practice into Policy*. Nottingham: Nottingham Trent University, 6 October.

Bell, D. (1974) *The Coming of Post-Industrial Society: A Venture in Social Forecasting*. London: Heinemann Educational.

Berg, I. (1970) *Education and Jobs: The great training robbery*. Harmondsworth: Penguin.

Berghman, J. (1995) 'Social exclusion in Europe: policy context and analytical framework', in Room (a).

Blackmore, L. and Heynen, M. (1998) *Evaluation of ACCESS 2000: Final Report*. Waterford: Waterford Institute of Technology.

Blehein, T. and O'Grady, M. (eds) (2000) *Community Education and Community Development: How it Happened in ACCESS 2000*. Waterford: Waterford Institute of Technology.

Blicharski, J. R. D. (1998) 'Disadvantaged youngsters: raising awareness, aspiration and access through summer school', in J. Preece (ed.) *Beyond the Boundaries: Exploring the Potential of Widening Provision in Higher Education*. Leicester: NIACE.

Blicharski, J. R. D. (2000) 'Targeting, tutoring and tracking potential undergraduates from disadvantaged backgrounds', in Thomas and Cooper.

Blunkett, D. (1999) *Social Exclusion and the Politics of Opportunity – A Mid-Term Progress Check*. 16th June 1999, London: DfEE HYPERLINK http://www.dfee.gov.uk

Bourdieu, P. and Passeron, J.C. (1977) *Reproduction in Education, Society and Culture*. London and Beverly Hills: Sage.

Bowles, S. and Gintis, H. (1976) *Schooling in Capitalist America*. London: Routledge and Kegan Paul.

Brennan, J. and McGeevor, P. (1988) *Graduates at Work: Degree Courses and the Labour Market*. London: Jessica Kingsley Publishers.

Brookfield, S. (1993) 'Self directed learning, political clarity, and the critical practice of adult education'. *Adult Education Quarterly*, 43(4), summer, 227–42.

Brown, P. and Scase, R. (1994) *Higher Education and Corporate Realities: Class, Culture and the Decline of Graduate Careers*. London: University College London Press.

Brown, P. *et al.* (1997) 'The transformation of education and society: an introduction', in Halsey *et al.*

Bruffee, K. A. (1995) *Collaborative Learning: Higher Education, Independence and the Authority of Knowledge*. Baltimore and London: Johns Hopkins University Press.

Bull, D. (2000) 'Overcoming social exclusion in higher education through the provision of a distance education enabling programme'. *Widening Participation and Lifelong Learning*, 2(2), 26–32.

Bulmer, M. and Rees, A. M. (eds) (1996) *Citizenship Today: The Contemporary Relevance of T. H. Marshall*. London and Pennsylvania: UCL Press Limited.

Burgess, R. G. (ed.) (1997) *Beyond the First Degree: Graduate Education, Lifelong Learning and Careers*. Buckingham: SRHE and Open University Press.

Bynner, J. M. and Roberts, K. (1991) *Youth and Work: Transition to Employment in England and Germany*. London: Anglo-German Foundation.

Callaghan, P. (2000) 'Equality, change and institutional barriers', in Thomas and Cooper.

Candy, P. *et al.* (1994) *Developing Lifelong Learners Through Undergraduate Education*. Canberra: AGPS.

Carmeli, A. (2000a) 'Social inclusion: a national example of good practice', in Thomas and Cooper.

Carmeli, A. (2000b) 'PERACH: A countrywide tutoring and mentoring scheme from Israel'. *Widening Participation and Lifelong Learning*, 2(1), 46–8.

Carter, J., Fenton, S. and Modood, T. (1999) *Ethnicity and Employment in Higher Education*. London: Policy Studies Institute.

Casazza, M. (2000) Keynote speech at the ninth EAN Conference *Access to Higher Education: The Unfinished Business: An Evaluation for the Millennium*. University of Santiago de Compostela, Spain, 3–6 September.

Charter, D. (2000) 'Degree of elitism persists at universities'. *The Times*, 6 October.

Clancy, P. (1982) *Access to College: Patterns of continuity and change*. Dublin: Higher Education Authority (HEA).

Clancy, P. (1982) *Participation in Higher Education*. Dublin: HEA.

Clancy, P. (1988) *Who goes to College?* Dublin: HEA.

Clancy, P. (1995) *Access to College: Patterns of Continuity and Change*. Dublin: HEA.

Clarke, L. (1980) *Occupational Choice: A Critical Review of Research in the UK*. London: Department of Employment, Careers Service Branch.

Clay, M. M. (1982) *Observing Young Readers*. Exeter, New Hampshire: Heinemann.

Coates, G. and Adnett, N. (2000) 'Higher education, performance indicators and gender inequality in the UK labour market: the case for female mature entrants'. *Widening Participation and Lifelong Learning*, 2(3), 7–13.

Coffield, F. and Vignoles, A. (1997) 'Report 5: widening participation in higher education by ethnic minorities, women and alternative students', in NCIHE.

Coffield, F. and Williamson, B. (eds) (1997a) *Repositioning Higher Education*. Buckingham: SRHE and Open University Press.

Coffield, F. and Williamson, B. (1997b) 'The challenges facing higher education', in Coffield and Williamson (op. cit.).

Coleman, J. S. (1988) 'Social capital in the creation of human capital', in *American Journal of Sociology*, 94 (suppl. 95), S95–S120.

Connor, H., Aston, J. and Blanden, J. (1999) *Making the Right Choice: An Analysis of the Scottish Applicants*. Brighton: Institute of Employment Studies.

Connor, H., Pearson, R., Court, G. and Jagger, N. (1996) *University Challenge:*

Student Choices in the 21ˢᵗ Century. Report 306. Brighton: Institute for Employment Studies.

Coolahan, J. (ed.) (1994) *Report on National Education Convention*. Dublin: Government Publications Office.

Costley, C. (2000) 'Work based learning: an accessible curriculum'. *Widening Participation and Lifelong Learning*, 2(2), 33–9.

Cotterill, P. and Waterhouse, R. L. (1998) 'Speaking confidentially, or "How long have I got?" The demise of the personal tutorial in higher education', in Jary and Parker.

Coupland, D. (1996) *Generation X: Tales for an Accelerated Culture*. London: Abacus.

CVCP (1999) *Briefing Note: Widening Participation*. Summer 1999. London: Committee of Vice-chancellors and Principals of the Universities of the UK.

Dahrendorf, R. (1987) 'The erosion of citizenship and its consequences for us all'. *New Statesman and Society*, 12 June.

Danermark, B. (1999) 'Including disabled students in higher education: a vice-chancellor's perspective'. Paper presented to OECD Conference on Higher Education and Disability, Grenoble, March 24–26. Paris: Organization for Economic Co-operation and Development.

Davie, R., Butler, N. and Goldstein, H. (1972) *From Birth to Seven*. Harlow: Longman.

Davies, C. (2000) 'National co-ordination through action on access'. Keynote speech at the conference *Action on Access: From Practice into Policy*. Nottingham: Nottingham Trent University, 6 October.

Davies, D. (2000) 'Lifelong learning in a global society: providential or pathological?', in Thomas and Cooper.

De Koning, K. and Martin, M. (eds) (1996) *Participatory Research in Health: Issues and Experiences*. London and New Jersey: Zed Books; Johannesburg: NPPHCH.

Dearne Valley Partnership (1995) *Dearne Valley Tour Guide*. Rotherham: Dearne Valley Partnership/City Challenge.

DEET (1990) *A Fair Chance for All: Higher Education That's Within Everyone's Reach*. Canberra: Australian Government Publishing Service.

Department of Education (Ireland) (1995) *Charting Our Education Future*. White Paper. Dublin: Government Publications Office.

Department of Education (Ireland) (1998) *Adult Education in an Era of Lifelong Learning*. Green Paper. Dublin: Government Publications Office.

DES (1973) *Adult Education: A Plan for Development*. The Russell Report. London: HMSO.

DETYA (1997) *Selected Higher Education Student Statistics: Preliminary*. Canberra: Australian Government Publishing Service.

DETYA (1999) *Equity in Higher Education*. Canberra: Australian Government Publishing Service.

DfEE (1998a) *The Learning Age: A Renaissance for a New Britain*. Cm 3790. London: The Stationery Office.

DfEE (1998b) *Action on Age: Report of the Consultation on Age Discrimination in Employment*. London: Department for Education and Employment.

DfEE (1998c) *Participation in Education and Training by 16-18 year olds in England: 1987 to 1997*, Statistical Bulletin 335/98. London: DfEE.

DfEE (1999) *Learning to Succeed: A New Framework for Post-16 Learning*. London: HMSO.

DfEE (2000) *Performance Tables 2000: GCSE/GNVQ Information*. HYPERLINK http://www.dfee.gov.uk

DfEE, IER, AgCAS and CSU (1999) *Moving on: short report on graduate careers three years after graduation*. London: DfEE.

Doncaster, K. (2000) 'Accrediting the experience of work-based learners: a case study'. *Journal of Access and Credit Studies*, 2(2), 269–77.

Dore, R. (1976) *The Diploma Disease: Education, Qualification and Development*. London: Allen and Unwin.

Douglas, J. W. B. (1964) *The Home and the School*. London: MacGibbon and Kee.

Duffy, K. (1995) *Social Exclusion and Human Dignity in Europe*. Strasbourg: Council for Europe.

Dugdale, K. (1997) 'Mass higher education: mass graduate employment in the 1990s', in Burgess.

Edwards, A. (1983) 'The reconstruction of post-compulsory education and training in England and Wales'. *European Journal of Education*, 1, 173–93.

Edwards, R. (1993) *Mature Women Students: Separating or Connecting Family and Education*. London: Taylor and Francis.

Eggins, H. (1997) *Women as Leaders and Managers in Higher Education*. Buckingham: Society for Research in Higher Education and Open University Press.

Essen, J. and Wedge, P. (1982) *Continuities in Childhood Disadvantage*. London: Heinemann.

FEDA (1998) *Programme: First Lessons for the Widening Participation Strategic Partnership*. Conference, held 18 November 1998. London: Further Education Development Agency.

Feetham, V. (2000) 'Working from where they are at: successful approaches to engaging the excluded with lifelong learning'. Paper presented at British Educational Research Association Annual Conference, 7–9 September, Cardiff University.

FEFC (1996) *Inclusive Learning: Report of the Learning Difficulties and/or Disabilities Committee* (Tomlinson Report). Coventry: Further Education Funding Council.

FEFC (1997a) *Widening Participation in Further Education Statistical Evidence*. London: The Stationery Office.

FEFC (1997b) *How to Widen Participation: A Guide to Good Practice*. Coventry: FEFC.

FEFC (1997c) *Identifying and Addressing Needs*. Coventry: FEFC.

FEFC (1998) *Annual Report 1997/8*. Coventry: Further Education Funding Council.

Ferrier, F. and Heagney, M. (2000) 'Dealing with the dynamics of disadvantage: Options for equity planning in higher education institutions'. *Widening Participation and Lifelong Learning*, 2(1), 5–14.

Finch, J. (1984) *Education as Social Policy*. Harlow: Longman.

Forde, C. (1996) *Making Education Work in Cork's Northside: A Strategy Statement*. Cork: Northside Education Initiative.

Freire, P. (1972) *Pedagogy of the Oppressed*. Harmondsworth: Penguin.

French Ministry of National Education, Research and Technology (1999) *Les Enseignants du Second Degre dans les Colleges et Lycées Publiques en 1997–1998*, 99(11), April.

Fryer, R. (1997) *Learning for the Twenty-First Century. First Report of the National Advisory Group for Continuing Education and Lifelong Learning*. London: DfEE.

Fryer, R. (1999) *Creating Learning Cultures: Next steps in achieving the Learning Age. Second Report of the National Advisory Group for Continuing Education and Lifelong Learning*. London: DfEE.

Fryer, R. (1999b) Keynote address at the conference *Access: The Changing Face of Further and Higher Education and Lifelong Learning*. Staffordshire University, April.

Galbraith, J. K. (1967) *The New Industrial State*. London: Hamish Hamilton.

Gallagher, A. *et al.* (1993) *Mature Students in Higher Education: How Institutions can Learn from Experience*. London: University of East London.

Gallie, D. (1994) 'Patterns of skill change: upskilling, deskilling or polarisation?, in R. Penn, M. Rose and J. Rubery (eds) *Skill and Occupation Change*. Oxford: Oxford University Press.

Gallie, D. and White, M. (1993) *Employee Commitment and the Skills Revolution*. London: Policy Studies Institute.

Gamarnikow, E. and Green, A. (1999) 'Developing social capital: dilemmas, possibilities and limitations in education', in Hayton (a).

Gibbons, M. *et al.* (1994) *The New Production of Knowledge: the dynamics of science and research in contemporary societies*. London: Sage.

Gillborn, D. and Gipps, C. (1996) *Recent Research on the Achievements of Ethnic Minority Pupils*. London: HMSO.

Gipps, C. (1994) *Beyond Testing: Towards a theory of educational assessment*. London: Falmer Press.

Gleeson, D. (1996) 'In the public interest: post-compulsory education in a postmodern age', *Journal of Education Policy*, 11(5), 513–26.

Glennerster, H. (1998) 'Tackling poverty at its roots? Education' in Oppenheim, C. (ed.) *An Inclusive Society: strategies for tackling poverty*. London: Institute for Public Policy Research.

Goddard, A. (1999) 'Access Bait Fails to Lure Poor', in *Times Higher Educational Supplement*, 4 June 1999, p. 1.

Goddard-Patel, P. and Whitehead, S. (2000a) 'The costs of "failure" in further education: the case of Bilston Community College'. Paper presented at British Educational Research Association Annual Conference, 7–9 September, Cardiff University.

Goddard-Patel, P. and Whitehead, S. (2000b) 'Examining the crisis of further education: an analysis of "failing" colleges and failing policies'. *Policy Studies* 21 (3), 191–213.

Goldthorpe, J. H. and Llewellyn, C. (1980) *Social Mobility and Class Structure in Modern Britain*. Oxford: Clarendon Press.

Gorman, T. and Fernandes, C. (1992) *Reading in Recession*. Slough: NFER.

Grace, G. (1984) *Education in the City*. London: Routledge and Kegan Paul.

Grant, D. (1989) *Learning Relations*. London and New York: Routledge.

Green, A., Wolf, A. and Leney, T. (1999) *Convergence and Divergence in European Education and Training Systems*. London: University of London Institute of Education.

Gregg, P. and Machin, S. (1997) 'Childhood disadvantage and success of failure in the youth labour market'. Mimeo.

Grimble, R. J., Aglionby, J. and Quan, J. (1994) 'Tree resources and environmental policy: A stakeholder approach', in *NRI Socio-Economic Series*, no. 7. Chatham: Natural Resources Institute.

Grimston, J. and Waterhouse, R. (2000) 'Students could pay £60,000 for degrees', *The Sunday Times*, 20 February, p. 6.

Guba, E. G. and Lincoln, Y. S. (1989) *Fourth Generation Evaluation*. Newbury Park, California: Sage.

Gutteridge, R. (2000) 'Evaluating the role of life skills in successful participation'. Paper prepared for the ninth EAN Conference *Access to Higher Education: The Unfinished Business: An evaluation for the Millennium*. University of Santiago de Compostela, Spain, 3-6 September.

Hager, P. (1998) 'Recognition of informal learning: challenges and issues'. *Journal of Vocational Education and Training*, 50(4), 521–35.

Hague, H. (2000) '1.2% of profs ... 11% of the UK workforce'. *THES*, 14 July, p. 20.

Hall, S. and Held, D. (1989) 'Left and rights'. *Marxism Today*, June.

Halsey, A. H. (1986) *Change in British Society* (3rd edn). Oxford: Oxford University Press.

Halsey, A. H. (1993) *Trends in Access and Equity in Higher Education*. Paris: OECD (Mimeo).

Halsey, A. H. (1995) 'Dons' decline reviewed', in F. Coffield (ed.) *Higher Education in a Learning Society*. Durham: Durham University School of Education for DfEE, ESRC and HEFCE.

Halsey, A. H. (1997) 'Trends in access and equity in higher education: Britain in international perspectives', in A. H. Halsey (ed.) *Education, Culture, Economy, Society*. Oxford: Oxford University Press.

Halsey, A. H., Lauder, H., Brown, P. and Wells, A. (eds) (1997) *Education: Culture, Economy and Society*. Oxford: Oxford University Press.

Handy, C. and Aitken, R. (1986) *Understanding Schools as Organizations*. Harmondsworth: Penguin.

Handy, C. (1985) *Understanding Organisations* (3rd edn). Harmondsworth: Penguin.

Hargrave, L. and Tudor, P. (2000) 'Community learning: experience in a deprived area'. Paper presented at British Educational Research Association Annual Conference, 7–9 September, Cardiff University.

Harrison, R., Fraser, L., Braham, J., Davies, C., Robinson, G., Scott, B. and Ryley, P. (eds) (2000) *Ideas for Inclusion: An A to Z for Practitioners*. National Task Group for Widening Participation, with support from HEFCE.

Harte, M. and Jordan, A. (1999) 'A new start: the regional educational guidance service for adults. Waterford Institute of Technology, Ireland'. *Widening Participation and Lifelong Learning*,1(3), 43–5.

Hatcher, R. (1996) 'The limitations of the new social democratic agendas' in Hatcher, R. and Jones, K. (eds) *Education after the Conservatives*. Stoke on Trent: Trentham Books.

Hayton, A. (ed.) (1999a) *Tackling Disaffection and Social Exclusion: Education Perspectives and Policies*. London: Kogan Page Ltd.

Hayton, A. (1999b) 'Boys and girls underachieving: Issues for 14+ education and training' in Hayton (op. cit.).

HEFCE Circular Letter 9/96 *Special Initiative to Encourage High Quality Provision for Students with Learning Difficulties and Disabilities*.

HEFCE (1997) *The Participation in Higher Education of Geodemographic Groups: A Research Report for the National Committee of Inquiry into Higher Education*. Bristol: HEFCE.

HEFCE (1999) (HEFCE 99/33 http://www.hefce.ac.uk).

HEFCE (1999) (HEFCE 99/66 http://www.hefce.ac.uk).

HEFCE (2000) 'New research findings on benefits of widening participation'. *Council Briefing*, February. Bristol: Higher Education Funding Council for England.

HEFCE Circular Letter 7/00 *Mainstream Disability Funding from 2000–1 onwards*. (http://www.hefce.ac.uk).

Held, M. (1998) 'Student Assistance Systems in 13 Western European Countries' in European Access News, no. 5, Spring, pp. 16–17.

Herman, R. and Stringfield, S. (1995) *Ten Promising Programmes for Educating Disadvantaged Students*. Baltimore: Johns Hopkins University Press.

Hirsch, F. (1977) *Social Limits to Growth*. London: Routledge and Kegan Paul.

Hirst, P. (1974) *Knowledge and the Curriculum*. London: Routledge and Kegan Paul.

HMSO (1994) *Competitiveness: Helping Business to Win*. Cm. 2867. London: Her Majesty's Stationery Office.

Hodgson, A. (1999) 'Analysing education and training policies for tackling social exclusion', in Hayton (a).

Hodkinson, P. and Sparkes, A. C. (1997) 'Careership: a sociological theory of career decision making'. *British Journal of Sociology of Education*, **18**(1), 29–44.

Hogarth, T., Macguire, M., Pitcher, J., Purcell, K. and Wilson, R. (1997) *The Participation of Non-traditional Students in Higher Education*. Warwick: The University of Warwick Institute for Employment Research.

Holtermann, S. (1997) 'All our futures: the impact of public expenditure and fiscal policies on children and young people', in A. Walker and C. Walker (eds) *Britain Divided: The Growth of Social Exclusion in the 1980s and 1990s*. London: Child Poverty Action Group.

Hopkins, D., Ainscow, M, and West, M. (1994) *School Improvement in an Era of Change*. London: Cassells.

Hostens, G. (1999) Director General of Secondary Education, Flemish Ministry of Education, Brussels, Belgium and Chair, Education Committee, OECD. Evidence submitted verbally to Skilbeck and Connell, 2000.

Howells, K. (1997) 'Funding after Dearing', speech to CVCP conference, 9 September, London.

Hurd, D. (1989) 'Freedom will flourish where citizens accept responsibilities'. *The Independent*, 13 September.

Independent Committee of Inquiry into Student Finance (Cubie Committee) (1999) Edinburgh: Independent Committee of Inquiry into Student Finance.

Institute for Employment Research (1999) *Moving On: Graduate Careers Three Years after Graduation*. Manchester: CSU Ltd.

Jackson, B. and Marsden, D. (1968) *Education and the Working Class: Some General Themes Raised by a Study of 88 Working Class Children in a Northern Industrial City*. London: Routledge and Kegan Paul.

James, M. (1994) 'Making choices: A New Zealand bridging program in action', in *Proceedings of Issues in Access to Higher Education Conference*. Portland: University of Southern Maine, pp. 213–19.

Jary, D., Gatley, D and Broadbent, L. (1998) 'The US community college: a positive or negative model for UK HE?', in Jary and Parker.

Jary, D. and Parker M. (eds) (1998) *The New Higher Education: Issues and Directions for the Post-Dearning University*. Stoke-on-Trent: Staffordshire University Press.

Jary, D. and Thomas, E. (1999) 'Widening participation and lifelong learning: rhetoric or reality? The role of research and the reflexive practitioner'. *Widening Participation and Lifelong Learning*, 1(1), 3–9.

Jary, D. and Thomas, E. (2000) 'Editorial: the case of Laura Spence: inequalities in entry to elite universities in the UK'. *Widening Participation and Lifelong Learning*, 2(2), 2–5.

Johnston, R. and Croft, F. (1998) 'Mind the gap: widening provision, guidance and cultural change in higher education', in Preece *et al.*

Jones, R. (2000) 'Analysis of the Kennedy Report: the idea of a strategic partnership', in PhD thesis (in progress). Institute for Access Studies, Staffordshire University. A version of this is to be published in 2002 as 'Restrictive practices? Critical reflections on collaboration'. *Post-compulsory Education, 7*(2).

Jordan, A. (1997) *'A New Start': an Integra Action Plan*. Waterford: Waterford Institute of Technology.

Jordan, A. (2000) ''Smartening up" or "dumbing down"? Academic standards in access courses', in Thomas and Cooper (op cit).

Joseph Rowntree Foundation (1995) *Inquiry into Income and Wealth*. York: Rowntree Foundation.

Kaneko, M. (1997) 'Efficiency and equity in Japanese higher education'. *Higher Education, 34*(2), September, 165–82.

Keen, C. and Higgins, T. (1990) *Young People's Knowledge of Higher Education*.

Leeds: Heist/PCAS.

Keen, C. and Higgins, T. (1992) *Adult's Knowledge of Higher Education*. Leeds: Heist/PCAS.

Kelsall, R.K., Poole, A. and Kuhn, A. (1972) *Graduates: The Sociology of an Elite*. London: Methuen.

Kennedy, H. (1997) *Learning Works: Widening Participation in Further Education*. Coventry: FEFC.

Kirton, A. (1999) 'Lessons from access education', in Hayton.

Kivinen, O. and Rinne, R. (1995) *The Social Inheritance of Education: Equality of Educational Opportunity among Young People in Finland*. Helsinki: Statistics Finland.

Kivinen, O. and Rinne, R. (1996) 'Higher education mobility and inequality: the Finnish case'. *European Journal of Education*, 31(3), 289–310.

Knowles, J. (2000) 'Access for few? Student funding and its impact on aspirations to enter higher education'. *Widening Participation and Lifelong Learning*, 2(1), 14–23.

Kommer, A. (1998) *Making it Work: National Report on Germany*. Working Paper. Bielefield: AUE-Hochschule & Weiterbildung.

Korten, D. C. (1984) 'Rural development programming: the learning process approach' in Korten, D. C. and Klauss, R. (eds) *People-centered Development. Contributions Towards Theory and Planning Frameworks*. West Hartford: Kumarian Press.

Kosuch, R. (2000) 'An access summer school: improving participation by young women in technology-related education', in Thomas and Cooper.

Lemlin, R. (2000) 'Access: past, present and future' in Thomas and Cooper (op. cit.).

Leney, T. (1999) 'European approaches to social exclusion', in Hayton (a).

Leney, T., Lucas, N. and Taubman, D. (1998) *Learning Funding: The impact of FEFC funding, evidence from 12 FE colleges*. London: NATFHE / Institute of Education, University of London.

Lipman, (1995) 'Caring as Thinking Inquiry', *Critical Thinking Across the Disciplines*, 15(1), autumn.

Lister, R. (1990) *The Exclusive Society: Citizenship and the Poor*. London: Child Poverty Action Group (CPAG).

Lovett, T. (1975) *Adult Education, Community Development, and the Working Class*. London: Ward Lock.

Lynch, K. and O'Riordan, C. (1998) *Inequality in Higher Education: A Study of Class Barriers*. Dublin: Equality Studies Centre, University College Dublin.

MacBeath, J. and Turner, M. (1990) 'Learning out of school: homework, policy and practice: a research study commissioned by the Scottish Education Department. Glasgow: Jordanhill College.

Macedo, D. (1994) Preface, in P. L. McLaren and C. Lankshear (eds) *Politics of Liberation: Paths from Freire*. London and New York: Routledge.

Machin, S. (1998) 'Childhood disadvantages and intergenerational transmissions of economic status', in Atkinson and Hills.

Mackintosh, M. (1992) 'Introduction', in M. Wuyts, M. Mackintosh and T. Hewitt (eds) *Development Policy and Public Action*. Oxford: Oxford University Press, in association with the Open University.

Mcknight, A. (1999) 'Graduate employability and performance indicators: first destinations and beyond', in *Moving On: Graduate Careers Three Years After Graduation*. London: DfEE, IER, AgCAS and CSU

Madden, N. A., Salvin, R. E., Karweit, N. L. and Dolan, L. J. (1993) 'Success for all: Longitudinal effects of a restructuring program for city elementary schools'. *American Educational Research Journal* 30(1).

Marginson, S. (1999) 'Young adults in higher education', in Dusseldorp Skills Forum (eds) *Australia's Young Adults: The Deepening Divide*. Sydney: Dusseldorp Skills Forum (pp. 169–88).

Marshall, K. (1999) *Are Older People Excluded from Higher Education in the UK?* Stoke-on-Trent: Institute for Access Studies, Staffordshire University.

Marshall, T. H. (1950) *Citizenship and Social Class and Other Essays*. Cambridge: Cambridge University Press.

Mayor, F. (1998) 'Foreword', in *Higher Education in the Twenty-first Century: Vision and Action*. UNESCO World Conference on Higher Education: Paris: UNESCO.

McLaren, P. L. and Lankshear, C. (eds) (1994) *Politics of Liberation: Paths from Freire*. London and New York: Routledge.

Metcalfe, H. (1993) *Non-traditional Students' Experience of Higher Education: A Review of the Literature*. London: Policy Studies Institute.

Millman, V. (1985) 'Breadwinning and babies: a redefinition of careers education', in *Just a Bunch of Girls: Feminist Approaches to Schooling*. Milton Keynes: Open University Press.

Modood, T. (1993) 'The number of ethnic minority students in British higher education: some grounds for optimism'. *Oxford Review of Education*, 19(2), 167–82.

Modood, T., and Shiner, M. (1994) *Ethnic Minorities and Higher Education: Why are there Differential Rates of Entry?* London: Policy Studies Institute/UCAS.

Monash Postgraduate Association Equity Project (1996) *Improving Women's Participation in Research Degrees*. Melbourne: Monash Printing Services.

Montgomery, R. (1995) *Enhancing Stakeholder Participation in Aid Activities*. London: Overseas Development Agency (ODA).

Mortimore, P. and Mortimore, J. (1986) 'Education and social class', in R. Rogers (ed.) *Education and Social Class*. Lewes: Falmer Press.

Mortimore, P. and Whitty, G. (1999) 'School improvement: a remedy for social exclusion?' in Hayton (a).

Mortimore, P. *et al.* (1988) 'The effects of school membership on students' educational outcomes'. *Research Papers in Education*, 3 (1), 3–26.

Moser, (Sir) C. (1999) *Improving Literacy and Numeracy: A Fresh Start*. London: Crown Copyright.

Murphy, B. (2000) 'An introduction to ACCESS 2000', in Blehein and O'Grady.

NACETT (1996) *Skills for 2000: Supplement to the Report on Progress Towards the National Targets for Education and Training*. London: National Advisory Council for Education and Training Targets.

NACETT (1996) Skills for 2000: Supplement to the report on progress towards the national targets for education and training. London: National Advisory Council for Education and Training Targets.

NCIHE (1997) *The Report of the National Committee of Inquiry into Higher Education*. London: HMSO.

Nexelmann, E. (1999) Ministry of Education, Copenhagen, Denmark. Evidence submitted verbally to Skilbeck and Connell, 2000.

O'Brien, A. and O'Byrne, M. (2000) 'Celtic kittens and fat cats', in Thomas and Cooper.

OECD (1995) *Our Children at Risk*. Paris: Organization for Economic Co-operation and Development.

OECD (1997) *Education at a Glance: OECD indicators 1997*. Paris: Organization for Economic Co-operation and Development.

OECD (1997b) *Industrial Competitiveness in the Knowledge-based Economy: The New Role of Governments*. Paris: Organization for Economic Co-operation and Development.

OECD (1998a) *Education at a Glance: OECD indicators 1998*. Paris: Organization for Economic Co-operation and Development.

OECD (1998b) *Redefining Tertiary Education*. Paris: Organization for Economic Co-operation and Development.

OECD (1999a) *Overcoming Exclusion Through Adult Learning*. Paris: Organization for Economic Co-operation and Development.

OECD (1999b) *OECD in Figures*. Paris: Organization for Economic Co-operation and Development.

Osborne, A. F. and Milbank, J. E. (1987) *The Effects of Early Education*. Oxford: Clarendon Press.

Osborne, R. and Leith, H. (2000) *Evaluation of the Targeted Initiative on Widening Access for Young People from Socio-economically Disadvantaged Backgrounds*. Belfast: HEA .

Paczuska, A. (1999) 'The summer maths scheme at South Bank University: a bountiful opportunity'. *Widening Participation and Lifelong Learning*, 1(2), 42–4.

Papadopoulos, G. (1994) *Education 1960–1990: The OECD Perspective*. Paris: Organization for Economic Co-operation and Development.

Papadopoulos, G. (2000) 'New resourcing strategies for an inclusive higher education', in Thomas and Cooper.

Parry, G. (1996) 'Access education in England and Wales 1973–1994: from second chance to third wave'. *Journal of Access Studies*, 11(1), 10–33.

Parry, G. (1997) 'Patterns of participation in higher education in England: a statistical summary and commentary'. *Higher Education Quarterly* 51(1), January, 6–28.

Parry, G. and Fry, H. (1999) 'Widening participation in pursuit of the learning society: Kennedy, Dearing and "The Learning Age"' in Hayton (a).

Parsons, D. and Marshall, V. (1995) *Skills, Qualifications and Utilisation: A Research Review*, Research Series No. 67. Sheffield: DfEE.

Parsons, T. (1959) 'The school class as a social system', in A. Halsey *et al.* (1961) *Education, Economy and Society*. New York: Free Press.

Pascall, G. and Cox, R. (1993) *Women Returning to Higher Education*. Buckingham: The Society for Research into Higher Education and Open University Press.

Patten, J. (1988) *Guardian*, 16 September.

Paul Hamlyn Foundation Report (1993) *Learning to Succeed: A Radical Look at Education Today and a Strategy for the Future*. National Commission on Education. London: Heinemann.

Payne, J. (1998) *Routes at Sixteen: Trends and choices in nineties research*, Report No 55, DfEE Research Briefs. London: DfEE.

Percy, K. A., Langham, M. and Adams, J. G. (1982) *Educational Information, Advisory and Counselling Services for Adults: A Sourcebook*. Lancaster: University of Lancaster.

Poole, M. *et al.* (1997) 'An international study of the gendered nature of academic work: some cross-cultural explorations'. *Higher Education*, 34, October, 373–96.

Poole, M. E. and Spear, R. H. (1997) 'Policy issues in postgraduate education: an Australian perspective' in Burgess.

Postle, G., Bull, D. and Clarke, J. (1997) 'Funding of equity: the Australian experience'. Paper presented to the sixth European Access Network Convention, University of Cork.

Postle, G., Clarke, J., Skuja, E., Bull, D., Batorowicz, K. and Cann, H. (1995) *Towards Excellence in Diversity: Educational equity in the Australian higher education sector in 1995*. Toowoomba: University of Southern Queensland Press.

Powell, F. (1999) 'Adult education, cultural empowerment and social equality: the

Cork Northside Education Initiative'. *Widening Participation and Lifelong Learning*, 1(1), 20–7.

Preece, J. (1999a) *Combating Social Exclusion in University Adult Education*. Hampshire: Ashgate.

Preece, J. (1999b) 'Difference and the discourse of inclusion'. *Widening Participation and Lifelong Learning*, 1(2), 16–23.

Preece, J. with Weatherald, C. and Woodrow, M. (eds) (1998) *Beyond the Boundaries. Exploring the potential of widening participation provision in higher education*. Leicester: NIACE.

Purcell, K. and Pitcher, J. (1996) *Great Expectations: The New Diversity of Graduate Skills and Aspirations*. Manchester: Association of Graduate Careers Advisory Services (AGCAS)/Higher Education Careers Services Unit (CSU).

Purcell, K., Hogarth, T., Pitcher, J., and Jacobs, C. (1999) *Graduate Opportunities, Social Class and Age: Employers' Recruitment Strategies in the New Graduate Labour Market*. London: Council for Industry and Higher Education (CIHE).

Putnam, R. D., Leonardi, R. and Nanetti, R. (1993) *Making Democracy Work: Civic Traditions in Modern Italy*. Princeton, NJ: Princeton University.

Ramsden, B. (1997) Paper from a seminar on Widening Participation in Higher Education held on 27 March 1997, cited in Coffield and Vignoles (1997).

Regional Office Staffordshire University (2000) 'Employees you can bank on'. *Regional Agenda @ Staffordshire University*, 1, Spring.

Reich, R. B. (1993) *The Work of Nations*. London: Simon & Schuster.

Robbins, D. (1993) 'The practical importance of Bourdieu's analyses of higher education'. *Studies in Higher Education*, 18(2), 151–63.

Robbins, L. (chair) (1963) *Higher Education*. Report of the Committee appointed by the Prime Minister under the chairmanship of Lord Robbins.

Robertson, D. (1994) *Choosing to Change: Extending Access, Choice and Mobility in Higher Education*. London: HEQC.

Robertson, D. (1997) 'Growth without equity? Reflections on the consequences for social cohesion of faltering progress on access to higher education'. *Journal of Access Studies*, 13(1), pp. 31–81.

Robertson, D. and Hillman, J. (1997) 'Widening participation in higher education by students from lower socio-economic groups and students with disabilities', in NCIHE.

Rogaly, J. (1988) 'The active citizen for all parties'. *Financial Times*, 5 October.

Ronayne, J. (2000) 'Creating a culturally diverse and inclusive higher education: an Australian example', in Thomas and Cooper.

Room, G. (1995a) (ed.) *Beyond the Threshold: the measurement and analysis of social exclusion*. Bristol: The Policy Press.

Room, G. (1995b) 'Poverty and social exclusion: the new European agenda for policy and research' in Room (a).

Roper, B., Ross, A. and Thomson, D. (2000) 'Locked out'. *Guardian Education*, 2 May, pp. 10–11.

Rowe, K. J. (1995) 'Factors affecting students' progress in reading: key findings from a longitudinal study of literacy'. *Teaching and Learning: An International Journal of Early Literacy*, 1(2), 57–110 .

Salter, B. and Tapper, T. (1994) *The State and Higher Education*. Ilford: Woburn Press.

Sand, B. (1998) 'Lifelong learning: vision, policy and practice'. *Journal of Access and Credit Studies*, 1(1), winter, 17–40.

Schnitzer, K., Isserstedt, W., Mussig-Trapp, P. and Schreiber, J. (1999) *Student Life in Germany: The Socio-economic Picture. Summary of the 15th Social Survey of the Deutsches Studentenwerk*. Bonn: Bundeministerium für Bildung und Forschung.

Schweinhart, L. J. and Weikart, D. P. (1997) 'The high/scope pre-school curriculum comparison study through age 23'. *Early Childhood Research Quarterly*, **12**, 117–43.

Scott, P. (1984) *The Crisis of the University*. London: Croom-Helm.

Scott, P. (1995) *The Meanings of Mass Higher Education*. Buckingham: The Society for Research into Higher Education and Open University Press.

Scottish Executive (2000) *Scotland the Learning Nation: Helping students*. Edinburgh: Scottish Executive. HYPERLINK http://www.scotland.gov.uk/consultations/lifelonglearning

Sharp, A. M. (1993) 'The community of inquiry: education for democracy thinking'. *Journal of Philosophy for Children*, **9**(2), 31–7.

Shaw, J. (1999a) 'Education and students with learning disabilities' in *Access*, February/March, pp. 23–5.

Shaw, J. (1999b) Personal communication, cited in Skilbeck and Connell, 2000.

Shirtliff, E, (1996) *Progression to Higher Education from Advanced GNVQ Business: A Case Study*. Leeds: Centre for Policy Studies in Education, University of Leeds.

Sinclair, H. and Dale, L. (2000) 'The effect of student tuition fees on the diversity of intake within a Scottish new university'. Paper presented at British Educational Research Association Annual Conference, 7–9 September, Cardiff University .

Singh, R. (1990) 'Ethnic minority experiences in higher education'. *Higher Education Quarterly*, **44**(4), 344–59.

Skilbeck, M. and Connell, H. (2000) *Access and Equity in Higher Education: An International Perspective on Issues and Strategies*. Dublin: HEA.

Slack, K. and Thomas, E. (2000) *Aiming High: Good Practice and Sustainability*. Stoke-on-Trent: Institute for Access Studies, Staffordshire University.

Smith, D., Scott, P. and Bargh, C. (1995) 'Standard systems, non-standard students: the impact of consolidation on access to higher education'. *Journal of Access Studies*, **10**(2), 120–36.

Smith, G. (1987) 'Whatever happened to EPAs?' *Oxford Review of Education*, **13**(1), 23–38.

Smith, J. (2000) 'Reaching out to the region: What works? Evaluating higher education strategies for widening participation in the context of a national policy initiative'. *Widening Participation and Lifelong Learning*, **2**(3), 23–31.

Smith, T. and Noble, M. (1995) *Education Divides: Poverty and Schooling in the 1990s*. London: Child Poverty Action Group.

Social Exclusion Unit (1998) *Truancy and Social Exclusion*. London: The Stationery Office.

Sommerland, H. and Sanderson, P. (1997) 'The legal labour market and the training needs of women returners in the UK'. *Journal of Vocational Education and Training*, **49**(1), 45–64.

Sowinska, S. (1993) 'Yer own motha wouldna reckarnized ya: surviving in the "knowledge factory"', in M. M. Tokarczyk and E. A. Fay (eds) *Working-class Women in the Academy: Labourers in the Knowledge Factory*. Amherst: University of Massachusetts Press.

Spedding, T. and Gregson, M. (2000) 'Widening participation: a missing curriculum? Some observations on the policy and practice of widening participation in further education in the UK'. Paper presented at British Educational Research Association Annual Conference, 7–9 September, Cardiff University.

Staffordshire Careers Research and Development Team (2000a) *Some Baseline Data about the First Year of the Education Maintenance Allowance Pilot Scheme in Stoke on Trent*. Stafford: Staffordshire Careers.

Staffordshire Careers Research and Development Team (2000b) *An Analysis of the Needs of Young People in Staffordshire including Stoke on Trent*. Stafford:

Staffordshire Careers.

Staffordshire Careers (2000c) *Staffordshire Careers Annual School Leaver Activity Survey*. Stafford: Staffordshire Careers.

Staffordshire Strategic Partnership (1998) *Making Learning Work for Staffordshire*. Bid submitted to the Further Education Funding Council (FEFC).

Stoll, L. and Fink, D. (1996) *Changing Our Schools*. Buckingham: Open University Press.

Storan, J. (2000) 'An analysis of HEIs initial statements on widening participation'. Keynote speech at the conference *Action on Access: From Practice into Policy*. Nottingham: Nottingham Trent University, 6 October.

Stringer, E. (1996). *Action Research: A Handbook for Practitioners*. California: Sage Publications.

Sutton Trust (2000) *Entry to Leading Universities*. Report by the Sutton Trust.

Taylor, G. (1999) 'Graduate recruitment and social class', *Update on Inclusion*, 2, 15–16.

Taylor, P. (1992) 'Ethnic group data and applications to higher education'. *Higher Education Quarterly*, 46(4), 359–73.

Taylor, P. (2000) 'The engagement of minority ethnic groups in higher education: experiences from the UK', in Thomas and Cooper.

Taylor, R. (2000) 'Continuing education practice, lifelong learning and the construction of an accessible higher education in the United Kingdom'. *Widening Participation and Lifelong Learning*, 2(3), 14–22.

Teare, R., Davies, D. and Sandelands, E. (1998) *The Virtual University*. London: Cassell.

Teichler, U. (1988) *Changing Patterns of Higher Education Systems: The Experience of Three Decades*. London: Jessica Kingsley.

THES (1999) 'Student entry to HE up, mature students down. *Times Higher Educational Supplement*, October 15, p. 20.

THES (2000) 'How many disabled staff at your university?' *Times Higher Education Supplement*, July 14, p. 20.

Thomas, A. (1996) 'What is development management?' *Journal of International Development*, 8(1), 95–100.

Thomas, E. (1996) *Barriers to Accessing Higher Education: A Study of Attitudes and Views*. Study carried out on behalf of the Dearne Valley Partnership, Barnsley and Doncaster TEC and Rotherham TEC. Sheffield: University of Sheffield Regional Office.

Thomas, E. (2000) ' "Bums on seats" or "listening to voices": evaluating widening participation initiatives using participatory action research'. *Studies in Continuing Education*, 22(1), 95–113.

Thomas, E. (forthcoming) *The Voluntary Sector: Social Policy and Evaluation*. Pearson Education.

Thomas, E. and Cooper, M. (eds) (2000) *Changing the Culture of the Campus: Towards an Inclusive Higher Education*. Stoke-on-Trent: Staffordshire University Press.

Thomas, E. and Jones, R. (2000) 'Social exclusion and higher education', in Thomas and Cooper (2000).

Thomas, E. and Slack, K, (1999a) *Aiming High: Evaluation Report 1998–1999*. Stoke-on-Trent: Institute for Access Studies, Staffordshire University.

Thomas, E. and Slack, K, (1999b) *'Money Matters' Evaluation*. Staffordshire Concordat. Stoke-on-Trent: Institute for Access Studies, Staffordshire University.

Thomas, E. and Slack, K. (1999c) *Staffordshire Quality Learning Service NVQ Scheme: An Evaluation of the Perceived Impact of Work-based learning for Support Staff in Schools*. Stoke-on-Trent: Institute for Access Studies,

Staffordshire University.

Thomas, E. and Slack K. (2000a) *Pupils, Schools and the World of Work: Preliminary Baseline Report*. Prepared for Staffordshire Partnership. Stoke on Trent: Institute for Access Studies, Staffordshire University.

Thomas, E. and Slack, K, (2000b) *Aiming High: Evaluation Report 1999–2000*. Stoke-on-Trent: Institute for Access Studies, Staffordshire University.

Thomas, E. and Slack, K, (2000c) *Staffordshire Universities Maths Summer School (SUMSS). Draft Evaluation Report 1: Improving the Process*. Stoke-on-Trent: Institute for Access Studies, Staffordshire University.

Thomas, E. and Slack, K. (2000d) 'Developing an evaluation framework: assessing the contribution of community-based and work-based approaches to lifelong learning amongst educationally marginalised adults'. Paper presented at the ninth EAN Conference *Access to Higher Education: The Unfinished Business: An Evaluation for the Millennium*. University of Santiago de Compostela, Spain, 3–6 September.

Thomas, E. and Slack, K. (forthcoming) 'Developing an evaluation framework: assessing the contribution of community-based and work-based approaches to lifelong learning amongst educationally marginalised adults'. Stoke-on-Trent: Institute for Access Studies, Staffordshire University.

Thomas, E., Jones, R., Johnson, M. and Spencer, P. (1999) *Staffordshire Strategic Partnership*. Stafford: Stafford College.

Thomas, E., Wyn Williams, S., Hallsworth, A. and Chilton, H. (1999/2000) 'Expanding the university interface: some recent initiatives in Staffordshire'. *The London Journal of Canadian Studies: Special Issue – Meeting Community Needs: Education in Canada and Europe*, 15, pp. 56–67.

Thomas, S. *et al.* (1997) 'Differential secondary school effectiveness: comparing the performance of different pupil groups'. *British Educational Research Journal*, 23(4), 451–69.

Tight, M. (1998) 'Education, education, education! The vision of lifelong learning in the Kennedy, Dearing and Fryer reports'. *Oxford Review of Education*, 24(4), 473–85.

Tizard, J., Schofield, W. and Hewison, J. (1982) 'Symposium: reading-collaboration between teachers and parents in assisting children's reading'. *British Journal of Educational Psychology*, 52(1), 1–15.

Tonks, D. (1999) 'Access to UK higher education, 1991–98: using geodemographics', in *Widening Participation and Lifelong Learning*, 1(2), 6–16.

Tripodi, L.F. (1994) 'Summer start: a program to equalize accessibility to higher education for 'at risk' students', in *Proceedings of Issues in Access to Higher Education Conference*. Portland: University of Southern Maine, pp. 64–71.

Trotman, C. and Pudner, H. (1998) 'What's the point? Questions that matter in community-based projects designed to counter social exclusion and increase participation in continuing education', in Preece *et al.*

Trotman, C. and Pudner, H. (2000) 'Higher education in the context of social exclusion: community collaboration at all levels', in Thomas and Cooper.

Trow, M. (1970) 'Reflections on the transition from élite to mass higher education'. *Daedalus: Journal of the American Academy of Arts and Sciences*, 90(1), 1–42.

Tuckett, A. and Sargant, N. (1996) *Creating Two Nations? Headline Findings on Lifelong Learning from the NIACE/GALLUP Survey*. Leicester: NIACE.

UNESCO (1998) *Higher Education in the Twenty-first Century: Vision and Action*. World Conference on Higher Education. Final Report. Paris: UNESCO.

UCAS (1997) *Annual Report*. Cheltenham: Universities and Colleges Admissions Service (see also HYPERLINK http://www.ucas.ac.uk).

UCAS (1998) *Annual Report*. Cheltenham: Universities and Colleges Admissions

Service (see also HYPERLINK http://www.ucas.ac.uk).

Wailey, T. and Simpson, R. (1999) 'Assessment of prior learning as a means of guidance on credit-based systems in higher education'. *Widening Participation and Lifelong Learning*, 1(3), 35–42.

Wakeford, N. (1993) 'Beyond educating Rita: mature students and access courses'. *Oxford Review of Education*, 19(2), 217–30.

Ward, K. and Steele, T. (1999) 'From marginality to expansion: an overview of recent trends and developments in widening participation in England and Scotland'. *Journal of Access and Credit Studies*, 1(2), summer, 192–204.

Waterford Institute of Technology (1999) *Looking for Something in the Dark.* Waterford: Integra.

Waterhouse, R. (2000) 'Science graduates earn best salaries'. *The Sunday Times*, 20 February, p. 6.

Waters, B. (2000) 'Addressing the under-representation of disabled students in higher education'. Keynote speech at the ninth EAN Conference Access to *Higher Education: The Unfinished Business: An Evaluation for the Millennium.* University of Santiago de Compostela, Spain, 3–6 September.

Watson, D. and Taylor, R. (1998) *Lifelong Learning and the University: A Post-Dearing Agenda.* Brighton: Falmer Press.

Watts, A. G. and Stevens, B. (1999) 'The relationship between career guidance and financial guidance'. *Widening Participation and Lifelong Learning*, 1(3), 11–19.

Whitburn, J., Mealing, M. and Cox, C. (1976) *People in Polytechnics.* Guildford: SRHE.

Whitty, G., Power, S., Gamarnikow, E., Aggleton, P., Tyrer, P. and Youdell, D. (1999) 'Health, housing and education: tackling multiple disadvantage', in Hayton (a).

Williams, F. (1989) *Social Policy: A Critical Introduction: Issues of Race, Gender and Class.* Cambridge: Polity/Basil Blackwell.

Williams, G. (1998) 'Current debates on the funding of mass higher education in the UK' *European Journal of Education*, 33, (1), 77–87.

Williams, J. (1997) 'The discourse of access: the legitimation of selectivity', in Williams, J. (ed.) *Negotiating Access to Higher Education: The Discourse of Selectivity and Equity.* Buckingham: The Society for Research into Higher Education and Open University Press.

Williams, S. (1999) 'Knowledge of the university, its provision and procedures: dispelling ignorance, inside and outwith the institution'. *Widening Participation and Lifelong Learning*, 1(3), 20–5.

Woodhead, C. (1996) 'Boys who learn to be losers'. *The Times* 6 March.

Wintour, P. (1997) 'Blair hits at "cynicism" as poll shows people's trust waning' *The Observer*, 23 November p.1.

Woodley, A. *et al.* (1987) *Choosing to Learn* : Adults in Education. Milton Keynes: SRHE/Open University Press.

Woodrow, M. (1998) *From Elitism to Inclusion: Good Practice in Widening Access to Higher Education.* London: CVCP.

Woodrow, M. (1999a) 'The struggle for the soul of lifelong learning'. *Widening Participation and Lifelong Learning*, 1(1), 9–13.

Woodrow, M. (1999b) 'Student finance: access opportunity'. Paper for the Independent Committee of Inquiry into Student Finance, October 1999.

Woodrow, M. (1999c) 'Commentary: student finance – fairness for the Future'. *Widening Participation and Lifelong Learning*, 1(3), 8–10.

Woodrow, M. (2000) 'Putting a price on a priority: funding an inclusive higher education'. *Widening Participation and Lifelong Learning*, 2(3), 1–5.

Woodrow, M. (forthcoming) *Poverty and Participation: From Elitism to Inclusion II: Widening Access to Higher Education.*

Woodrow, M., Feutrie, M., Grieb, I., Staunton, D. and Tuomisto, J. (2000) 'Lifelong learning to combat social exclusion: policies, provision and participants in five European countries'. *Widening Participation and Lifelong Learning*, **2**(2), 6–17.

Index